Theatre as Alter/"Native" in Derek Walcott

Nirjhar Sarkar
Raiganj University, India

Series in Literary Studies

VERNON PRESS

Copyright © 2023 Vernon Press, an imprint of Vernon Art and Science Inc, on behalf of the author.

All rights reserved. No part of this publication may be reproduced, stored in a retrieval system, or transmitted in any form or by any means, electronic, mechanical, photocopying, recording, or otherwise, without the prior permission of Vernon Art and Science Inc.

www.vernonpress.com

In the Americas:
Vernon Press
1000 N West Street, Suite 1200
Wilmington, Delaware, 19801
United States

In the rest of the world:
Vernon Press
C/Sancti Espiritu 17,
Malaga, 29006
Spain

Series in Literary Studies

Library of Congress Control Number: 2022935706

ISBN: 978-1-64889-653-8

Also available: 978-1-64889-431-2 [Hardback]; 978-1-64889-581-4 [PDF, Ebooks]

Cover design by Vernon Press. Cover image by JL G from Pixabay.

Product and company names mentioned in this work are the trademarks of their respective owners. While every care has been taken in preparing this work, neither the authors nor Vernon Art and Science Inc. may be held responsible for any loss or damage caused or alleged to be caused directly or indirectly by the information contained in it.

Every effort has been made to trace all copyright holders, but if any have been inadvertently overlooked the publisher will be pleased to include any necessary credits in any subsequent reprint or edition.

Table of contents

	Foreword	*v*
	Acknowledgements	*vii*
	Introduction	*ix*
Chapter 1	**Alternative Morality and Ethics of Self-fashioning in Walcott's Early Plays**	1
Chapter 2	**Native "difference" and Elemental Man in *Dream on Monkey Mountain***	39
Chapter 3	**Staging Classics at the Interface of Creation and Criticism**	67
Chapter 4	**The Vision of Plurality and Collaborative Politics in Walcott's Late Plays**	95
Chapter 5	**"Creole-Continuum" and Radical Disruption in Theatre**	115
	Conclusion	*131*
	Bibliography	*137*
	Index	*147*

Foreword

Accidental examiner of a PhD dissertation – this is how I saw myself when I first met Nirjhar Sarkar at North Bengal University where he was going to defend his thesis. So often this is how one comes to examine dissertations as the institutional head's random pen lights on a name in the panel of examiners. Nirjhar was the youngish, harried scholar, apparently charged with all the responsibilities of the day's rituals, hoping for an eventless defence, a seal of approval on his thesis and a relieved goodbye to the external examiner.

The subject of the dissertation itself intrigued me. Walcott was not an easy choice. How had he come to select him? Why had he selected the plays? How was he negotiating the theoretical minefield that he seemed to have taken on with author and genre? That the defense was successful, that he received his degree and went back to his life as an English teacher – this is the story of hundreds of PhD scholars in English departments across the country. But for Nirjhar, obviously, this was not the end. The choice of Walcott, his quiet passion for the area he had studied for several years, and a recognition of what it means to find a lifetime's work in one's author and context pushed him to do something that all Indian scholars of English perhaps dream of, but only a few successfully manage to do – transforming the dissertation into a book, for which there is now a publisher and a waiting readership.

This book develops around a number of key aspects of Walcott's work. Walcott's "mulatto aesthetics" is presented as a formidable challenge to colonial cultural discourses of Western origin and to an answering Afrocentric aesthetic which merely guarded borders and erased all local/native differences.

Walcott's position, that West Indian militancy lies in its art, is basic to this book's examination of the plays, as is the theatre's revision of identity, agency, and selfhood. For Nirjhar's work, Walcott is someone who represents the unrealized aspirations of postcolonial intellectuals – the urge to step out of the grip of revenge historiography and aesthetics, and to find in local cultures the sources of both theory and creative practice. But perhaps most importantly, Walcott's is that exemplary literary sensibility that translates local ethos so wonderfully into thematic and style. The determinedly Caribbean flavor of Walcott's work, its creolization of the theatre and the process of "de-Westernization" of Trinidadian drama are all displayed with care and attention by Nirjhar, as he builds on the emphasis of his title to show what an alter-'native' theatre can be.

The book brings to its readers one more example of literary work as cultural nationalism and is a valuable addition to scholarship on Walcott, and to theatre as a tool and site of resistance.

Prof. Nanadana Dutta
Guahati University

Acknowledgements

Ever since the submission of thesis in North Bengal University, I was encouraged to believe that it may be expanded to a full- length book. Words of appreciation from the senior scholars and academics and my unabated interest in Derek Walcott prodded me to undertake a more comprehensive revision of the dissertation in this monograph. At that stage, I was lucky enough to have the serious comments and observations of Prof. Nandana Dutta (of Guahati University), Prof. Ashis Sengupta and Prof. Ranjan Ghosh (at the University of North Bengal), Prof. Chidananda Bhattarcharaya (of Rabindra Bharati University). Let me record my gratitude to noted Walcott scholars like Prof. John Thieme of East Anglia University and Paul Breslin for their mail response to my queries. My earlier research publication in the journals like *Anthurium- A Caribbean Studies Journal* and *Post-colonial Text- A Journal* provided the impetus for a further critical investigation into the individual plays. My students and young researchers at Raiganj University have always provided me with intellectual stimulus. Among them, a special thanks go to Mr. Subham Ganguly for all his technical assistance and Pankaj Kumar Das for active support during the preparation of my manuscript. My sincere thanks to the brilliant editorial team of the Vernon Press and anonymous reviewers for their constructive feedback.

My daughter, Sanskriti, and wife, Debasri, have always been the biggest support of all academic ventures. It is their unconditional love and understanding that have mattered most in finishing my project.

Introduction

This present monograph is intended to complement, develop and update the thesis I had submitted at The University of North Bengal in India towards the end of November 2016 on Derek Walcott's Plays. This academic focus reflects my growing critical interest in Derek Walcott, the playwright whose drive at initiation of the cross-cultural performance to the Caribbean stage has often been, sadly, lopsided. Robert Hamner, in a review essay (*Modern Drama* Vol. 39, No.1), mentions how Walcott himself lamented the meagre critical attention offered to his plays. Long way back in nineteen ninety-two, in an edited volume of essays, titled *Post-colonial English Drama Commonwealth Drama since 1960* Bruce King had noted that Derek Walcott's plays still have not had a book while his World-famous contemporaries like Wole Soyinka and Athol Fugard received full-length studies. However, King's own critical study —*Derek Walcott and West Indian Drama* has proved to be a work of painstaking scholarship and of singular importance in this direction. After King's pronouncement, only two monographs followed, entirely devoted to his plays—Julia. D. Davies's *Derek Walcott: Dramatist- creole Drama for creole acting-* (2008) and Dark Sinnwe's *Divided to the vein? Derek Walcott's drama and the formation of Cultural Identities* (2001). There is no gainsaying that the complex, diverse postcolonial theatre landscape has owed much to Walcott and his famous Trinidad Theatre Workshop- a highly productive association which spanned over three decades. An artist as astoundingly prolific as Walcott has always generated fresh interpretations and evaluations. This book seeks to explore how within the ambit of performance, the cultural entanglements and dialogues can be re-read in a more comprehensive and theoretically informed way.

Throughout his long and exceptionally prolific career of more than four decades, the poet-dramatist Derek Alton Walcott (1930-2017) has paid tribute to his beloved birthplace - the island of St. Lucia. It is his hallowed native land, his native community, displaced and dispossessed people in their peculiar cultural situation that have remained the nub of his creative enterprise. In fact, he has consecrated literary imagination to his island community– impoverished but culturally rich – a potpourri of race, language, religion and culture. This artistic debt is eloquently acknowledged in his Nobel acceptance speech, too (in 1992).[1] The cultural riches of the "unscripted" folk lives not

---

[1] "This is the benediction that is celebrated, a fresh language and a fresh people, and this is the frightening duty owed," he said. And added in the name of the Caribbean people "I stand here in their name, if not their image."

only surrounded him but sustained dramas since his juvenile years. This cultural competence and authority, a form of Bordieuan *cultural capital*, is a counter to the inflow of global capital in the Caribbean archipelago. Though shackled with debt and heavily dependent upon tourism West Indies has continued to produce a plethora of artists, like musicians, poet, painters. At a very young age, the St. Lucian playwright Derek Walcott felt inspired to pursue "prodigious" creative ambitions; hailing from a colonial backwater, he had faced an acute dearth of resource for publication. In his essays and interviews, Walcott has left well-documented pictures of a struggle for literary productions in the small islands. His dedicated enterprise of staging a Caribbean theatre had to flourish against severe material constraints. Walcott knew well that theatre as a cultural product of historical, geopolitical and ideological conditions could map the Caribbean region notwithstanding the schism of language, religion and race. By exploring the inter-dependence of world, text and performance, the theatre could become "a crucial part of the entire process of decolonization and understanding of modernity" (Thiong'o XII).[2] Theatre, with a new "creole" architecture opened the way to interrogate the existing structures of power and knowledge.

In the fifteenth and sixteenth centuries much of the native population in the Caribbean archipelago had shrunk due to slave labour and imported disease. With the virtual disappearance of the native population in all the islands of West Indies, the territories were gradually filled with the population of African descent and indentured, migratory Asian labours. The common experience of colonisation under the European powers like Spanish, British and French resulted in miscegenation or racial mix. These historical events resulted in "a body of literature exhibiting an extraordinarily robust and heterogeneous archive of discourse on involuntary displacement, courageous journeying, the pining for home and the ambivalence of return" (Bucknor and Donnell 245). The void created through ethnic cleansing or genocide and subsequent settlement of a huge diaspora population paved the way for heterogenous cultural formations, which I will call Alter/"Native"; it is the fulcrum of my main argument that weaves the five chapters, here. In the heterotopic space of theatre, the Caribbean alterity is not only fore-fronted, but theatre gestures towards becoming an alternative itself – a postcolonial leeway out of Manichean and polar politics. Walcott's in-between racial and cultural location has shaped dialectical approach to culture–his deep involvement in myths, rituals, legends, popular performances of all diasporic communities

---

[2] Ngugı wa Thiong'o has contributed a Foreword titled "Placing theatre at the center of postcolonial theory and modernist Discourse" in Awam Ampka's critical study *Theatre and Postcolonial Desires*.

and his abiding fascination with Western classics and English language. As every performance emanates out of a particular cultural life and fosters a new cross-cultural theatrical reality, the 'everyday theatre' could prove to be an important marker of self-apprehension as well as the springboard of Walcott's creative writing. King observes: "Efforts to create a theatre about lives, written by local dramatists were and to an extent remain, international with producing classical and contemporary foreign plays" (3). In her brilliant study, *Theatre, Space and World Making*, Joanne Tompkins calls the space of theatre a space of alternate ordering because in such spaces the imaginative ordering resonates with the real. Also in Walcott's corpus, the imagined ordering of reality had a mooring on the socio-political context of his time. The singular events of post-independence days in the islands had deeply impacted Walcott's creative journey. His rich *oeuvre* of over 30 plays (with quite a few unpublished) and musicals testify to the stage product as a liberatory, vibrant cultural counter which can contest strident claims of nativist politics. His unfettered creative practice mounted challenge at the empty rhetoric of political nationalism. At its nascent stage, theatre could open up a terrain charged with creole energy and imbued with trans-continental influences: "From the *Ramayana* to Anabasis, from Guadeloupe to Trinidad, all that archaeology of fragment lying around, from the broken African kingdoms, from the crevases of Canton, from Syria and Lebanon, vibrating under the earth but in our raucous, demotic streets" (Walcott, Nobel lecture transcript).[3] The "demotic" lives of streets in his birth place, the daily, open-air performances and the rituals had inspired him; what he inherited from the Trinidadian cultural life were translated into signs of theatre. And within the ambit of performance, a complex interplay of several cultures managed to explore a "trans" zone. This imagined world of alternatives (in terms of narrative, architectural design of theatre and dramaturgy) has survived the "nightmares of History" and nurtured the "adamic" vision of green beginnings. And permanently altered the theatre landscape of the Caribbean.

Theatre at the Crossroads

In the early fifties when anti-colonial sentiment and vision of pan-Caribbean culture were widespread and prevalent, Walcott set out to espouse a radical and alternative representation in the forum of theatre. Seeking a voice for his people and geography of his place he attempted to establish a distinctly native literary tradition. This cultural and literary identity could be asserted in

---

[3] In "The Antilles" (1992) - a transcript of his Nobel lecture repeatedly stresses that performance in the Caribbean emanates from transcontinental influence and transcends the specifies of language, race and history.

performance and rituals because theatre is empowered with strong transformative and emancipatory energy. As he was surrounded by "theatricalities of our lives", his dramatist's vision ignored all boundaries between society as the objective reality and theatre as a subjective, constructed, actional representation (mimesis). These two interrelated realms have always shared his stage representation. Walcott embarked upon producing plays at an important historical juncture–the end and withdrawal of colonial powers and the beginning of political independence in some of the West Indian islands. In the islands held still under the yoke of colonial rule, the burgeoning attention to theatre movements attested to the key role of theatre as powerful political engagement. Belonging to such an island, Walcott considered theatre to be the most appropriate medium for negotiating the politico- historical realities. From the beginning of his creative career, like Soyinka, Walcott was tirelessly involved in directing, teaching actors, scripting, conducting workshop and forming theatre groups. He worked towards creating a theatre company, often compared with Brecht's theatre ensemble[4] which became a travelling company in the islands and beyond. To realise his long-cherished goal, he had founded Trinidad Theatre Workshop (1959) - an expansion of Little Carib Dance Company. Despite paucity of all logistics and infrastructural set up, theatre proved to be an effort of immense faith, dedication and discipline. It rose to prominence with native and international productions. But when Walcott parted with the Company, it was exposed to vulnerable conditions. When the claim and promise of sovereignty joined hands with the rapid advance of modernity, in the eventful moment of transformation, theatre and performance had a very significant intervention to make. In dramaturgy, methods and perspective, it appeared to be a complete indigenous practice, a powerful cultural tool which can break down the tyrannical web of representations and mute "the noisy commands of colonial authority" (Bhabha 12).[5] While finding a new form for the age, he felt that a style of performance had to be evolved that is global in its ambition and also critical of local political actions. A significant body of Walcott's plays reflects the traumatic displacement of transatlantic slavery, the forced voyage of migrant Asian indentured labour and conquests of colonial powers and their settlement. And as a consequence, it proved instrumental in negotiating the complex, overlapping cultures and "intertwined histories" of his native land. The defining features of the region have been identified by Benitez Rojo

---

[4] In an exhaustive chapter titled 'The Theatre of Our Lives': founding an Epic Drama (208- 228)" Paula Burnett draws an analogy between Walcott's Trinidad Theatre Workshop with Brecht's theatre *ensemble*.

[5] See, "Signs Taken for Wonders: Questions of Ambivalence and Authority under a Tree Outside Delhi, May 1817" *Critical Inquiry,* 12 (1), 1985.

as: "its fragmentation; its instability; its reciprocal isolation; its uprootedness; its cultural heterogeneity; its lack of historiography and historical continuity, its contingency and impermanence; its syncretism etc" (1). Without a single, homogeneous Caribbean identity and without a centre to what is called the "Caribbean", the New theatre could map the region and 'stage' the essential plurality of West Indian experience.

Premier among the Anglophone playwrights, Derek Walcott did not have much of a theatrical legacy worth the name. In "Discovering Literature in Trinidad", C.L.R. James comments that he did not "know much about West Indian Literature in the 1930s—there wasn't much to know" (James 73). Though rich in cultural diversities, the Caribbean theatre had no well-developed tradition to rest upon. Notwithstanding this limitation, in the mid30s, James's own Haitian plays, no doubt, heralded a new era in producing Caribbean theatre. To him belongs the credit for recording and staging that "history from the below" in a passionate attempt to present the colonised as subjects of their own history. Walcott, also, had virtually no such tradition or model to resort to; beside dance, carnival, steelbands, there was hardly any mention of theatre. He lamented in his seminal essay "What The Twilight Says: An Overture": that though theatre was ubiquitous in the Caribbean society, it was never "solemnised into cultural significance" (*Essays* 7). In his *The Pleasures of Exile* (1960), George Lamming discusses the lack of a Caribbean audience and the sense of "inadequacy" and "irrelevance of function" consequently felt by many Caribbean writers in their own societies. But theatre activities also met with very frugal state support and lack of institutional validation in his time. Finding an acute dearth of interest in drama or rich theatrical experience in the archipelago, he had to forge his own way. Against the established practices, Walcott envisaged drama to be a powerful cultural force and an ideal national theatre to be a major cultural institution. Like his famous contemporary, Errol Hill, he stressed on post-colonial nation-building and its concomitant reflection in fashioning national theatre. Though West Indian fiction had ascended into prominence in the metropolitan literary circles, Walcott felt that the drama would not be lagging in finding a wider audience; as a truly egalitarian artistic form in the midst of the conditions of low literacy and poor educational opportunities, it will not fail to thrive. It was no wonder that local and particularistic drama entailed the audience at home as poetry did not. Staging and performing, like any other writing, claims the space for affirming selfhood beyond the rigid binary of "Self-Other". As an enlightened response to oppression and oppositional politics, the drama could explore the interface and continuity between old antagonists and fix up the breach in history and culture. In the domain of performance, the natives could break away from the subjugation and interrogate the privilege of certain signifying systems. Walcott was convinced that it could offer fresh cultural ideas for literate and non-literate countrymen alike. By generating performance experience, theatre did not only bind them into an imaginary collective but constituted them "as a temporary community with a shared ideology and identity" (Gaskell 233). Whatever theatre was there in the islands under colonial rule, it had little vision and power to shape opinion or open up the scope for collective participation and representation. As a reflector of sociocultural reality, the institution of theatre could attract cultural cohesion entailing all ethnic diversities and class differences; by articulating various socio-political formations, it could aspire to transcend geopolitical boundaries. It is this re-imagining in the stagespace that could supplant the cohesion conceived by the political structures like fledging West Indian federation. In the post-independence days, Walcott knew that the play-world could actualize a sense of solidarity and community and act as a site of resistance to government policies. With this conviction to bring art to the community, Walcott organised the theatre group in the late 50s and early 60s - "theatre and performing arts", as Bruce King notes, "were the cements needed to bring the various peoples and places of the region to a shared culture" (*Derek Walcott* 494). As an initiator of local drama and local production, Walcott had stated in explicit terms the unique responsibility of the playwright or theatre artist because his was the vocation to create "not merely a play, but a theatre, but its environment" (*Essays* 6). Walcott derived artistic inspiration from his father's background in painting and his mother's interest in Shakespeare. In the Catholic-dominated society, the twin Walcott brothers – both, aspiring playwrights– were banned by the Catholic Church, in 1958. The St. Lucian society in its parochial ways sought to limit the artist to race, ethnicity and social class. With the Methodist background of his family, Walcott did cultivate his anti-authoritarian stance and reposed faith upon poems and plays to generate a cultural consciousness which will break free from the clutches of the popular political, religious and cultural discourses of his time. Since the loci of the Caribbean cultures are numerous and widespread, there can be no single overarching cultural form. When the Caribbean colonies were on the brink of decolonisation, the cultural public spheres were found in need of mobilization to recover the indigenous voices. And theatre could integrate manifold cultural expressions popular in the Caribbean and, through this cross-pollination, become more egalitarian. Walcott knew well that new drama will entail local presence and community of actors, producer, designer and audience. And its audience will be a combination of the elite and the common mass. Walcott's dramatic literature and practical theatre eased the clutches of Western otherization and local and nationalistic sentimentality with its radical overtones. This alter/"native" form has remarkably assimilated modernity to local and contemporary context, classical and creole acting to contravene neo-colonial modernism. The present study affirms how this radically different, alternative ways of staging, in the face of oppositional choices, suggests a new ethics of hybrid and mulatto lives.

Identity formation and Theatre

"all cultures are involved in one another; none is single and pure, all are hybrid, heterogeneous, extraordinarily differentiated, and unmonolithic." (Said 1993: xxi)

> "After the white man, the niggers did not want me
> When the power swing to their sides
> The first chained my hands, and apologize, 'History'
> The next said that I wasn't black enough for their pride"
>
> (*Collected Poems* 350)

Ever since the earliest moment of colonial venture in 1492, i.e., Columbus's arrival in San Salvador and subsequent exploration of the lesser Antilles in 1493, the European contact with the original people had made it difficult to name the region; since then, the process of subject-formation began to move along self-other dynamic. The counter-image of Caribbean alterity was produced to maintain the civilizational superiority of the West. Following Middle Passage, slavery and indentureship, the colonial racism was reflected in the "black skin, white mask" dichotomy. The process of identity or subject formation was occluded by undifferentiated categorization, based upon sameness. By the eighteenth century, as the historian Kathleen Wilson argues, the Caribbeanness was associated with ineffable otherness. Both Naipaul and Froude voiced deeply pessimistic views about the region's banality, non-achievement and its harsh legacy. The wealthy planters represented forms of vulgarity, backwardness and degeneracy that inverted the standards of English culture and civilization. Faced with such reductive, dismissive stereotypes and stringent cultural purism, Walcott's plays exude fresh confidence to initiate a process "by which objectified others may be turned into the subjects of their history and experience" (Bhabha 178). All cultural boundary was rendered permeable by "Creole" theatre practices. As in a creole register, here, the colonizer and the colonized occupy several speaking positions while the cultural authority is denied to the both. In the site of drama conflicting legacies and cultures fused into a new eclectic mode and the notion of a homogeneous and unified imperial Britain is downplayed; it could, also, elide the divisions and tensions in a creole society. The future-oriented theatre sought to pay attention to the creolized New World, to cope with the place in its own cultural terms—mimicry, appropriation and assimilation — a variety of ways which could produce an altered, fresh views. When Brathwaite called cultural artifact as "something torn and new" (*Arrivants* 269-270) could displace the old, parochial notions of identity and nationalism. It sought to repudiate the conviction of the British historian Froude about the failure of an imagined community in the West Indies as he was of the view that Africa and Asia will not mix.

For Walcott theatre was a syncretic alternative to cultural monolith and creative counter to all the painful experiences of colonialism. As an opaque medium, his creole theatre could absorb all components without relinquishing one's own dimension. Without limiting to "hybrid" practice in sheer neglect of material realities it could pay adequate attention to economic, political and social inequities.[6] It may be read as "the sign of the productive emergence of new cultural forms which have derived from apparently mutual "borrowings", exchanges and intersections across ethnic boundaries" (Brah and Coombes 9). It serves as a conduit between the "local" and the "global" bringing together disparate themes ranging from imperialism to subject formation. This process also facilitated new narratives of becoming and emancipation which will be the focus of my discussion in the opening chapter. The totalizing narrative had long colonized modes of thinking and production of knowledge. The events in local world threw into disarray the grand narrative of Western modernity and critique trenchantly the encroachment of global capital in the poverty-ridden islands. The theatrical misrepresentation had prodded the disfigurement and dehumanization of the "native". At the observance of the centenary year of the British rule, two of L.O. Inniss's works, *Carmelitta, the Belle of San Jose and The Violet of Icacos* extolled the British rule and completely denied the presence of the Africans, the group that constituted almost eighty percent of the population. Many other plays were informed with discourses of "othering", as Gay in *Polly* perpetuated imperialist and mercantilist dependencies upon the construction of the very identities so dispossessed by the Power. Another remarkably successful play *The West Indian of Cumberland* staged the glorification of the English identity and romanticization of the Caribbean life. In the eighteenth century, local military groups and travelling companies from England and America visited the Caribbean islands, regularly. There is no denying that since the nineteenth century and well into the early decades of the twentieth century, Caribbean theatre remained merely a reflection of English and European, British, and occasionally French and American play houses. And these performances were

---

[6] In her study *The Caribbean Postcolonial,* Shalini Puri argues that "hybrid" is a misleading category and refuses to see it as a panacea to the exclusionary notion of cultural purity.

mostly attended by the upper-class society, like the planters, merchants, military and naval officers, govt. officials and civic leaders. Some performance activities like song, dance and masquerade though, were conducted by the migrant indentured labourers and free workers. Walcott's new theatre refused to adhere to any of these models and moved towards making theatre truly demotic and egalitarian– a point where high and low culture converge and where theatre ceases to be a ghettoized cultural experience. As a syncretic model with alternative theatrical idioms, it could play out "the masses of Caribbean peoples traditionally misrepresented in master script but to the very mechanisms that continue to erase and denigrate, enslave and encrypt" (Canefield 297). Laurence Breiner has noted that like Brathwaite, Walcott never ceased to ask how the West Indians could divest themselves of the attributed identity of being Africans, Asians and Europeans and pursue their fate as West Indians only. Hence, building a self- image was a serious imperative for all West Indian artists. It was drama, in particular, which could effectively contravene the Western imagining and unmoor itself from Eurocentric anchorage.[7] As the Caribbean world was not merely an outpost of empire the artists were bent on transforming it into a self-invented world. The non- European performances by the slaves and indentured workers sought to retain the tradition of the distant homeland. But as practitioners, Walcott and Hill were forging more community-based theatre — theatre "as means to raise the social, political and aesthetic consciousness of the people through what has been called the theatre of collective creation" (Banham et al. 142). Rather than linear history, their imaginative narration could fill the void and deepen the awareness and significance of the Caribbean world. The spirit and sensibility of the age could best be reflected in new theatre rather than in political discourse or rhetoric of propaganda. And the aesthetic consciousness could best be generated by community-based theatre.

Leaving behind derivative and bland imitativeness of the eighteenth and nineteenth century, West Indian literature was entering a new epoch towards the establishment of a literary canon; it was facilitated by the institutions like the University of West Indies, the Caribbean voice of BBC, magazines like *Bim* and the Caribbean Artists' Movement. Beside the leading role of The Beacon, quite a few little magazines and literary journals fostered the new writings and exerted the influence beyond the collapse of the Federation. The Rockefeller Foundation played a key part in starting modern West Indian theatre in the 50s and 60s and made supportive contribution to theatre groups of adequate

---

[7] In an interview with Edward Hirsch, Walcott said, "to me there are always images of erasure in the Caribbean – in the surf which continually wipes the sand clean..." (*Critical Perspective* 74).

promise. His early verse plays like *The Wine of the Country, Henri Cristophe* opened at the Dramatic Theatre of the University College of the West Indies where the University Players put up spirited performance. Under the aegis of the Little Theatre in Kingston, the Jamaican school of Drama was established in 1969, a permanent home for the school that was erected in 1976. This is the only theatre school in the English-speaking Caribbean which brought together theatre practitioners from all over the region. With all these institutional and organizational supports the West Indian literature claimed an independent space for itself and as a cultural agency it moved outside the homeland. In the 1950s, the novels of Lamming, Selvon and Naipaul, had brought to the notice of metropolitan readers the range, depth of creative imagination of the diasporic West-Indian artists. Kenneth Ramchand has singled out that West Indian literature is one among the three cultural institutions which have kept alive the inchoate idea of the federation. The political federation and the emerging nationhood of various islands were closely tied to the growth of independent literary writings and many such intellectual enterprises. The literary establishment set off a flurry of anthologies as "Federation meant a way out of the parochialism of the individual is lands, meant larger audiences, and better communication among writers" (Breiner 95). Walcott belonged to a generation stirred by West-Indian nationalism, with federation struggling to take shape and the Empire on its last leg. Inspired by the provincial aesthetic- cultural, his mission was to fashion theatre as a home-grown cultural product, appealing to an indigenous as well as to the non-indigenous audience of the metropolis. It was an era of literary writings which combined anti-colonial perspective with new values and beliefs. Notwithstanding all the local differences, a vision of unified Caribbean was taking shape to subsume all experiences, local differences and contraries. The practice of indigenous theatre could promulgate cultural resistance to the Euro-American cultural homogenization and "imperial humanitarianism" which justified the expansion of European power. When poetry and novel were striding ahead, drama too did not lag far behind in asserting Caribbean identities.

Fanon was deeply sceptic of belief in "authentic" cultures and identity which in a very simplified way, impedes the growth of international consciousness in a writer. As a corrective to the "purist", oppositional aesthetics, Walcott had espoused "mulatto aesthetics" because it eschews "the groan of suffering, the curse of revenge" (*Essays* 39). By brushing off the poetics of anger, revenge and recrimination or remorse, Walcott sought to reassemble the legacies of all his ancestors. Unburdened by any cultural baggage, most of his plays form an intricate web of cross-cultural and trans-historical influences. Like Achebe and Brathwaite, the sound colonial education and intimacy with classics in school years moulded Walcott's plays of his juvenile, apprentice period. Despite avid consumption of the canonical works, they wrote back to the strategic ideological control of the "centre". By fashioning new creolised plays, Walcott could assimilate all cultural values and belief patterns and eliminate negative patterns of race-based politics. He himself was a progeny of mixed-race and his mixed ancestry provided the impulse for mulatto aesthetic; its ceaseless cross-cultural dialogue could redefine the native Caribbean form. The ideological programmes of Black Power, Negritude Movements tended to efface the plurality of colonial cultures and the racial diversity of the colonized. They championed homogeneous, all-embracing black culture grounded upon the awareness of specific national communities. Walcott knew that no single aesthetic agenda could evince the multiplex reality of the Caribbean. As a postcolonial hybrid Walcott knew "a myth of shared origins is neither a talisman which can suspend political antagonism nor a duty invoked to cement a pastoral view of black life that can answer the multiple pathologies of contemporary racism" (Gilroy 99). He sought to extend the Caribbean frontier beyond geography into culture and reorient the promises of cultural nationalism.

Described as the leading light of Caribbean theatre, Walcott knew that the creole aesthetics would reinvent the New World. Such aesthetic evinces appropriation of all possible sources and influences and shrug off all the illusions of the Old World. A new insight could be added to non-colonial and non- white cultural sources and it looked set to part with the practice of high literary idiolatry. In his much-cited essay "The Muse of History", he has paid homage to the poles of his ancestry- black and white – both of which had their best offerings and gifts to cultivate for the young artist "like the halves of a fruit seamed by its own bitter juice ..." (*Essays* 64). His postcolonial theatre negotiates between the ancient tradition of drama and its immediate political objective which evolved into a "new model" (Burnett 211). Such theatre was intended to be a local praxis to emerge from the interface of cultures and assert the origin of theatre as multiple and non-singular. At a time of intense cultural flux and repositioning, it could explore the legacy of colonial histories and postcolonial subjectivities. It set out to respond to the challenges attending to the cultural imaginary of distinct national agendas and characters. Particularly in the seventies, in the heydays of Afrocentric demagoguery, Walcott's polyphonic theatre took up a new dimension, seeking an elimination of the discrete identity categories which were promulgated in adversarial discourses. In his numerous articles and interviews, he had vented his deep annoyance with art committed to the causes of chauvinism and narrow nationalism. He dismissed the nativist railing against Western worldviews as a reductive formulation. In a total dismissal of Revenge aesthetics, the proposed alternatives of theatre brought to the fore the jarring juxtaposition of multiple cultural heritage- "creole- continuum" and European classics, informal language, street *patois* and sublime poetry and diction of Elizabeth verse. It was committed to

> "forging of a language that went beyond mimicry, a dialect which had the force of revelation as it invented names for things… (*Essays* 15)

Such language, Walcott was convinced, will be most enabling for creating an oral culture of chants, jokes, folk songs, and fables. To the region's emerging cultural habits, this theatre offered a new artistic experience as it reconciled all disparate heritages. For scant experience of serious theatre and relatively small size of educated theatre-goers, the Walcott brothers- Derek and Rodney were spurred to make forays into local theatre without the blemish of provinciality. Together they had established the St. Lucian Arts Guild, performing both the local and canonical plays. In a way, they responded to Shaw's famous instruction to reclaim a space for the home-grown theatre and get rid of the habit of mimicking Western styles of performance. Because the touring troops were disconnected from the place of its origin and its local moorings. In these years, the protest plays of Amiri Barka stirred a new fervour in America about black consciousness and claimed an elimination of white supremacy. But Walcott was strongly sceptic of the politics of hatred, bitterness, rage and fuming protest and no wonder that his new theatre carefully evaded straightforward political affiliation. For him, resistance of performance and (re) action of speech, acts and gestures could generate a new consciousness beyond victim-victimizer duality. Art serving only radical, militant agenda, for Walcott, is bound to be ethnocentric and non-egalitarian. As he famously proclaimed, "the future of west Indian militancy lies in its art" (*Essays* 16). Therefore, his creole theatre mounted a strong challenge to absolute valourization of the black and absolute denigration of the white. Walcott's immediate predecessors like C.L.R James and Marcus Garvey initiated local dramas which would vent the spirit of anti-colonial movement. His dramatic narratives were couched in highly symbolic language and its rich verbal and visual qualities were particularly appealing to the native folks. The local drama groups and entertainers sought to exhibit more folk entertainment and deployed dialects in a far more dignified way. The focus on indigenous culture brought to the fore native comedians, notably Ernest Cupidon of Jamaica and Sam Chase of Guyana, both of whom wrote and performed comic sketches before admiring popular audiences. In the Hispanic Caribbean, too the 50s was the decade of the flowering of drama and greater visibility of local aesthetic and artistic parameters.

In its formative days, Western-styled education had enriched the theatrical form and content of the Caribbean plays. And the African plays enlivened the stage with sophisticated use of music, mime, masquerade. Before Walcott, Louis

Bennet had prioritized folk songs, stories and *patois* in order to develop Jamaican sensibility and identity. Beside Little Theatre Movement, St. Lucian Theatre Guild significantly contributed "to promote essential Caribbean drama to dethrone the gods of Prosperan masque as they tore away the masks of colonial theatralizations" (Canefield 297). C.L. R James had already recommended the practice of the melding of master script with the plays about "vododoo" — an interstitial form between high art and popular. The post-independence drama was intended to be grounded in West Indian reality and experience and rooted in local cultural experiences. Errol Hill's *Man Better Man* used the frame of Calypso drama, peppered with creole songs. Calypsonians, lower classes and folk cultures continued to supply the material for Hill and fertilized the imagination of the artists of the succeeding generations. This coupling of melody of Europe and rhythm of Africa lay at the heart of such indigenous productions. Thus, newly- fashioned West Indian theatre sought to undo "ideological maneuver through which imagined communities are given essentialist identities" (Bhabha 294). Like Soyinka, Walcott depended upon Western cultural practices without being burdened by them. By his self-definition, Walcott was a natural assimilator – he knew the literatures of the empires Greek, Roman, British through their classics; both "the *patois* of the street and the language hid the elation of the discovery" (17). Grounded upon mulatto aesthetics, his performance became an alternate to dominant styles of representation where unexpected combination of belief systems embodies composite affiliations, cultures and identities. Robert. D. Hamner in his essay "Exorcising the planter- devil in the plays of Derek Walcott" analyses how Walcott has produced something marvellously new out of the synthesis of African and European heritage. It parted with the mimetic realism of Western texts and oppositional "Black" aesthetics to shore up the fragments of multiple cultures and customs. It sought to undo mere Afrocentric black difference and all its stable ideological position. His preferred alternate was "tough aesthetics of the New World"- one that is succinctly analyzed by Olaniyan as "The aesthetics proper to this space calls… "mulatto", neither purely black, nor purely white; a hybrid aesthetics free to speak in creole, English or both, or appropriate forms from the diverse cultural traditions that make up the Caribbean- European, African or Asian" (199). Such theatre aesthetics was capable of navigating all spatial and temporal distances.

Emergence of alternative (s) in theatre

> "Culture is a discourse, a language, and as such it has no beginning or end and is always in transformation, since it is always looking for the way to signify what it cannot manage to signify"
>
> *The Repeating Islands* (20)

With more and more totalitarian cultural forms gaining ascendency in the midst of plural life worlds, theatre offers a forum for imagining the alternative world. In such alter/native worlds, the dualisms like local/global, North/South, Centre/Periphery crumble to open up spaces for new narratives of "becomings". Spearheading the theatre movement in the Caribbean region Walcott's plays have re-imagined collectives like tribe, community; through alternative and disruptive performative styles they have recovered the rags and patches of dissonant space called "nation". The "native" which became a code for subordination and pathological deficiency for the colonialists and an expression of racist pride for the advocates of the Nativist discourses, had stimulated deep antipathy in Walcott. By de-coding "native" as a construct and its precarious relation with "origin" and "belonging", we will inquire into indigene subject position; it will help us explore further the key issues of community, home, root permeating all his major plays. He has described his plays "open in form and tribal rather than individualistic".[8] It is suggestive of the elemental, earthy Caribbean life, vibrant with dance, music. No wonder then that the thumping language of national pride, collective and group passion, sentimental yoke of distant homeland wese jettisoned by Walcott as his career evolved in different directions. He wrestled with "re-membering" broken lives, shattered histories of indigenous lives or what Bhabha calls "rags and patches of daily living". By registering the diversity and particularity of several diasporic experiences and their cultural cross-pollination, the creole artist can hope to transcend national and provincial limits and affirm culture's changing multi- locationality across time and space.

In the post-independence years, the euphoria over political gerrymandering of republics into federation and emerging nationalisms had assumed what Anderson has described "a near pathological character"; it spread its roots "in fear and hatred of Other and its affinities with racism" (129). As in the African countries, the Caribbean archipelago also witnessed a surge of nationalist and radical movements. As in America, there was a strong mobilisation of international black consciousness which inspired cultural products to turn imperial hegemony upside down. Since the nineteen thirties, as the Black Power movements, Negritude movements and Garveyism were gathering momentum, the notion of pure cultural practice took hold of the popular consciousness. There was a proliferation of claims which used race, nation as the categories of identity-analysis. They asserted their being in reclaiming African heritage and passionately exalted African cultural values. Along with

---

[8] In an interview published in *Parisan Review* Walcott criticized American theatre as "closed and shuttered", as antipode to the indigenous Caribbean theatre - cited in a chapter contributed by Renu Juneja.

Africanist identity formation, they reified racial polarity and monocultural identity. A common agenda that informed such cultural insularity was to resist the politics of assimilation and recognized colour as the source of common cultural heritage and origin. Conceived as rival to the European Great Tradition, it asserted an equally homogeneous cultural condition which was grounded on the mythically satisfying past known as Africa. As Laurence Breiner says quoting C.L.R James in *An Introduction to West Indian poetry*, "The road to West Indian national identity lay through Africa" (142). It underscores the idealization of Africa as a counter-sign, the flipside of European cultural hegemony. Passive, subservient relationship to dominant culture and implacable hostility between the native and the invader failed to appeal to the native artists like Lamming, Harris or Walcott.

Released from the chimera of past and historical degradation Walcott proposed an alternative approach to nationalism which repudiated the linear, time-bound historiography through creative, individual expression. Simple allegorical representation of Non-White lives will encourage "revenge aesthetics" and will proceed further to produce "inverse colonialism". The radical aesthetics and Ideology of oppositionality like hatred and revenge, permeating through the Protest Poetry or Negritude writing, could never redeem the condition of servitude. It only resulted in decisive closure – replacement of one system with another. Afrocentrism was a cultural remedy for the wounded Black psyche, disoriented by centuries of Eurocentric historical presumption and arrogance. It was natural then that the Caribbeans should re-align themselves with the cultures of pre-colonial Africa. According to Brian Crow and Chris Banfield, such movements were only but "the ideological banner waved by reactionary nationalism, or the tattered cloak that conceals the nakedness of corrupt, incompetent and exploitative politicians" (10). Therefore, the attempts of nationalist agenda to find a reciprocal relation between race and nation proved to be an impediment to the creole theatre. From the beginning, Walcott countered the hold of monolithic culture; local literary tradition could only flourish by giving free reign to the imperceptible process of creolization whereby two or mere cultures merge into a new mode. Hence, the Caribbean Man could find identity in what Said has called "a geography of other identities, peoples and cultures, and then to study how despite their differences, they have overlapped one another through unhierarchical influence" (*Culture and Imperialism* 8). Though Brathwaite had found in Black Power Movement a scope for forging transnational solidarity, uncritical acceptance of oppressive raciologies would have locked the natives as mere victims. As singularity of black experience for the Caribbean would have promoted the victimhood Walcott inveighed against artificial continuity between distant African homeland and present Caribbean state. In his view, such aesthetic orientations only help in the "reproduction of dominant structures insubordinate languages, thereby recreating the hierarchical mechanism" (Chambers 73). But such artistic imperative, as Walcott believed, was accommodative of ideologically convenient mythology. Instead of harking back to the ancestral memories of some ethno-racial origin, Walcott was more drawn to the difference of culture; he espoused a theatre aesthetics which cross-cut the divisions commonly made between the particular and general, the individual and the collective, the one and the many which help us redefine the emerging Caribbean subjecthood. As he always held to the belief "this earth is one/island in archipelago of stars" (*Star-Apple Kingdom* 20) the stage space could articulate the ideal of mutual sharing.

To free identity from the boundaries of particularism, from the space of nativist discourse and Western representation, Walcott set out to unleash a polyphonic and syncretic theatre. Walcott was quite outspoken against the strategic essentialism of Nativist ideology and all its affiliated movements as they lacked the vison of plurality and the energy of mobilizing the subjugated Caribbean people. Beside excoriating Afrocentric demagoguery in politics and art he redefined the Caribbean alterity as a polysemic sign. As new intellectual horizons began to unfold, the model of static, rigid culture began to wear out; it was found incompatible with the complexities of Caribbean cultural fabric. Drama and theatre have drawn sustenance from the reality of Caribbean culture and its combination of differences has proved effective for symbolic narratives. The performative space of theatre was organized in a way that it could reflect, enunciate and criticize the contemporary reality. Walcott belonged to a generation stirred by West Indian nationalism with post-independence and post-federal disenchantment. As Breiner says, "Federation meant a way out of the parochialism of the individual islands, meant larger audiences, and better communication among writers" (95). Walcott's aesthetic vision ran counter to the agenda of political decolonization and in practice, it moved beyond the displacement of the discursive apparatus of eurocentricism. Like Cesaire, Walcott believed "Theatre should evoke the invention of the future" (184, ibid); in the emergent postcolonial nation-state drama could prove to be a powerful cultural tool of politico-cultural transformation. The attempts of cultural self-assertion mainly by reclaiming "African" heritage in the West Indian cultural landscape had evolved within the wider context of American Black Power, transatlantic Negritude. But adversarial nationalism, Walcott knew, would be "a transitional and transitory moment in the decolonizing project" (Gandhi 122). Walcott's unflagging opposition to the notions of "authentic", "native", "original", "return" was prompted as he knew that the "erasure" of historical memory as part of the Caribbean experience will only end up in futile nostalgia. This violently inflicted condition of "desire to forget" or "will- to- forget" (Gandhi 4) dismantles the cultural and idealist "return to roots". Such cultural quest for lost roots propped up the totalizing ideologies of Nativism and Black consciousness. His artistic mission has always been to celebrate the entangled web of stems and roots of a network, analogous to rhizomatic network. As the heavy presence of black, African population fuelled the strive for cultural recuperation, a communityism. In his articles for *Trinidad Guardian*, he vented his growing annoyance with "abuses of nationalism as an excuse for chauvinism in the arts" (Breslin 27). In a review of Federal Arts Exhibition, Walcott wrote: "I think there are many bad amateurs who are getting a great many fancy notions about nation alart without getting rapped on knuckles. They are dangerous and superfluous" (6). Such instances of cultural nationalism, Chinweizu argues, only railed "against the cultural hegemony of the West, the nativists are of its party without knowing it…the cultural nationalism remain in position of counter identification…which is to continue to participate in an institutional configuration-to be subjected to cultural identities they ostensibly decry…Time and time again, cultural nationalism followed the route of alternate genealogizing" (170). Hence Walcott felt that new narratives, multiple in time and ensemble of different worldviews and customs must be forged to articulate what Bhabha calls "the heterogeneity of its people". Walcott conceived "nation" to be far from a homogenized artifice and identity as processual, contingent and heterogenous. His plays reveal the radical contingency of identity and refutes the unitary, pre-given identity in a land where the native is far from a homogeneous Other. Described often as a "meta-diaspora" the region is unstable and suspended between cultures and conflicting identities, irreducible to the illusory vision of one language, one race. His poet-persona Shabine's proclamation sums up in an inimitable way: "I have no nation, but imagination".[9] The effective way of reimagining identity and nation formation remained a major obsession with Walcott from his very early works. It is in the performative space that identity is positioned and re-positioned and undergoes the "play of history and culture"- as Stuart Hall phrases in his canonical essay "Cultural Identity and Diaspora" (1996). Both Gilroy and Hall contended that in the act of probing the dynamics of race and nationalism the artists must repudiate the singular, essential Caribbean identity. As identity is not ahistorical or immutable, no diasporic community can inhabit any single dominant national identity. For the Caribbean society, with its wide array of experiences like colonialism, slavery, globalization, the discontinuous history has rendered the grammar of identity obsolete. Extreme belligerence between West-Indians of African and Asian descent, people of colour and mulatto and their cultural polarities made impossible

---

[9] This often quoted line of *The Schooner Flight* included in *The Star-Apple Kingdom* remains Walcott's most cogent expression of sundering of ties to nation and race while undertaking a quest for selfhood.

the reflection the general, shared cultural codes and common historical experiences of "a people" (Hall 111). At a time when language and race-based nationalism was prevalent and popular a new form of drama and performance could exhibit the entanglement of "heterogeneous selves and subjectivities" (Radhakrishnan 752). Walcott was convinced that the divisions and vicissitudes of the Caribbean history could be reflected in the stage and the cultural personality of the Caribbean could be defined only by demythifying it from the fixation of colonial discourses.

The transcultural encounter of theatre has always undermined the borders erected by the Nativist politics or other forms of ethnic nationalism. As Shalini Puri observes, "The philosophical burden of the concept of cultural hybridity in the post- modern academy has been to correct purist, essentialist, organicist conception of culture" (19). The assertive claim of cultural nationalism rooted in Power, Walcott knew, was merely "political" (*Essays* 21). To contravene all the pretexts of political power, Walcott sought to enunciate cultural certitude; rearticulation of New World aesthetics and diaspora identity had, no doubt, offered him an artistic advantage. The proliferation of commercial performance in the post-independence days only debilitated the West Indian culture and identity. Walcott wove Calypso, steel band, carnival into the fabric of his play texts very deftly in his indigenous theatre to expose the vacuity of commercial elation of tourist entertainment.[10] Deriving from both Western tradition and non-Western models, Walcott's play texts collapse the distance between periods and cultures. Wilson Harris, Walcott's another famous contemporary, also believed that cross-cultural dynamic bridges the divides in Manichean paradigms of cultural superiority and holds the possibility for humanizing sensibilities. Similarly, Walcott's deep commitment in theatre and performance stirred further cultural awakening. It was the imaginative ventures which underscore "the unique condition of being a Caribbean "the era of the struggle for independence was marked by a corresponding eagerness to distinguish West Indian theatre from English literature, to establish the former identity as an on-going concern" (Breiner 101). By emptying consciousness from both European and African schemata and old automatized patterns and perception of belief, the dramatic narrative could powerfully free the subjects from the straitjacket of psycho-somatic identification.

Through local rendering and non-proscenium stage performance it confronted hierarchies of colonial knowledge and values. It is in what Harris calls "theatre of Creolity" that the New World artists find the alternative praxis

---

[10] In "What the Twilight says" Walcott, sadly notes, "These popular artists are trapped in state's concept of the folk form, for they preserve the colonial demeanour and threaten nothing."

Introduction xxvii

– a source of elation and exuberance and a promise to be redeemed from "dreadful secondariness" (Said 207). By radically separating from Europe, it was the dramatist's vision to make an amalgam of all disparate traditions which could assert as "absolutely new ways of living and thinking" (Lyotard qtd. in Gandhi 7). Their disparate performance styles and conflicting cultural legacies bear witness to "any given culture would appropriate individual elements of other traditions and weave them into its own theatrical fabric in order to expand its possibilities and means of expression" (Fischer-Lichte 114).

Walcott's quest for an alternative in theatre aesthetics and practice was also prompted by the disregard of the state in funding the fledgling institution of theatre and its indifference to recognize theatre as national institution. He resented, "In these new nations art is a luxury and the theatre the most of superfluous of amenities" (*Essays* 23-24). The impoverished communal life that surrounded him did not occlude his creative energy; rather, the cultural potential embedded in daily life deserved to be "scripted" to the non-Caribbean audience. Moreover, it had to grapple with the prevalent state-sponsored folk-tourism, fetishization of popular shows as adjunct of active touristic entertainment. In the post-independence years, the prevailing philistinism, the strong hold of seasonal carnival on popular minds had disappointed Walcott. No wonder then, Walcott's plays from the outset had been fiercely critical of the commodification of the native culture by the tourism industry and bastardisation of folk-culture catered for passive consumption of cultural commodities. Like most post-colonial theatres, they hold up to scrutiny the imperial system of governance, social and economic structures of power or local post-independence regimes. The stage performance could effectively negotiate the contemporary cultural and political needs, promises of budding nationhood. Especially in his seminal essay "What the Twilight Says", he took to task the appropriation of folk culture by the government. Appropriated by the state, the folk art appears as a sign of "carefree, accommodating culture" and the figures like steelbandman, calypsonian and limbo dancers became stock popular entertainers. These typically Caribbean performers in the era of multinational capitalism persist in catering to the tourism industry. Some of his later plays (discussed in the final chapter) register the tension of the traditional, indigenous life and onslaught of modernity with hype of progress and development. The network of globalization and local government's complicity with corporate capital surfaced in Walcott's later works. His counter-narratives dismissed the stereotype of sunny Caribbean paradise to probe into poverty, unrest and political uncertainties. In the process, the political and hegemonic definition of "native" is destabilized. As "native" refuses to be assimilated into Anglo-European norms and converted into a radical sign of aggressive particularism of Caribbean nationhood, this theatre came to "mean a symbolic interpretation of social reality that facilitated communication, socialization, and community" (Awam 5). The social sphere, therefore, was thus reconfigured for accommodating new theatre. In the 70s, after his disconnection from Trinidad Theatre Workshop Walcott invested his energy in the U.S. theatre scene, staging plays in St. Croix, New York and Los Angeles. It exposed his production to wider global recognition. His newly created forms of theatre benefited not only from the Western canonical writings but also from Oriental entertainment forms and performance style as well. It is strongly evident when he was commissioned to write a play on Homeric epic immediately after he clinched the Noble Prize in 1992. By extracting the cultural potential of different islands, he proved that the cultural pastlessness or historylessness is a privilege and the empty slate can be reinscribed with new notation of cultural redemption (Fischer-Lichte 3).[11] Theatre thus becomes a product of multivocal modernity in the Caribbean. The five chapters arranged in the following order will probe into syncretisation of existing cultural patterns and attempt to find how alter/"natives' can be self-defining and self- affirming. They aspire to offer a scope of fresh evaluation of the plays that have been heavily commented upon.

The **first chapter** discusses three early short St. Lucian plays (*The Sea at Dauphin, Malchochon, Ti-Jean and His Brothers*) where a process of self-fashioning, a self- overcoming form "centuries of servitude" are explored in the small, unheroic simplicities. Walcott's vigilantly "Caribbean" stories with their earthy vulgarity animate the "un-storied" Caribbean zones, inhabited by the degraded, destitute like wood-cutter, charcoal burner and sailors. No longer stereotyped subjects, in the face of repressive mechanism, they maintain dignity and pride and overcome "slavish" and "weak" morality. Scripting and staging the story of Caribbean "everyman" identity in these works appear to be immanent "becoming" and they no longer appear to be transcendent, fixed entity. With a new theoretical approach and framework of Nietzsche, this chapter will attempt to explore the Caribbean personhood as an experience of "becoming".

The **second chapter** is concerned with Walcott's masterpiece, the signpost of his career *Dream on Monkey Mountain*. It carried forward Walcott's quest for artistic and cultural freedom to overcome the mechanism of inferiorization and static framework of identification within the prominent socio-historical and politico-economic context. It portrays "back to Africa" and Revenge on White Masters issues in the light of fantasy, the dream sequence. Its ostensibly "illogical and contradictory" structure affirms the Monkey Mountain as the

---

[11] "Performances grew out of these confrontations and interactions between artists and audiences, each seeking to make claims about their cultural identity".

original home of Makak, the Caribbean everyman and redeems the chronic condition of homelessness.

The **third chapter** analyses how Derek Walcott's major stage adaptations produce their alter/native, counter-discursive space. In the Caribbean islands, Homer, Defoe and Shakespeare were familiar icons and also a stubbornly foreign presence. As he's often called "Caribbean Homer", Walcott had set out to explore, interpret and translate classics into (an) other language and culture. In his later career, ambivalent dialogue with canon and its British and Greek classics resulted in the recasting of the masterpieces of Homer, Synge and Defoe into dramas. As imaginative challenge to the hegemony of colonial institutions and practices, his stage space initiated cross-cultural dialogue and cross-pollinations of different performance styles which proved compatible with creolizing theatre and process of "de-Westernization" of Trinidadian drama. Walcott never ceased to insist that the fluidity of myth rather than historicist time, as was a productive concern for the "New World" artists. This chapter rereads three major rewritings of Walcott, *Pantomime, Odyssey- A Stage Version, A Branch of Blue Nile* – and inquiries into the process of translation of fictional narrative and epic of Defoe and Homer into play. What we find here is the slippage of "translation"-an act between fidelity and betrayal, loyalty and treachery. This chapter aims to understand Walcott's dialogue with the ante-texts and how it "un-writes" and "rewrites" their cultural codes to transform the "other" into an ambivalent, aporetic space.

The **fourth chapter** probes Walcott's heteroglotic profusion of idiolects, deployment of standard English and Creole register to offer a medley which rebuts linguistic hegemony. The comprehensive creole continuum, informed by coalescence of picong, English, French creole and island *patois*, has a rich, deterritorializing potential to forge alternative theatrical idioms. His lifelong romance with English, however, did not preclude his narratives to downplay the centrist assumption. Brathwaite's recommended "nation language" proved inadequate for the Caribbean stage as it foregrounded only a consolidated form out of several dialects. The graceful heterogeneity of language enables an experiment with alternative register; it portrays an artist's struggle to maintain pride, thwarting shame and humiliation of the native speech. The code-switching, deformation of accent, amorphous register in his later plays become a potent marker of "difference" which Walcott knew "could command attention without pleading" ("What the Twilight Says").

The **fifth and final chapter** examines how post-Trinidad Workshop plays portray the volatile political reality in the wake of the breakdown of the federal state. Here, Walcott's plays have re-imagined collectives like the tribe, community through alternative and disruptive performative styles which attempt to bring to the fore the rags and patches of dissonant space called "nation". Tending towards non-totalitarian and non-hegemonic theatricalities his *oeuvre* has spelt possibilities of emancipation from the yoke of collectives and re-placed it with the ethics of "being- in- common". Focusing on three important late plays *The Last Carnival*, and *Remembrance, Beef, no Chicken*, this section inquiries into creole theatre's questioning, re-assessing and challenging of national values, priorities, the inheritance of multiple legacies and neo-colonial ventures.

Chapter 1

Alternative Morality and Ethics of Self-fashioning in Walcott's Early Plays

> To stride from the magnetic sphere of legends, To change the marble sweat which pebbled
> the wave blow of stone brows for the sweat-drop on the cedar plank,
> for a future without heroes,
> to make out of these forests and fishermen
> heraldicmen!
>
> -Derek Walcott

> Turbulence is at work everywhere ... (millions of simple folk) have now become the subject of their own history, engaged in a global war to liberate their own villages, rural and urban, from the old encirclement of poverty, ignorance and fear...This is the most fundamental battle of our time, and I am joyfully lucky to have been made, by my work, a soldier in their ranks.
>
> -George Lamming

> ... this past, this endless struggle to activate and reveal and confirm a human identity, human authority, yet contains for all its horror, something very beautiful.
>
> -James Baldwin

Within a brief period between 1957 and 1959, the years between New York experience and the founding of Trinidad Theatre Workshop, Derek Walcott produced several one-acters which ushered West Indian drama into greater visibility. Undeterred by the span of interest of his home audience, he found in them a scope of "enterprise of recovering and uncovering the contents and forms of the consciousness of the people" (Lazarus 8). The narrative and the stagecraft deployed in these "folk" plays are fostered by local rituals, customs and carnivals. To give an authentic voice to his people, to his emerging society was a major artistic imperative for Walcott. The nineteenth-century theatrical texts on the Caribbean basin were replete with myths and negative stereotypes which occluded the process of self-definition for the local people. Their misrepresentations perpetuated the illusion for the European sovereignty and dominance. To these "un-storied" lives Walcott dedicated his stagecraft; in them, the innate theatricality of daily life was imaginatively transformed into counter-narratives of (in)subordination. Cultural representation of the non-Western "other" lay at the core of imperial discourses. Walcott firmly castigates such representations: "Our myths are ignorance, theirs are literature" (*Essays* 39). The creative expressions of Achebe's novels often centre around unrecorded customs, beliefs, magic and rituals, legends of the Ibgo society.[1] These home-spun narratives and mythologies of folk imagination could mount a challenge to dominant narratives of acculturation and "civilizing mission" promulgated by colonial practices. Set in a milieu of low cultural self- regard theatre could articulate alternative heroism of the Caribbean "heraldic men" - their ability to register what Walcott phrases as "the sacred urge of the actors everywhere" despite "the anguish of race" (5).[2] When formalized on stage the theatre embedded in the quotidian experience could be pressed to the service of the oppressed, subjugated humanity. These early plays were rooted in "insignificant" lives and "its people as a counter to metropolitan marginalization" testified to the building alternative self-image (Burnett XI). Unlike Naipaul's contempt for the "half-made society" and "borrowed culture" of Trinidad, Walcott found the inner reality of the Caribbean experience rewarding. No wonder then, his plays endowed the Caribbean common man with an enriched self- knowledge. In non-literate communities which formed the majority of the West Indian population, stories had a central place to maintain and sustain its culture. While the songs, legends and stories bespoke of the rich cultural life in the region, they, profoundly, represent the heterodox Caribbean cultural reality and offer its artist a new way of seeing. Stylistically, he resembled Achebe's deft interpenetration of Igbo folktales and proverbs with Western literary tradition; for the African and Caribbean playwrights, such fusion of the oral and scribal traditions proved to be a useful springboard in fashioning a new art form which could confront the touristic debasement of "folk" as an adjunct to tourism; he excoriates the state initiative to trade every cultural form, a form of bastardization of "folk" (*Essays* 7). For Walcott, a potent alternative to the grand narratives in the "history-orphaned islands" (8) was the unscripted and unperformed stories of the wood-cutter, fishermen. They inspired rather than hindered his aesthetic sensibility. In the Caribbean archipelago, the coercive

---

[1] The world of Achebe's fiction has often been compared with Thomas Hardy's Dorset and Faulkner's Mississippi as vast Igbo population is portrayed with unfailing accuracy.
[2] Acting and performance were so germane in the Caribbean society that Walcott found them in What the Twilight Says: An Overture "sacred", a staying power against the anguish of deeply impoverished conditions and dehumanizing mechanism they suffered.

mechanism of colonialism could not rob the grace and dignity of the "dispossessed" lives; therefore, Walcott anchored his narratives on their struggle to throw off the burden of servitude and the weight of insults, they underwent down the ages. As a theatre-practitioner knew theatre to be a socially committed vocation; as a cultural form and product the theatre could affirm the cultural substance of subjugated people and reinforce a collective cultural identity. The rhythm and beauty of life in St. Lucia gave him an impetus for finding/claiming a counter-discursive space to the historical narratives and narratives of empire – an opportunity to break free from all ideological constraints. The three short plays discussed here, extracted from his first major collection, *Dream in Monkey Mountain and Other Plays*, no doubt, sum up how "Walcott's foundational contribution towards a West-Indian theatre was rooted in the experience of the common people, drawing on their arts of performance, including their language, and that in the context of the colonial experience of the region" (Baugh 58).

The vitality of the folklore and the scope of communal participation through the indigenous narrative had also inspired artists like George Lamming and Wilson Harris. The West Indian villages, often inhabited by an indentured cane-cutters of Asian and African diasporas continued their seasonal ritual with gusto. By ingenious appropriation of both the Western and non-Western aesthetic models, Walcott wanted to develop a drama within a limited orbit of reference, allusions and beliefs. In his essay "Tradition, The Writer and Society", Harris emphasised the essential role of the West Indian writer to awaken his countrymen from the oppressive legacies of racism and colonialism, to generate a truly revolutionary life in them.[3] Walcott also set himself the task of imaginatively transforming the "unheroic" lives mired in poverty; he sought to place the marginal locus at the centre of his texts and add new insights to Caribbean culture. As he states in his commentary on the politics of theatre-making in the Caribbean in his prefatory essay to the Volume *Dream on Monkey Mountain and Other Plays*, titled "What the Twilight Says: An Overture": "Poverty seemed a gift to the imagination, necessity was truly a virtue, so we set our plays in the open, in natural, unphased light, and our subject was bare, unaccommodated man" (7). He was always aware that theatre could generate a representation for heightening politico-cultural awareness as the dominant systems of knowledge refused to heed the marginal, "oppressed, disempowered voices". But he was strongly sceptic of political measures in redeeming from dire poverty. Long objectified

---

[3] As a literary innovator Wilson Harris's lectures and essays have encompassed cross-culturality as an imaginative venture to reflect upon tradition, legend in the West Indian writings.

under the Western "gaze", the St. Lucian people required a narrative space from which they could speak and act as subjects. It took the intervention of the artists to recognise the resilience of the subjects who plied their daily activities within the limits of the imperial power. With *The Sea at Dauphin* (1954), Walcott left the youthful ardour for Haitian revolution - an event of great magnitude which exercised a strong fascination for many creative artists. The lacuna of "single heroic warrior figure" in West-Indies is addressed with the stories of wood-cutter, charcoal burner or fishermen- the "unaccomodated man" and solitary figures who captivated the imagination of the dramatist when he was exploring new grounds for imagining the alternative world. His early protagonists of these "folk plays" are derived from local legend, popular folk tales or even village scandals. In the apprentice days Walcott's preoccupation was with what Lamming has described in *The Pleasures of Exile* as "lives of men and women who were never thought to be sufficiently important for their thoughts and feelings to be registered" (5). Though they belonged further down the scale of hierarchy, the St. Lucian peasants had an exceptional moral courage and immense relish for life. The scar of subjugation, the plight of communal life and bleak future are placed at the heart of Lamming's novels; still, he asserted in *The Pleasures of Exile* (1992) the possibility of restoration of the peasants to the true status of personality. It was his conviction that they will act as the agents of collective action and recognize and understand the world around them. In drama Walcott had found an imaginative scope to enter and share the insider's experience of life, redeem the sufferers from a position of non-entity vis-a-vis their cultural and economic plight. Theatre proved an effective tool to confront the structure that had made their "naked, pessimistic life" (*Essays* 15) a daily ordeal. Walcott's upper middle-class status and Methodist background had denied him a direct experience of the down- trodden lives. He sadly witnessed how the West-Indian mass met with the indifference and contempt of the politicians in the days of neo-colonial encroachment. But what stood out was the rich variety of the performance, the passion and untiring struggle that underlined the cultural survival. Like Ngugi Wa Thiong'o, he set the artistic goal to articulate the right to name the world as a part of communal self-determination. Walcott consciously shunned legends and myths; the orbit of his plots was the communal predicament of fishermen, woodcutter and charcoal burner. His native disenfranchised masses were "the common people, the salt of the earth" who provide an obvious basis for defining national identity ("a new people") (Breiner11). The chapter twelve of Walcott's lyrical masterpiece, *Another Life*, opens with the memorable image of a carpenter, the craftsman who compels the admiring gaze of the poet: "I watched the vowels curl from the tongue of the carpenter's plane" (*Collected Poems* 294).[4] The present chapter pays attention to both "suffering" and "solidarity", the redeeming qualities of degraded lives as embodied in Walcott's imaginative responses to the blights of colonialism. It was Walcott's conviction that by "story-ing" their lives, by transmuting them with the fire of their artistic imagination could a writer undo the colonial structure of awareness. In his Nobel lecture, he asserts provocatively that "in the Antilles poverty is a poetry with a V, *une vie*, a condition of life as well as that of imagination". Their wretched daily lives also demonstrate "compassion, mutual support, and solidarity" (Burnett 55) notwithstanding stark, hostile conditions. The asymmetrical relations of power, coercive mechanism cannot undermine what Fanon calls "basis for hope" (*Black Skin* 25). In *Drums and Colours*, the emerging nation is embodied through such plebian figures- Ram, Pompey, Yette, Yu, epitomizing bond of all races and classes. As Paula Burnett describes them, "They are poor and chaotic, but they are well motivated and deal with adversity with wit and wisdom" (232).[5] Although Walcott denies poverty as a virtue, he recognizes a latent mobility in the poor who cannot escape their island conditions and overcome violent oppression and dehumanization. The popular folk tales often supplied him with raw material, and Walcott knew they could expose the fantasy of power and control besides celebrating the vital earthiness. The wretched, abject native lives is bestowed with vitality to offer resistance to dehumanization. Robert. D. Hamner in his essay "Mythological Aspects of Walcott's Drama" highlights this dominant concern of early Walcott: "He delineates the innermost character of a people, the essence of what it means to have been born West Indian" (35). And in so doing, the playwright can address the aporias of cultural representation and rebut Freud's stricture that the West Indians have "no character".

These brief early plays mostly engage with myths and archetypes, embodying the timeless values, the emotional realities of Caribbean life and its primeval association between man and nature. Walcott firmly believed that the racial and cultural blight of several centuries of trans-Atlantic slave trade have failed to undermine the dignity of New World individual and communal life or taint the vernal space of cohabitation of man, nature and animal. Sometime classified as folk plays, also, Walcott's early works valourize how the

---

[4] Walcott finds the artist's craft strongly analogous to daily labour of carpenter in his Crusoe poems.

[5] In this play the historic figures are counterpoised by the presence of a non- heroic group in which figures from Indian, Afro- Caribbean, Chinese and mulatto community- a miniature of Caribbean community.

average people continue to assert cultural freedom notwithstanding the crippling blows of history. Rather than fostering the spirit of anti- colonialism, they affirm the resistance to the structure of domination. In post-independence days, the Caribbean artists were resolved to explore new ways to inveigh the constraints and controls of colonial authority. The hardship of dismal poverty of his homeland and the brunt of racial injustice are poignantly described by Plunkett in *Omeros* as "[t] here's is too much poverty below us" (63). Their existential struggle was noble and affirmative and enabled their personhood: "to save the salt light of the island, to protect and exalt its small people" (*Another Life* 56). In order to exalt the "small people" and their earthy simplicities, Walcott sought to develop the Caribbean stage differently from the proscenium of Western drama, in a bare setting, unconventional spaces as theatre suffered acute dearth of enclosures. In a clear rejection of stylized performance of the tourism industry Walcott turned to the minimal stage arrangement in open, natural settings. Quite appositely, Breiner has described them as "poor theatre" in terms of material resources – stripped of lavish *mis- en- scene*, costumes or decorative establishment. The entire action of *The Sea at Dauphin* is set in the open, littered beach with bamboo poles and a canoe named *Our Daily Bread*. It is here that the actions start two hours before sunrise. Spanning from early dawn to sunset hour, the dramas of the life of fishermen take place in natural light. While in *Ti-Jean and His Brothers*, the action alternates between the hut and the wood; in these bare settings all the encounters take place between the brothers and the devil. Here, again the open, bare natural setting embodies the lives of stark necessities. Also, in *Malcochon or, The Six in the Rain* the action is set in "A disused copra house" on the edge of a bamboo forest. All these remind us of eminent Indian dramatist Badal Sircar's version of an unadorned performance, reduction of stage props, set, costumes and reliance on the movements of human body embodied in open-air performance.[6] Like Walcott, Sircar also fervently believed in the role and responsibility of the writer as the initiator of change and development in his own community. If the world around us is a world of constant change and irreducible diversity, it is no doubt, a world of becoming, also. Around 500 B.C. Heraclitus wrote "Everything flows and nothing abides; everything and nothing stays fixed"; in the late nineteenth century, Nietzsche developed the vision of a chaotic world in perpetual motion and change which undermined the notion of a fixed, sovereign

---

[6] Sircar was a populariser of street theatre or courtyard stage performance in upholding his egalitarian theatre. His stage environment was no doubt a path- breaking devise in Indian theatre.

subject.[7] The concept of 'becoming' in philosophy is connected with two: movement and evolution, as becoming assumes a "changing to" and a "moving toward". Becoming is the process or state of change and coming about in time and space. From the early days, Walcott's focus was on little places, the backwaters, a place like Dauphin which Afa finds heartlessly hostile.

For Walcott, the very adverse conditions to which they are born, the very parochiality of their lives proved to be an enabler of producing culturally vibrant forms. The earthy simplicities of life, the elemental conditions they wrestle with elicited Walcott's heart-felt admiration: "A woodcutter or charcoal burner. To me this figure represented the most isolated, the most reduced, race-containing symbol" (*Essays* 48). They merited an alternative stage/space, a theatrical language that "went beyond mimicry" and entail in the creole texture the oral practices of chants, jokes, folk-songs and fables (17). Naming the "New World", its landscape and people was a very strong artistic imperative for Walcott. "Faith in elemental man", rather than the splendour of ruins– was a quality that informed the artistic visions of New World Poets, like Neruda or Whitman. St. Lucian life in its regional rawness, cultural dispositions, folk customs, carnivals, local legends, story-telling had endowed upon his dramaturgic practice a new, creole significance.[8] By staging local lives, custom, local legends he issued a rejoinder to the charge of cultural mediocrity often levelled at the West-Indian subjects. The dramatic narrative and heightened language were apt for narrating the life of a "Haitian king" or "fisherman"; his theatrical idioms were capable of sharing the "torture" of articulation of these lives (*Essays* 17). With these tortured voices, ordinary heroes interrogate unequal power relationship and shake the very basis of ascriptive identities. The present chapter pays attention to how life can be made worthwhile and how the peasants or working-class characters exemplify "the process of self- discovery and self-renewal" (Dabydeen and Wilson-Tagoe 89). While living in the midst of adverse natural and social

---

[7] According to tradition, Heraclitus wrote a treatise about nature named "Περὶφύσεως" ("Perìphýseōs"), "On Nature", in which appears the famous aphorism πάντα ῥεῖ (*pantarhei*) translated literally as "the whole flows [as a river]", or figuratively as "everything flows, nothing stands still".

[8] "It is this awe of the numinous, this elemental privilege of naming the New World which annihilates history in our great poets ... They reject the ethnic ancestry for faith in the elemental man"- "The Muse of History", p. 40)

environment they embody what Schopenhauer calls "affirmation of will".[9] In *Omeros III*, Walcott avowed to celebrate the moral and spiritual strength of those who were discarded and erased by history:

> ... Look, they climb and no one knows them; they take their copper
> pittances and your duty
> From the time you watched them from your grandmother's house as a
> child wounded by their power and beauty
> is the chance you now have, to those feet a voice. (69-74)

The ordinary, earthy lives of coal-carrying women, revolving around the arduous toil, are emblematic of collective suffering which had preoccupied Walcott in *Another Life*. In the early plays, he has left behind the figures like Dessaline or Cristophe of the early plays- the commanding figures of grandeur, size and mania and gripping stories of their rise and fall. Rather his or "home-grown heroes" (Baugh 58), are lauded as "herladic men"; they displace the mythic "heroes" – as Edward Baugh describes: "A central motive in this endeavour was to address the apparent or supposed absence or dearth of home-grown heroes" (45).

To negotiate with this absence, Walcott, like Brecht, chooses ordinary, resilient and often non-conforming individuals as heroes who relentlessly interrogate the structures of domination. In Soyinka's early tragedies like *The Swamp Dwellers* (1959) or *Camwood on the Leaves* (1969), the youthful antagonists are overpowered by the structures of powers, the authoritative figures, an apparatus of oppressive regime. Modelled on folk-tale heroes or Anancy figures of cunning and wit, they impress as challengers to the dictatorship and tyranny – emerging from the deep, dark shadow of non-entity. Though his characters do not encounter the vices of the town life, Walcott's dispossessed inhabitants demonstrate moral and spiritual strength and their culture survives and thrives despite the traumatic wounds of Middle Passage. With youthful ardour gone for the slave-heroes, he reposed faith upon the deeply neglected figures as they demonstrate more affirmative personhood. From the earliest days of artistic career, Walcott's creative works, like that of Synge and Lorca sought to translate the language of the fishermen, peasants or ballad singers. In "What the Twilight Says" he states that bereft of History there were no heroes in the Caribbean and amidst daily life

---

[9] Schopenhauer, in his magnum opus *The World as Will and Representation*, stresses that the will, the aimless undercurrent of all things in nature that constantly strives for greater realization and prolongation of itself, reaches its highest form in the human being; in this form, the will finally is able to reflect upon its own essence and existence and thereby come to know itself.

experience of poverty, hunger and unemployment around, they sought to glorify racial "revenge" only. Determined not to idealise "poverty" or produce strident protest in the social forum of drama, Walcott took up the "theatre of daily lives" of the rural peasantry, the small drama and all its minutiae. When he undertook the production of "serious theatre" with Caribbean Theatre Workshop, Walcott attempted a trenchant critique against the White Lord, God, planter who devised the mechanism of oppression. In dismissing history, Walcott sought to dramatise "the history of emotion", which welled up through the cravings for elemental necessity. Both aesthetically and thematically, these narratives are rooted in indigenous material and cultural contexts. Always sceptic towards the meta-discourse of modernity, "history" and its "great actors" he reinstated the small narratives of struggle and survival which can interrogate the consensuality of political discourse or identity paradigms. If grand narratives promise knowledge secured on the basis of recorded or empirical reality, little narratives show how knowledge may be decentralized and localized within its restricted scope.

In the early plays, the performance is rooted in native traditions, or local ritual and superstition. By passionate engagement with true imaginative rendering of "local" and "folk" culture Walcott was resisting the neo-colonial appropriation of them: "The folk arts have become the symbol of a carefree, accommodating culture, an adjunct to tourism, since the State is impatient with anything which it cannot trade" (*Essays* 7). Walcott was relentless in his strictures against the effects of neo-colonialist and imperial practices; he scathingly repudiated the practice of adding ethnic flair to some indigenous cultural traditions for the consumption of the nations of North. His was the challenge to what Naipaul had lamented in *Middle Passage* as the failure of West-Indian writers to articulate his own place and position. In an atmosphere of cultural degradation. Walcott was keen to share the Brechtian view of man as determined by social and material forces but not overdetermined by them. Walcott's famous contemporary, Errol Hill's dramas articulated lower class West-Indian oral tradition, street communities and street festivals in the early sixties. The essential motivation may be summed up in the words of Benitez Rojo: "In the Caribbean, we are all performers [...] we try to act the roles our skin reads to us" (236).

Ti- Jean and His Brothers

> "The print of hunger wanders in the land.
> The green tree bends above the long forgotten.
> The plains of life rise up and fall in spasms.
> The huts of men are fused in misery"
>
> *University of Hunger.* Martin Carter

The gloom and despair of poverty could not thwart Walcott's literary ambitions; his plays and poems were preoccupied with the poverty-ridden conditions of average Caribbean life. The narrative of his early plays is premised upon a simple allegorical structure of colonial binary - the unmitigated antagonism between "white rulers" and "black natives". By foregrounding a native style, a medley of story-telling, song and dance, Walcott espouses a new theatrical style. *Ti-Jean and His Brothers*, written in the extremely prolific decade of the fifties, thematizes the transformation of life under the colonial lordship and reclaiming of dignity in the midst of adverse material conditions.

One major thematic focus of the plays is social/racial inequality in the human and the non-human world under plantation system and experience of subjection and brutality that permeated the colonial society. A family that ekes out by collecting woods from the forest is exposed to the harshness and severity of the elemental conditions. Legend and fable emerge as a narrative framework to demonstrate the restorative unity of Man, Nature and Animal and issues a glimpse of the new vision of humanity. Stripped of the basic sustenance they wrestle with the formidable enmity of the plantation lord. Read from the perspective of Mother, the story affirms power over oneself than power over others, which underlies the asymmetry of race and gender. The plot is constantly marked by tension between the material and spiritual claim to supremacy. Towards the end, it is the figure of Bolom, a disfigured fetus who celebrates his birth towards the end:

> "I am born, I shall die! O the wonder and pride of it! I shall be a man!"
>
> (17-19, 164)

> The quality of compassion, the ability to feel human emotion can also redeem the devil and help him achieve humanity as he listens to Ti-Jean's singing, inspired by the death of his mother (21-23, 162-163).

Long after it was written, *Ti-jean* was described by the playwright himself as his "most-West-Indian play".[10] Walcott must have meant it to be distinctively and recognizably West- Indian in form and content. Set in motion by the bird-beast narrator, the plot plunges us into harsh actualities of the lives of the West-Indians, the "naked, voluble poverty" that surrounded Walcott's own childhood experience. When the Bird asks "How poor their mother was?" the Frog describes their nest as unprotected where four members live in a bare

---

[10] In an article for the *Trinidad Guardian* in 1970, Walcott recalled, as the editorial note put it, "how he created what he calls his 'most West Indian play,' and the source of its creation Walcott, "Derek's 'Most West Indian Play,'" 7.

condition and eke out their living, collecting from the wood and sustaining (13-25, 288).

A four-member family in a hut, they struggled with extreme hardship and natural adversities. The everyday experience of impoverished life is an important thread that weaves these small plays. Exposed to severe cold and rain, the mother or the old woman struggles hard to fend off hunger and save the family from starvation. She is left with meager hope to alleviate the melancholic life; in the dialogue of Frog and Cricket, her plight is foregrounded in stark, vivid details. While inside the hut, the homely conversation of mother and three sons, also, centres around the regular experience of hunger, starvation.

In the beginning, Gros, the elder brother returns without procuring wood from the forest, as they were dampened by the weather. And Mi-Jean also returns empty-handed from the fishing venture. This "starving" condition and struggling are attributed by the mother to the planter's exploitative system; a stark contrast is outlined between the plantation labour and estate owners; the starvation of inmates of the hut is pitted against the planter's rich ways of life.

This grim picture suggests how serious inequality has created a wide rift by the plantation economy. The cricket describes her little house on the brow of the mountains where it was so cold that it would not only make the frog stop singing, but all the creatures stopped acting and behaving normally. As the Frog narrator tells us, their hardship is exacerbated by the presence of the Devil living in close vicinity of the mountainside. Their life is perpetually tormented and insecure as the Devil uses to appear in a different guise as emissary of death. He claims to be the owner of half the world and the seat of evil, intrigue and destruction. And Bolom, also, introduces him as the prince of the "kingdom of night".

The estate of the planter is a symbolic antinomy to Mother's hut which exudes love and warmth. As Gros Jean walked up through the bush, he encountered a large field. Estate-like, a big white house where the devil lives (109). He accuses the planter as "big, white man" (109), cold and inhuman who coerce the black slave to most gruelling toil. Like his mother, he has portrayed the planter devil as the possessor of land, house, all the riches and as the supreme authority over the labouring blacks. Resentful, he notices how the black people are deprived of rest and in the canefield workers are over-exploited mercilessly (7-8, 148).

The overt binary structure of black/white, man/devil and their confrontation is often said to have been a literary analogue of the slave revolt. On the moral plane the three encounters, here, embody the shortcomings of brute power or bookish knowledge and also underline the triumph of practical wisdom and earthy common sense. Gros Jean feels slighted to be considered a "common man" and asserts that he can prove to be powerful and reminds him "all could be mine". It attests to adversarial or oppositional politics which professed the blacks to be in the first place as equal of white. In the course of verbal duel, the Planter continues to call him by names like Mac, Jo, Gross Chien, Horace, Hubert, Benton and Francis, despite his repeated reminder of his original name. This violence of naming is central to the mechanism of colonial authority. Kamau Brathwaite states in his essay "World Order Models" that the erasure of name works as a metonym for crossed-out identity. The Caribbean islands were named after the name of the Christian saints like St. Martin, St. Lucia and St. Vincent as their native names were cast out. Violence, fraud and erasure of the name were the signs of imperialist pedagogy which Bhabha calls "the right to signify" through "the power of naming".[11] Paul Breslin in his nuanced analysis, has read the play as the story of successive attempts to respond to colonial oppression. The first contender of the Devil is the eldest brother, Gros-Jean, who is over-confident about his "arm of irons" and is subject to more oppressive toil dictated by the planter. Mi-Jean follows him and as he is a proud intellectual, in his oratorial passion, he has shown signs of identification with white culture. He has no respect for the native animals and birds. Like all mimic man, he continues to beat the masters at their own game with the self-awareness to assert the "difference". In this allegorical tale of the brother-devil encounter, sheer physical strength or intellectual ability– both have proved too inadequate responses amounting to empty blast only.

The last challenger of the White Planter is the youngest of brothers, Ti-Jean who immediately strikes with a humble and courteous gesture. His name Ti-Jean is symbolic of a West- Indian little man, ordinary but rich in practical wisdom. As he leaves behind the hut, unlike others, he listens attentively to his mother and also asks for his blessing. He is befriended by animals and birds. While his brother Gros set out by kicking away the frog as a slimy bastard (104). He refuses to laugh at the base voice of the frog. And the Frog assures him to help in the hour of need. When he meets the Devil disguised as Old Man, he vaunts that what counts in this world is money and power, expressive of a quintessential ethos of every colonial venture and global market economy. It is a strident claim for the mechanism of material exploitation. Ti-Jean is empowered with common and native wit and he does count on them only to overcome temptation. But capitalistic proclamation, exploitation of nature and environment are triumphed over by the rapport of

---

[11] Bhabha offers a brilliant analysis Walcott's poem *Naming* to contend that the pedagogical process of imperial naming was an effective cultural strategy to possess the Caribbean islands (331-37).

Ti-Jean with the bird and beast; they recreate the vision of the ordered universe. As Albert Ashalou observes, "Fully equipped with his mother's advice and blessings, the knowledge acquired from the smaller animals, his humility and natural instincts, and an invincible determination, he successfully beats the devil in his own game, outwitting him at every point" (*Critical Perspective* 123). The recognition of the ties between the beast, man and birds has always claimed attention to the cultural reality of the Caribbean lives.

Ti-Jean is much more sensitive to the call of the beasts and birds as friends and seeks their help to reach the estate of the old man. Contrasted to him, the Devil curses all "fish, flesh and fowl". When Ti-Jean eventually wins the battle, it attests to the victory of qualities like pity and fellow-feeling; it is very much antithetical to the dehumanizing proclamation of the Devil at the beginning to give him a child for the dinner (89). It is his song that finally moves the Devil to tears. Edward Baugh observes: "Ti-Jean enacts the humanity and personhood of the Caribbean subject in the response to the tradition of discourse that would deny him or her those attributes" (77). No longer a messenger of the Devil figure, when Bolom appears as a newborn child, it symbolizes the emancipation of the slaves from the iron-clutches of the devil. Its coming into life is suggestive of emerging West Indian consciousness - to get rid of the yoke of subjugation. A miscegenated offspring, an embodiment of white male's response to the allure of exotic sexuality is described as "child of the Devil" (94). A recurrent figure of the West-Indian folklore, this unborn fetus living in the corner or near the bed usually harm at the command of its master. Possessing the folk values in abundant measure or guided by instinct, he outwits and humbles the Devil. Greed and exploitation will be replaced by native and liberatory stratagem capable of ushering "green beginning". Such celebratory and highly affirmative moments can be said to effect transmutation of consciousness in which the essentialised categories of identity look to be worn-out. The triumph of the little man is ensured with "the advice of his aged mother (experience) and of lowly animals (instinct) from whom he learns to respect nature and to use his wits" (Hamner 47). Native wit, compassion, earthy common sense can overturn the politics of domination and expansionism. In such figure, the West- Indian man "possesses the possibility of complex and integrated self which is his by virtue of his experience" (285). True to his name, Ti- Jean's victorious feat becomes "little man's triumph over the power groups in society and h e proves to be "fool like all heroes". Regenerating the myth of native heroism, the play proves to be "an allegory of the dispossessed of the Caribbean peasantry's fight for survival under colonialism and gradual movement towards the independent consciousness represented by Ti-Jean's stance" (Thieme 60). Through vibrant and colourful performative strategies, punctuated with song and music, it humanises the ruthless Devil.

Most of the critical readings of this play have shed little light on the figure of the Mother, so far, casting it as a morality play – a narrative of the encounter between three young black sons and the white planter. But she deserves comments as a strong presence, a blend of frailty and staunchness beside all male figures; she is far from a stereotype in Walcott's overwhelmingly male art world. Feminist critics like Elaine Savory in an article entitled "Value Judgements on Art and the question of Macho Attitudes: The Case of Derek Walcott" takes Walcott to task for his clichéd, stereo-typed and negative portrayal of women. She notes that Walcott's women are shorn of individuality, playing an auxiliary part only to the male-centred drama. She contends that as passive creatures, they await male appreciation and with their condescending roles, they help re-enforce the male hegemony. Much later, Patricia Ismond, in a kind of rejoinder in "Woman as Race-containing Symbol in Walcott's Poetry", argues that in the work of the late 70s, Walcott began to cast women in a more positive light and in a more active role. But here much earlier in this play of 1959, appears the figure of Mother whose home-bound persona speaks in a dignified voice. She is the perpetuator of myths and stories and communicator of feelings. African and Caribbean literature celebrates mother figures, those who nurture, protect and also possess secret knowledge. Catherine Obianuju Acholonu argues that the mother is at the spiritual heart of the African family with the abiding power of love, tolerance and service. The spirit of motherhood, here, prevails over male antagonism; her motherly part is a symbolic counterpoint to the lust and greed of the devil. In the absence of her husband, the mother epitomizes authority and dignity; she is the centre of the mother-headed family. They carry well as a family unit and interact with each other to hold out against the threatening surrounding. For her, home is an extremely vulnerable place, far removed from the place of safe, secure living. She can hardly be read as a victim figure; her instructive role in posing a spirited challenge to the Devil as they face him in succession compel our attention. Like the heroine of Armaha's *The Beautyful Ones are Not yet Born*, she is the "symbol of patient suffering". Though a victim of plantation society, she is without any victim complexity. In this play, the Frog and Cricket introduce her as the centre - a widow dwelling insecurely in the mountain side and finding her existence embattled. Denied of minimum subsistence, she stands out as a composed figure - rock-solid in defence against the threatening devil. To quote Patricia Ismond, "Walcott here extends into the plight of women at the extreme pit of disadvantage and degradation in the society to project the image of woman as its arch-victims and underdogs" ("Theatre" 9). When her sons get locked in an argument, she interferes. She keeps up the hope that "God will send us something" (92) against the irreverent attitude of her sons. It is she who senses the Devil's approach, crying out "Death is coming nearer" (94). When

Bolom accuses one mother of the deformed condition, she consoles her with the words of wisdom:

> "Look, perhaps it is luckiest
> Never to be born,...
>
> (1-4, 96)
>
> it resonates with the line of Sophocles:
> "Never to have been born is best".

The Greek God Silenius taught that life is not worth living. It is the extreme standpoint of pessimistic outlook that stresses the futility and pointlessness of human existence. Voltaire even believed life to be a bad joke, not preferable to nothingness. Schopenhauer never ceased to stress that suffering is not only inevitable in fact, an essence of life.[12] She clearly understands that elimination of poverty and misery in this world is impossible and therefore it is better to wish not to have been born at all. To be born is to experience decay, decrepitude, disease and eventually death. In spelling out this ultimate futility of human existence she does not appear to be a starkly a "nay-saying" character who must negate all values of life.

Guided by experience, age and wisdom, she corroborates an independent role in the male-dominated world of drama. In his *In The Castle of My Skin* Lamming also emphasizes on the role of the mother in maintaining paternal authority in the absence of the father at home.[13] In Walcott's *magnum opus*, *Omeros*, Ma Kilman embodies an organic connection with natural life-science, as a human personification of the very landscape. She is the fostering mother and provider of the herbal magic potion to the festering ankles of Achille. Like her, the Mother of Ti-Jean, is moulded by her native soil and her earthy wisdom. She is, to quote Patricia Ismond, "embodiment of a regenerative, nurturing landscape" ("Theatre" 84). She is not beaten down by the loss and worries but makes a fine adoptability as she tells Gros Jean, "Woman life is so. Watching and Losing"; but it does not confirm her as a defeatist (102). Over the years, she has maintained the grace and dignity of maintaining family values. Love is her very forte against the fear and terror

---

[12] In *On the Suffering of the World*, Arthur Schopenhaeur allows himself to pose the question regarding the fate of the human species, the role of suffering in the world and the rift between the self and the world that increasingly has come to define the human existence.

[13] Father-absence is a major concern of this novel. This void is filled by the mother who is a stern, ambitious, tenacious figure in full command of her family.

that surrounds her hut as Bolom sums up, keeps it warm from the cold wind and rain (14-16, 98).

Despite her ill-fate, she is not a mere withdrawn, self-effacing figure. Rather she represents the West-Indian solidarity with the earth as the coal carrying women of *Another Life*, carrying loads down its "hemophilic hills". In a life plagued by appalling poverty and undiminished suffering, her loving, protective care and earthy common sense resist the greed, violence and exploitative stratagems of the Devil. Ti-Jean is for her "last of my chickens" (6, 132) as after the loss of two sons her fate is on tenterhooks. But it is Ti-Jean who reminds her how she taught them to be strong in adversity and be in love of god. She does not only pray for the safety of Ti-Jean but wishes "let him die as a man" (10, 158) The way she maintains her dignity marks her out as formidable, iron-willed mother figure. In the course of action, her role appears affirmative and instructive as her sons set out to encounter the devil. She reminds Gros to praise God and seek the help of bird and insects. Eminent French thinker, Helene Cixous consistently upholds the view that women inhabit a pre-civilizational world which is closer to the pulse of nature and the rhythm of sensuality. She has staked a claim for true female identity by linking women's position with that of people outside Western culture. Moreover, the mother warns her sons about the various impersonations of the Devil by which it beguiles its opponents. And Ti-Jean profits from her practical suggestions on his way to confront the devil. Thus, she manages to overcome the inhibiting conditions of self-realization. As the simple tale of tortoise and birds is the paradigm for the rise and fall of Okonkwo in *Things Fall Apart*, the legend of devil and three sons and Bolom, here, bears out the force of Anancy myth in Walcott's most West Indian play *Ti-Jean*. Like other plays about St. Lucian people, here, too, Walcott has explored how such marginal lives were rich in practical wisdom.

Malcochon or Six in the Rain

> "I am morality itself, and nothing beside is morality"
>
> -Nietzsche: *Beyond good and Evil*, 202

> "Thus nobody up to now has examined the value of that famous of all medicines which is called morality; and the first step would be—for once to question it. Well then is precisely is our task"
>
> -*Gay Science*, 345

> "Under what conditions did man devise these value judgements good and evil? And what value do they themselves possess? Have they

hindered or furthered human prosperity? Are they a sign of distress of imperialism, or the degeneration of life? Or is there revealed in them, on the contrary, the plentitude, force and will of life, its courage, certainty and future."

(*Genealogy of Morals*. Preface, 3)

In *Malcochon or Six in the Rain*, the plot swivels around conflicting interpretations of sin and crime borne out by the murder of Regis, the planter and the violent end of Chantal, the protagonist. Most of the scholars of the play have stressed the overt influence of Akira Kurosawa's classic *Rashomon*; its bare setting in a forest and the "unaccommodated" lives had inspired Walcott's. This section will focus on how Walcott's treatment of the murder episodes here unsettles the moral considerations as determinative and how the contrasted views and belief systems suspend the finality of judgment. The framework of Nietzsche will help us understand more clearly the issue of moral relativism as it might be described as a process of "revaluation of all values" and "self-overcoming of morality", Moreover, my reading finds how the life of instinct, drive and energy in the illiterate communities is foregrounded to destabilize the commonplace notions of "truth", "value", "savage", "civilized".

Morality as "an everyday cultural phenomenon" (Leiter 252) guides our conduct in a very systematized and codified way. And these conducts of daily lives are binarized in moral terms which have become entrenched in our value systems, like "good" and "evil", "savage" and "civilized", 'saved" and "fallen". A passionate philosopher of skepticism and scathing critic of Christian morality, Nietzsche, in the second half of the nineteenth century, sought to free human beings from the clutches of normative systems and their propagation of universal moral codes and moral hierarchy. Moral values, as Nietzsche argued, are thoroughly self-interested and are binding only on those whom they promise to provide some relief from the sufferings of life. According to him, morality is a menacing system, a "danger of dangers". *On the Genealogy of Morals*, he strongly argued that a process of moralization has traditionally upheld the foundational concepts like "good" and "evil" in order to motivate people into herd-like quiescence. He also observed that the evaluative distinction between good and evil originated within the noble class or society- that is, among those who enjoyed greatest privileges. Morality, as Nietzsche firmly believed, poses obstacles to human flourish. He urged modern Europeans to re-evaluate the origin of all ethical belief at a time when the morality of the herd had become only morality and began to prevail over all other forms. This herd morality inhibits the drives and desires and turns one into an ethically dependent person. As Nietzsche maintains in *Beyond*

Good and Evil "there is a hierarchy between human and human and therefore between morality and morality as well" (186). Since morality is incorporated into our basic ways of thinking, feeling and living, Nietzsche urged a revision of this scenario. As Leiter puts it, "Morality, Nietzsche holds, is a surface phenomenon that requires a meta level of interpretation in accordance with a different, superior set of extra-moral values 'beyond good and evil'" (18). This narrative of crime, justice and punishment expresses reactive and relativistic views to understand truth and value and offers an alternative perspective to a murder story. The plot of his early masterpiece, *Malcochon,* unfolds a process of inquiry into the reality of a murder and gradually unsettles the popular legend of Chantal's inhumanity. In so doing, it not only asks for thoughtful scrutiny of fixed moral values or moral categories like "savage"/"civilized", man/beast but prods the readers, also, to scrutinise the need for "revaluation of values" (*umwerthungaller Werthe*).

At the centre of Walcott's expansive artistic imagination lay his inexhaustible attachment to his own earth and history. The Caribbean Sea and its wild landscape strengthened his spiritual connection with the people and added order and harmony to his creative vision. The provincial St. Lucian life fed and nurtured his artistic imagination and also afforded him the scope to probe into the community, society, and the issues like humanity and morality and God. It is from the marginal, wretched lives and earthy vulgarity that Walcott articulated the "native" spirit in rejoinder to the Western version of heroism. These "unaccommodated" lives were reconfigured with the colour of his artistic vision. Walcott's early 'home-grown' heroes are "obscure" and insignificant but fascinate with non-conformity and fearless expression.[14] Ostracized, these heroes inhabit an extra-moral space; without yielding to misfortune, they struggle to overcome the surrounding and stand out "from the crowd, the many, the great majority" (*Beyond Good and Evil* 26). Friendship or affection is unknown to them. Used to acts of violence and cruelty, they stand at the farthest remove from the image of a "moral man" because moral considerations override all competing considerations. Their plight underscores the experience of living in a world devoid of religious and metaphysical certainties. The experiences of subjugation, crime, brutality, dire poverty fail to thwart their survival instinct. By giving vent to energy and drive and instinct, Walcott's early heroes spurn ethical doctrine and wilfully

---

[14] In their scholarly studies on Walcott's early heroes John Thieme and Edward Baugh have stressed them as solitary figure and how in the narratives their personhood and subjecthood are asserted despite all material hardships. The stories of the lives have also mounted challenge to the conventional moralizing and affirm a process of self-fashioning subjecthood are asserted despite material hardships. The stories of the lives shed also mount challenge on the conventional moralizing and affirm a process of self-fashioning.

affirm their independence from external constraints. They refuse to follow what Nietzsche has called "weak and slavish" morality. The burden of traditional law and custom fail to prevent them from their resolved course of action consistent with their ethics of "self- making". These heroes' clamour for *ipse*, the self that gives itself its own law and can be the sovereign of it by subverting established communal laws. The moral tradition may condemn their actions and behaviours as repugnant, but the narratives smash the cherished assessment to bits, holding up guilt, conscience as well as justice to question. The plot attempts to understand the outmoded moral parameters, which attempt to understand the action and passes judgment. They exhibit a spirit because the misery of experience cannot be mitigated by blind striving or withdrawing from the ordeals. Their ethical imperative is to realize the self to its fullest potential and by so doing, articulate the "affirmation of will". *Malcochon or Six in the Rain* initiates a process of "re-evaluation" and cancels out reactive morality of "good" and "evil". Unsettling the conventional moral assumptions through an act of murder, it prompts us to take, what Nietzsche describes in *Rebaptizing Our Evil*, "fresh look at actions that have traditionally been dismissed as whole categories and assessing them in the context of particular situations" (410). Nietzsche castigated herd morality as it proffered moral dictum to proscribe the instinctual energy of individual and desires. Here the disempowered group undermines the hold of life-denying morality.[15]

In the story of a maligned wood-cutter, Chantal, the question of external constraints and conventional moralities are called into question. It problematizes the presupposition of value and easy division between "man" and "beast". Like its cinematic intertext, Rashomon, this play sets out to investigate the nature of truth and justice. It proffers a life beyond the established ideals and fixed moral dichotomies of "good" and "evil". Chantal is a defiant opposer to the inflexible moral laws; instead of parasitic dependence on the traditional value system, his actions re-examine the moral binaries like "good" and "evil" or "slayer" and "victim". Like Afa and Makak, he leads a solitary life without family; inhabiting a pre-socialized realm, he mounts challenge to the custom and its ethos. Like them, he's bitter and scornful against the institution of judiciary and religion; his responses are not merely reactive responses of a helpless victim in the face of repressive power. Against all stigmatizing, he asserts the will force in a way that all assumptions about his "social identity" demand urgent revision. Instead of seeking comfort and contentment, he plunged into saving the deaf and mute Moumou from the

---

[15] In all his major works, Nietzsche has advocated moral skepticism and urged to "re evaluate" our cherished values. He bemoaned how the Christian indoctrination of slave morality has undermined the life of instinct and passion of the heathen Greeks.

fatal blow of the ruthless planter. Demonized as the "tigre", "beast", Chantal is an animalized solitary with an association with petty theft and murder of Regis, the planter. In the world of jungles, the threats posed by the animality are inseparable from the "dangers posed by the hidden native" (Punter 145).[16] Colonial narratives abound in such fantasies of connection between natives and their "assignation to the animal" (145), their recourse to violence. Chantal, as Theodre Colson describes, "is a perpetual fugitive, with a reputation of violence and crime, a man whose name has been used to frighten the children" (128). Like them, he pours out scorn against all forms of authority- divine or secular. As a recluse, their perspective and experience of the social world collide with dominant ideology or normative authority; he is averse to the domineering structure of social institutions. The society built on Christian ethics and political ideologies seeks to produce a dull, non-conformist society. But in Afa's Dauphin or Chantal's forest life, the mechanism of oppression and injustice face an audacious challenge: "But blessed are they that hungry for righteousness' sake…" (176). Such communities suffer unmitigated deprivation, oppression and violence in their daily life. But Walcott's narrative is not a recounting of victimology; condemned to live without prestige, honour, and wealth, Chantal lashes out at those who are at the helm of power. Chantal's self-introduction stamps him as an offender, a violent challenger of the law and system of justice which is somewhat akin to Makak's smashing of the café and taken to jail (13-16, 172).

To recognize 'evil' in oneself is a long-standing practice in the Christian tradition. Nietzsche reminded us that violence and cruelty "condemned as uncharitable and unchristian", are also part of a broader economy of life in producing "a higher type of man" (*Genealogy* 94). Murder and cruelty are acts which the moral traditions reserve to downright moral condemnation. In the conventional system of justice when someone breaks the law or makes violent transgression, the society can exact punishment. By adaptation of the anti-natural morality, Nietzsche knew, all individuals were to be forced into mediocrity or a "herd man". Herd morality finds comfort in mediocrity and instructs adherence to certain abstract and absolute values which Nietzsche famously argues in *The Birth of Tragedy*. The characters who meet fortuitously at the copra house to find outcast Chantal are fundamentally weak and mediocre and have fixed assumptions regarding "truth" and "false". Their perspective on reality is found to be universally and objectively true. Against

---

[16] In a chapter titled "Becoming Animal, Becoming Woman", Punter argues how the colonial narratives foreground the threats posed by animals is equivalent to the "dangers posed by the natives". Such narratives abound in fantasy images of bestiality and natives.

this soul-killing "herd morality" or moral world view, Nietzsche upheld unimpeded expression of instinct and energy, especially in the pre-Christian Greeks, men who actualized themselves by adopting what Christianity forbids. Because as an ideology, Christian morality "encourages a belief in the repression of the instinct, and thwarts creative energies" (Robinson 27).

As the legend has it, Chantal is an outlawed and demonic figure- "historically discredited Caribbean person, the floatsam of history, historyless" (Baugh 73). The Nephew recalls the scandal that surrounded Chantal as a woodcutter and madman of the forest who would terrify little children (1-2, 181). He is described variously by those who proclaim them to be sane and civilized as "madman", "enemy of god", "Tarzan of the apes", "Tiger of the Forest" (195). In the course of the plot, Chantal's popular identification in stories and folk tales — all the common appellations are subjected to intense scrutiny. The meeting in the disused house in profuse rain and the chance meeting with Chantal climaxes in a startling revelation of the murderer of Regis the planter. The process of *moralization* challenges the inseparable association of violence and cruelty with the image of an immoral man; Chantal by common consensus is an ostracized, scandalized figure. As the plot begins to unfold, it confutes the cherished values of "truth", "justice" and their eternal validity; through a chance meeting the figures from mainstream society reveal in moral censure and disapprobation. Instead of upholding truth as the highest standard, Nietzsche urged the individuals to develop their own power of judgment and produce ideas and ethics that will strengthen and help them live. Far from being immutable, moral values are a historical product, contingent creations of particular group of people; they are designed to serve the power and coerce every individual of the community. As suggested by Walcott's use of Sophoclean epigraph, the plot of Malcochon sets out to mount disquieting challenges to the normative belief systems:

"Who is the slayer, who
the victim? Speak!"

Nietzsche also contended our every act to be finally "unknowable". Intention and consequence are not an absolute determinant of any action to be "good" or "evil". He contended that which is conventionally regarded as good and evil in fact are relative rather than discrete categories. Finding the ethical implication analogous to the final part of the Greek tragedy, Thieme observes, "there is a movement beyond a cycle of crime and punishment, as Kurosawa's moral relativism".[17] The intention of two murders— one that of the Planter that took place before the start of the action and one that takes place at the end and murder of Chantal are acts of saving rather than brutal aggression. Since both the acts were directed towards protection, they unsettle the "slayer"-"victim" dualism. Nietzsche claims, "an action is in itself perfectly devoid of value: it all depends on who performs it. One and the same crime can be in one the greatest privilege, in another a stigma" (338). The Conteur who introduces the play seems to present us with the widely popular folk tale or local legend of the murder of Regis, the white planter by Chantal, the brute and also asks not to believe every word they heard or read (6-8, 171).

Violence and cruelty are always deemed as uncharitable and unchristian and they govern our moral assumption to indict the perpetrators of this act. When Conteur, the traditional West-Indian story-teller appears it is not without a grain of doubt. Truth and values are man-made and more often than not, they are absolutist in their claim. And human beings ever create truths for themselves that are useful and help them survive as species.

Chantal is a degraded wood-cutter and like Makak condemned for being unruly and outlawed; indulging in petty theft or larceny, he appears to be the threatening "other" of civil society. Even bearing the stigmata, he can demonstrate positive force of will and strength. He is maligned to have been monstrous, uncanny and ferocious and when he passed through the village he was jeered and chased by roaring children: "Tigre, tigre chou brule; tigre, tigre chou brule" (177). Though some of his utterances are overtly hostile and hateful against the power structure of the society, they are underlined by extreme dismal material conditions which drives him to petty theft (28-30, 176).

Chantal's instinctive and passionate ways defy every restrictive measure against his drives. In *The Sea at Dauphin*, Afa appears for the most part as a confirmed cynic, having found no possibility of organizing life around some ultimate purpose like 'God' or social justice'.[18] In the Nietzschean sense, Chantal actualizes himself in ways that the 'herd morality' of Christianity forbids. Christian ethics or political ideologies seek to produce a dull, conformist society; seeking to enforce harsh punishment and discipline for non-adherents. In the dying minutes, Chantal refuses to be comforted by the priest or his mediation before his final journey (7-8, 204). He will die with the peace of soul inside the forest, rather than leaving it. The vision of "home" in

---

[17] John Thieme in the third chapter of his monograph titled "Founding a West Indian Theatre", touches upon the issues of moral relativism that informs the ending of many Greek tragedies.

[18] For his vituperative reaction against "God" and purveyor of traditional religion like priest Walcottian unlettered hero throws challenge at the spiritual authority.

the Monkey Mountain awaiting to greet Makak is anticipated in Chantal's wish in the dying minutes. Though an anti-social solitary, he finds to his heart's content a glimpse of nature's beauty before his death. Finding final peace to be laid in the forest, he mutters how the sun light shines upon the wet leaves, the abiding beauty of the forest holds him in thrall to the end (6-8, 205). For the downtrodden West-Indians, forest or Mountain is the locus of final rest, an alternative home which is more spiritual than physical. Displaced and rootless, the West Indian man finds alternative 'home' with an affirmative zeal. As Artaud's "theatre of cruelty" forces the spectator to confront the harsh facts of a cruel world and his or her isolation, Walcott's heroes, also, travel back to their solitary dwelling after a brief encounter with the world outside. Artaud believed that civilizations had turned humans into a sick and repressed creature and the true function of these theatres was to redeem the humankind of these repressions and liberate each individual from repressed instinctual energy. Eugene O'Neill's hero, Yank, in *Hairy Ape*, victimized by a process of dehumanization, has been interpellated as "ape" and led up to the zoo having failed to cope with the technological, modern society. At that state, he is a man free of class or clan and has some kinship with some primitive relatives only. And in losing contact with nature, he has deviated from simplicity and natural goodness. In the Caribbean islands, the pariahs like Makak or Chantal explore the contradictions and hypocrisies of bourgeois society and give free rein to the "primitive" impulses. And they also confront the received identarian categories like "savage", "cruel". Like in life, in death also, Chantal is left alone, discarded and cast 'outside' the pale of society.

Like the earlier play *Ti-Jean and His Brothers*, here, all the characters are afflicted with poverty and hunger and they are victims of the material exploitation. The nephew, soon after his appearance, bitterly describes his own condition as "hungry like hell". Chantal has spent three weeks in the forest, eating bird, small animal and green plantain (176). Now assembled inside a copra house they face a harsh spell of storm and rain making it intolerable particularly for the old people. They discuss how the experience of poverty, one of the damaging legacies of the plantation economy has afflicted them. As the Nephew sings:

> "One, two, three, the white men have plenty,
> When thunder roll is a nigger belly empty" (14-16, 173).

The contrast of white man and nigger underscores how the question of race is implicated in the formation of the class. By all moral considerations, Chantal is a notoriously "bad" man; "As a bad man, one belongs to the 'bad', to a mass of object, powerless men who have no communal feeling" (Nietzsche 47). By opting for a self-chosen course of life, by defying the shared values of society,

Chantal is the maligned "other"; all other characters find him to be a potential threat. Though verdicts were passed upon him even before the beginning of the action, he assumes the role of a judge in a play-within-the-play before whom the errant wife and the old man confess their past. The six characters that have assembled in the forest shed are to face moral judgment beyond the societal legalities. As the old man enunciates his view that in the middle of a forest, men may meet and encounter the darkness of sins which becomes a soul-searching experience (1-3, 180).

All those who have assembled in the copra, seeking shelter from rain and storm- nephew, uncle, husband and wife get locked in bitter acrimony. They openly accuse each other and bring a charge of infidelity. Such serious moral issues are cross-examined by Chantal who calls himself the "other" of law; he finds that they fail to face up to the "truth". It is he who uncovers the hypocrisy of other law-abiding, good citizens and their sinful behaviors are exposed to his judgemental gaze. This role-playing contravenes the normative codes underpinned by ethical ideology. Julia Davis, in her study on folk plays, makes a very important observation, seldom noticed by early critics and scholars; "the reality is that Chantal disturbs the value of western culture, by stripping the veil off the other 'good' citizens. He stands morally above the searchers of truth... he is the symbol of the superior moral values of the truly honest self-accepting man" (64).[19] Thus, the plot charts Chantal's internalization of a new evaluative scheme to confront dominant ethics. Himself an object of condemnation, the "old stinking tiger" (197), Chantal arranges a mock trial and assuming the role of a judge manages to elicit the truth long hidden in the past; he asks all to kneel down and face the trial in the forest, thus collapsing the binary of the judge and criminal. Walcott's wood-cutter hero is an outright challenger to all moral dichotomies (2-4, 196).

No sooner the trial begins, the nephew and the husband start to panic and tremble. In the brief trial episode, in course of a battle of arguments "truth" recurs no less than six times and "lies" no less than three times. Madeline, threatened with a cutlass, confesses her adultery. Charlemagne also let it out how he has committed adultery with his brother's wife and resultantly, he incurs the wrath of the boy. In the mock trial, he's managed to extract a truth which ends in an acquittal of those who lived in the mainstream society. This self-reflexive technique effectively interrogates the credentials of a judiciary process.

The intention of his crime hardly discussed is left suspended till the plot reaches its climax. The vortex of the action - the murder of Regis, the planter

---

[19] In her discussion of folk plays Julia Davies points out how these early plays disrupt the conventional binary like action/intention, Slayer/Victim and their hiearchization.

and the motif reveal what runs counter to public knowledge. "Sometimes, instances of behavior and attitudes deemed 'evil' by the moral tradition are better understood as symptoms of vitality instead" (Higgins 410). It was carried out to save the deaf-mute Moumou who stole the silver spoon from the brutal white planter. Conventional morality too easily condemns the act of murder; if the violent act were motivated by a spiteful and resentful will, then the violent act is contemptible, but if it were motivated by a healthy will, then the violent act is possible. Here both the murders are acts of saving rather than aggression; they do not elicit our moral disapproval or condemnation. Nietzsche denied that he wants to recharacterize categories of action hitherto deemed "evil" as desirable across the board. Before all are given a hearing, or any indictment is passed, Moumou plunges the knife all of a sudden on the back of Chantal. He misread the intention of Chantal and posed to be the savior for all those who were present there. Thus, the intention and action are found to be at odds which obstructs moral judgment. It is Chantal who aptly expresses it: "You see how a man can have good meaning and do the wrong thing?" (202). In *Beyond Good and Evil*, Nietzsche contended what we think of as the conscious intention behind a moral act may be examined further. The final judgment is suspended to the end as Chantal's final utterance echoes the Sophoclean epigraph in his dying moments: "Who is the murderer, who the dead, eh, tell me...what use the truth is?" (13-14, 203). At the tragic climax with the death of Chantal, the slayer-victim opposition completely blurs; he is killed by Moumou whose life he himself had saved by killing Regis. But the mute and deaf, Maumou plunges the knife to in a hasty, unthinking elimination of Chantal. Here again, a rupture takes place between a positive intention and action, which leaves us undecided about the categories like right/wrong. What is sometimes taken as a morally repulsive act has some ambiguity about it, too. The commonplace understanding of truth, grounded upon a moral ideal, the absolutist notion of "right" and "wrong", was castigated by Nietzsche: "truths are illusions of which we have forgotten that they are illusions, metaphors which have become worn by frequent use and have lost all sensual vigour, coins which, having lost their stamp are now regarded as metal and no longer as coins" (1999, 146).

To sum up, the play offers a vision of a life beyond moral values, an alternative to the habit or custom of value judgment. In *The Will to Power*, Nietzsche had contended truth to be merely provisional and untruth as a condition of life which passes beyond what is merely good and evil. Chantal's final moments in the company of the Old Man corroborates what Nietzsche writes in section 552 of *The Will to Power*:

> Truth is therefore not something there, that might be found or discovered- but something must be created and that gives a name of

process or rather a will to overcome that has in itself no end- introducing truth, as a process or rather to a will to overcome that has in itself no end- introducing truth, as a processes in infinitum, an active determining- not a becoming conscious of something that is in itself firm and determined. (298)

In the final moments, the Old Man comes forward to take pity on dead Chantal calling him brother instead of convention identity of beast. Again, the beast-man dichotomy is problematized as the moment of discovery dawns upon the Old Man. When all other witnesses slip away from the site, only the Old Man stays with him. It illustrates the quality of understanding suffering and compassion:

"The rage of the beast is taken for granted,
Man's beauty is sharing his brother's pain." (7-8,206)

In his final comments, the Conteur again questions the validity of "beast", "man" dualism; the tragic end of Chantal and the compassionate stay of the Old Man teases all the characters and the audience out of the comfort of passing the final verdict. The closing moment throws new light on the crimes committed and underscores the need to re-investigate "innocence" and "guilt" as absolute moral categories.

Kurosawa's classic *Rashomon*, also, presents mutually contradictory, conflicting versions of rape and murder and leaves the audience with multiple truths rather than over-arching, absolutist version of the truth. In this play, both Maumou and Chantal believing them to be saviours, commit murder. Finding Chantal in the throes of death, the Old Man discards his early description as "small dog" and even calls him "my son" with a good heart. Thus, Chantal seems to have fulfilled what Nietzsche demanded of "free spirits" - to have the robust spirit to overcome this restrictive morality, to move beyond the out-worn social structure and thus create *extra-moral* values. He questions the validity of the establishment and urges to revalue all values – values that are merely projected onto the world. By accepting his ill-fated end, Chantal has confronted the "proven wisdom of the tribe" (Nietzsche 67). Here the revaluation consists precisely in the creation of the freedom to shape oneself, maintains an ethical care without a reactive feeling of hatred. Chantal like Afa or Makak demonstrates the freedom of will, independence from the stranglehold of moral lives. By suspending judgment, it forces us to present equally weighty question on both sides of the issue of guilt, offence and justice and eliminates the unequivocal version of truth. As each case is different, each decision must pass through a kind of Derridean "undecidability"[20] and justice is always "to come" in the future. The tangled relationship of truth-falsehood, beast-man, as unknotted in the end, validates Nietzsche's insistence that no single viewpoint can help us comprehend absolute truth. In *Beyond Good and Evil* he argued profoundly that the opposites like "good and evil" or "truth and false" are interdependent and imbricated with each other. In a way, Walcott's masterpiece *Malcochon* also addresses the need to revalue all our moral values and assumptions and confront the mechanism of dehumanization in the context of the general poverty of the West Indian mass.

The Sea at Dauphin

> I am content to live it
> all again And yet again.
>
> -W. B. Yeats: A Dialogue of Self and soul

> Was that life? I want to say to death. Well then! Once more.
>
> -Nietzsche

> We, however, want to become those who we are- the ones who are new, unique, incomparable, self-legislating, self-creating.
>
> -Nietzsche.

As the earlier play was modeled on a Kurosawa classic, this play was directly modelled on Synge's classic Irish tragedy *Riders to the Sea*. Walcott has ostensibly proclaimed Synge's play to be its "ante- text" and the fishing community, the antagonistic sea, their ill-fated encounter in the fishing village of Dauphin here, have a strong resonance with the Irish sea- faring life. The existential crisis and hardships of living on the margin have been portrayed vividly; here, the dismal lives of the Aran islanders are translocated in the grim battle of the Caribbean fishing community. The tension between religious hope and nature's hostility, between negation and affirmation, weakness and strength of the characters animates the plot here. The present section aims to study his one-act play *The Sea at Dauphin* as a creative affirmation of pain and suffering and seeks to validate how the harshness of

---

[20] Derrida in addressing the tension between law and judgement has re-signified "decision". In texts like *The Gift of Death, Deconstruction and Possibility of Justice*, Derrida argues that a decision requires a "leap of faith" beyond the sum total of facts.

the realities of this fishing community's life becomes a metaphor for calm acceptance and fortitude. The play interprets a mode of being that affirms values like will, strength, endurance and in extolling a strong life, it undermines the ethos of Christianity. And it aims to show how like the Aran islanders, the grim sense of fatality has been overcome by a stoic acceptance here, too.[21]

At the heart of the play lies the life of fishermen mired in the "naked, voluble poverty" in the remote village of Dauphin. In "What the Twilight Says: An Overture" (1970) Walcott posits the fisherman at the centre of "New Aegean race": "And the fishermen, those whom Jesus first drew to his net, were the most blasphemous and bitter of all races. Theirs was a naked, pessimistic life, crusted with the dirty spume of beaches. They were a sect which had evolved its own signs, a vocation which excluded the stranger" (16). Without any organizing principles, illusion and promises are denied in their lives. They not only fall short of ideals but struggle to live without bare necessities. The protagonist of the play, Afa, is very commonly read by Walcott scholars as "bitter" and "misanthropic". But to cast him as a sheer despiser of all positive things and values, a mere "nay-sayer", will be extremely reductive. Far from being the voices of *resentiment*, god-denying, hard-hearted race, the fishermen compel our attention by mastering the wild, destructive sea and evince an ethical imperative to lead a life which cannot be dismissed as merely unjust or miserable. In *Thus Spake Zarathustra*, Nietzsche contended that life is a continuum of creation, entwining past, present and future. By sermonizing firm denial of life, Christianity, drains away all life-enhancing drives. Nietzsche emphasized that it is in the ways of continuous change and passing that our earthly life may be constructed and re-constructed. In *The Sea at Dauphin* what permeates the plot are the experiences of death and mishaps: for the local fishermen, every new sailing strike terror. Finding a means of survival often becomes a death trap for them as they regularly put out to sea and get exposed to hostile seas. Here, the plot seeks to create a meaning and value in an existence in which hopes of redemption and transcendence have fallen away. Stripped of security and dignity, the fishing community of the Dauphin embodies the spirit of self-overcoming. Inhabiting the cold, inhuman world, the unaccommodated fishing folk do not merely figure as some victims of some nihilistic disorientation or a group of mute sufferers in the face of perilous seas. It is in a grim, daily encounter with

---

[21] In his seminal essay "What the Twilight Says," Walcott reflects upon the formidable challenge of deprivation, destitution, and West-Indian poverty to the nascent literary and other art practices, especially drama which called for melding the interior life of poetry and outward life of action and dialect.

hostile elemental forces they re-define life as the ongoing process of "becoming". Though most of the critical readings over-emphasize his bitterness and fuming rage of Afa, my reading argues that as the domineering figure of the fishing folk, he seems to succeed in creating alternative values.

The sea as a symbol is all-pervasive in Walcott's corpus; "The sea carries things between continents and casts them arbitrarily into new worlds. Its tides wash beaches and make them new as if continually starting again [. . .] It is the sea as a medium, then, a medium like art in its capacity to transform, that supplies Walcott with an endless metaphor" (Tagoe 177). The life of the fisherman has been one of the thematic foci in Walcott's *magnum opus Omeros*. In the poem, the epic battle is scaled down to the vying between local fishermen for a local, beautiful maid Helen. Though identified more as West Indian "nobody", Walcott's creative interest was spurred by the dispossessed lives of this fishing folk. Within the daily encounter with terror, pain and anguish, Walcott's play attempts to enunciate the spirit of a people who maintain dignity and values refusing to be swallowed by the darkness in their lives. Life, as described by the pre-Socratic philosopher Heraclitus, is eternal war, polarity and tension. Willing and striving are the essences of all living and as Schopenhauer believed, "willing is a sufficient condition of suffering, because all the acts of willing arises necessarily from a want or deficiency, and to experience a want is to suffer" (42). The life of the fishing community is an uphill struggle as Afa reflects how the children are left to starve and suffer and without means to buy new sail and twine (58). This nothingness of human struggle and existence reminds us of Nora's brooding in *Riders to the Sea*: "And isn't it a pitiful thing when there is nothing left of a man who was a great rower and a fisher but a bit of an old shirt and a plain stocking" (101). But the fishing community's life in Walcott's play is not a tragic story in a negative sense, ending in failure and frustration. Instead, it is affirmatively tragic in revealing that human lives are not designed or pre-scripted, but a process of "becoming".[22] The fishermen can transcend the pointlessness of existence and by leading life "now" and "innumerable times more" as they will return knowing that "there will be nothing new in it", rather than adhering to Christian ethics of preparation for an afterlife. While the weak might have discovered worthlessness and loss in such life, Afa and his mates, a gritty band of sailors, demonstrate readiness to embrace all inevitable return of all past experiences in the haunting memories of the loss of their fellow sailors. Looking at the sea, he reflects on how his comrades were swallowed by the sea- Annelles, Bolo, hounakin; hence, they lead a deeply uncertain life. (17-

---

[22] With the ancient philosopher Heraclitus, the notion of radical flux or "becoming" became ontological contrast of "being" popularized by Parmenides.

18.80). What is spelt out here is no mere apprehension of an aged sailor or a mere defeatist submission. Facing up the strictures against mortality, Afa and his mates do not only oppose the subjection of life but also steer forward without hope, promise or end. Instead of an unhealthy obsession with the past, his rumination stresses how times are knotted together: how the present never leaves behind its past and how it is also tied to a fated future. By reminding them of the finitude of life, by stripping them of illusions can they embrace all the past experiences and negotiate with the chaotic world. Resignation, defeat and clear submission to fate mark the ending of *Riders to the Sea*, but here the ending transforms the experience of suffering into something ennobling and positive, a spur to further action rather than withdrawal and passivity. Dauphin's life described by Afa is bleak and hopeless, which catches up all in an existential cycle of toil, pain, frustration and failure; the regular travails of sweat and salt and the stinking hover over them (53).

In his study of Nietzsche's doctrine of "over-coming nihilism", Bernard Reginster finds the action of Sisyphus of pushing the rock on the mountain as life-affirming, rather than futile.[23] Dauphin people are regularly subjected to both physical and psychological torment; battered by loneliness, hunger, life appears a never-ending struggle. In life, as Schopenhauer has also contended, it is far more correct to regard work, privation, misery and suffering, crowned by death, as the aim and objective of our life. Two hours before sunrise, in the "sleep-tightened village", the fishermen arrive barefooted, tattered- cloaked. Little late to arrive is Hounakin, appearing picture of weakness and misery, devastated from the recent loss of his wife. The wind is 'savage' and the early October chill at the daybreak face them with an inhospitable climate. They are hurrying for an early departure with their canoe, significantly named Our Daily Bread. Almost photographically truthful and brutal in realism, the central inspiration of the story is the ordinary lives of ordinary people. Before they set out to sea, their body is exposed to inclement conditions, wants and necessities; for the dirty women and children no prayer avails. Impoverished, they long for friendship only.

Here Afa indicts life as painfully inadequate as it offers no hope of deliverance or redemption. Poor and outcast, Afa is lonely, without wife or children and is unrelenting, facing many adversaries- Sea, God, Church and

---

[23] Bernard Reginster invites this comparison in his study of overcoming nihilism in *Affirmation of life: Nietzsche on Overcoming Nihilism* which he considers to be an overarching project of Nietzsche. The sixth chapter of this study entitled Dionysian Wisdom discusses suffering as constitutive of affirmation of life and Nietzschean postulate of suffering as desirable.

White man. Trapped in hostile circumstances, life, more often than not, appears sordid and disgusting. He pours out bitterness against all who surround him; sometimes with unslackened hatred he sounds almost a "nay-sayer" trying to come to terms with a nihilistic crisis. A veteran sailor, Afa broaches hard, fatalistic view of life; he broods over defeat at the hands of external forces, which epitomizes human predicament in general and the most existential question of death. Every time they put out to sea, the sea faces them as a destroyer of human and family relations. With every sailing, they stand on the edge of disaster. Here the sea stands as a symbolic reminder of the "timeless repetition of life and death". The narrative oscillates between affirmation and negation, between hope and frustration. It does not proceed towards any closure or a teleological end; rather, it implies a cycle, a motion without end. Afa asks Augustin, "Because one old man dead, the sea will stop?" (75). The mood evoked here is akin to the last line of *Omeros*: "When he left the beach the sea was still going on". The ever-flowing sea, evoking a counter version of linear time, creating "a tenseless space" may be taken as a metaphor for the Cyclical nature of existence. The sailors embody different ethics from the individuals who come and pass and leave behind only a faint memory. It testifies to the unshaken faith to the earth, rather than craving for otherworldly realm. This 'eternal return' is a major ethical imperative for Afa and his mates. The central exhortation of Nietzsche in *Thus Spake Zarathursta* is this: "I beseech you, my brothers, remain faithful to the earth, and do not believe those who speak to you of other worldly hopes!" (3).

In this poverty-ridden life organizing life around some ultimate, transcendental purpose like "God", or "Truth", "Justice" is impossible to be meted out. Afa appears, for the most part, a confirmed cynic, an opponent of authority, divine or secular. Through most of his actions, he savagely attacks Christian morality and the falseness of the Christian doctrine. And scathingly opposes prayers, ritual and reverence. His God is not "dead", missing or lost but rather "a big fish" eating "small fishes", an inflictor of pain, a pitiless authority. The land of Dauphin, as he describes, is hard (61) and the unforgiving conditions of the land they inhabit permeate through the narrative. In stark deprivation and dismal daily existence, he lashes out at the mechanism of oppression and injustice, whether it is conducted by the God or the white rulers. Immersed in pain and toil, he hits out at religious teachings and transcendental hope offered by Christianity. He has the audacity to curse "God" for all the ill-fate his people undergo. In an altercation with the young priest, he bursts out in deep scorn against church and the vocation of the priest and all moral values they propagate. Without taking recourse to moral values he lives in alienation, comparable to the sages only. When it comes to putting out to sea, he is fearless enough to proclaim that he will venture alone and find no one to accompany him (61). When Augustin accuses him that he has no respect for man, animal, sea or God (61); he also explains how years of experience have turned him hard-hearted (61). Only with a fiercely independent streak, this spirited individual can distance himself from the surrounding world. By vigorously repudiating the general and abstract system of values, he takes an important stride towards complete self-assertion or what Nietzsche calls the spirit of *ressentiment*. As a non-conformist, he questions the validity of conventional moral categories like "good"' and "evil". As a self-determining man, he spurns the values of "slave" morality. Saddened and distressed by the news of Hounakin's death, he proclaims that no prayer or ritual can palliate the distress of such lives. His gesture of defiance, of tearing a scapular from his neck and hurling it to the ground (73) in the presence of the priest is no doubt irreverent. This sacrilegious act is suggestive of disaffiliation from ecclesiastical order, a transgressive gesture to the dictum of pious life, recommended by the Church and the priest.

The hope of salvation, as Nietzsche contended in *Beyond Good and Evil*, will only rob the individual of a free spirit. A true noble spirit can defy the established ideal of good and evil and remain indifferent to slights and injuries. Without being guided by norms or spiritual values he is a self-determining man; Afa stands apart to decide his course of action and create his values. Nietzsche believed that only noble nature can impose its own values in the world as they are spurners of conventional morality or "herd morality". It is here that the powerful beings can separate them from the weak and virtuous. As Lee Spinks observes in his commentary on *Beyond Good and Evil* "the noble nature, by contrast, is not made for pity "because it has the strength, spontaneous to affirm its own nature" (90). in the course of the plot, all of Afa's words and acts may be said to "take a moral formula in a supra moral sense", a sign of Nietzschean higher man. Afa picks up a quarrel with the young priest once he mentions that the old man (Hounakin) had God". Christianity's espousal of death as a gateway to enter into the blessed life of eternity is strongly refuted by Afa. In a more blistering speech, he equates God with the white man:

> "God is a white man. The sky is his blue eye, His spit on Dauphine people is sea" (9-10.61).

As Afa curses "God", it is quite obvious that his unmitigated aversion is directed at both religious and secular authority. Ziauddin Sardar in his *Orientalism* contends: "White men as God syndrome" (55) was fairly common in the colonies, especially in such recorded events as when Captain Cook was greeted by the native Hawaiians as the God Leno, upon his arrival on the shore.[24] It seems fairly reasonable to say that the thrill and wonder associated with those events are subverted by Walcott's sailor protagonist. The colonial fantasy that equates white man with God is subverted when he describes them to be in a league, wielding the tool of oppression. Thus, the wonder and valediction at the arrival of white people have been held up to question. What it stresses moreover are the values associated with God or "white men"; like all values, they are foisted upon the dispossessed. He argues that hardships of quotidian life cannot be redeemed by any spiritual salve. Anxiety and terror are so inextricably familiar that they seem to be experiencing what Empodcles calls "un-life". Both Afa and Garcia demonstrate the worth of life in negotiating with the phenomenal world of ceaseless striving and pain, rather than resenting pain. One way to overcome contingency and pain, as Richard Rorty has stressed in *Contingency, Irony and Solidarity*, is to recognize it. Now it remains to be answered, how may life be affirmed in the depth of abyssal suspicion? How can one go on loving life with so much scorn or affirm a communal life bereft of divinity? What practices guide them through the chaotic and disenchanted world? How can an individual cobble together meaning out of the nothingness of existence? This section attempts to find an answer by scrutinizing parts of Afa and Augustin in the play. The futility of life has been so overwhelming that Afa scornfully rejects any moral or ethical position. But his is not merely the voice of all resentful or frustrated sentiments. As opposed to falling into resentment, he maintains dignity in venting his own views. As he has no regret and remorse, he will not be immured by the past acts and decisions. Afa never appears apologetic for all his gestures and actions; his moral stance is never that of a pessimistic rejecter of life. He promises to stand by his old East-Indian sailor friend in his crisis and loss; he does not only console him in a moment of grievous loss but also advises how he will regain self-control to overcome this personal tragedy. He advises him to return to his daily chore, to talk to a priest, take care of goats or drink white rum (10-12.64). Unlike the earlier impressions of his remorselessness, he sounds tenderly caring and compassionate. By forging creative unity of nature, individual and society, life may be redeemed or made more worth living. Such small gestures of compassion help us see him involved in the process of self- formation, bringing new values into being. After the day's sailing, he even returns with a pail of fish and Augustin with a shell for their mate Hounakin. To call him a cynic to the extreme is to endorse

---

[24] It places Edward Said's contribution in an appropriate historical context, examines the work of his critics, and explores the postmortem future of orientalism. Ziauddin Sardar provides a highly original historical perspective and shows how orientalism was reworked and reinvested during the Middle Ages, the Enlightenment, colonialism and under the impact of modernity.

Augustin's observation that he is irreverent, a stranger to all common human emotions without a family, child or God (6-8.51). In *Beyond Good and Evil*, Nietzsche contended that goodness is often defined in terms of moral terms like self- restraint. The positive moral virtue that society upholds is identified with weakness.[25] More often than not, it is the weak and insecure people who stay content with traditional belief. While being good often demands the suppression of free will and instinct. Nothing can tame Afa into a "civilized animal" or curb his drives and passions. Weakness and humility are morally justified and the young priest describes Afa and his community as "hard race" (74) and in need of spiritual help. Morality is said to be "the residue left when the constant battle of the contraries is rigidified into the religious and life-denying opposition of good and evil". Afa is deeply distrustful of inflexible moral laws as they only subordinate the being of "man" to mere abstraction or dogma. Asserting himself over ethical restraints, Afa embodies powerful individuality of instinct and passion. All his bitterness and disgust and a certain degree of ruthlessness do not undermine love and compassion: "The compassion and tenderness that cannot be altogether suppressed by Afa's hardness are crucial markers of his humanity" (Baugh 69). Hounakin, a recent widower, has surrendered to the chaos and confusion of his personal life; unable to shake off the despair, exhaustion, he kills himself. But what prevails over loneliness and perpetual suffering of the community lives is the vision of bonding between the fishermen- reflected in their daily recreative hours of jokes, rum and meeting at Samuel Café after return from the daily chore of fishing. With an intensification of fellow feeling, life can be redeemed from meaninglessness and the sense of futility. The painful end of Hounakin cannot blur such glimpses of fraternity and bonding. The endemic condition of poverty can forge a bond among the powerless, which may be read as a counterpoint of solidarity advocated by the ethics of globalization: "… poverty can remind us that we share a predicament with our neighbour, and it confirms the importance of compassion, mutual support and solidarity" (Burnett 55). Such solidarity can only warm up the early morning chill of October. When Afa motivates the boy Jule, the son of Habal to join them in the future expedition, a contrasting vision of a new beginning emerges. Hounakin's self-destructive end is redeemed in Jule's decision to step in his father's shoes. As the day moves towards the close, old challenges give way not to a new day of untroubled calm and security but to greater hazards. Death, loss can be counterbalanced by the eternally recurrent patterns and customs in life. Nietzsche upheld the Dionysian point of view which regards suffering

---

[25] In *Thus Spake Zarathrustra* III, though he admitted pain and evil, Nietzsche never bore disgust towards life and avoided saying "no" to life and the world.

as desirable and pain as an enabling condition for the affirmation of life. The real dignity of life is not in empty vanity of pleasure and happiness but in striving, toils and struggles. The Greeks also upheld the values of *pathei mathos* ("learn by suffering") in social life. It is the closing moments of the action that is the centerpiece of the whole work as it interfaces death and life, stasis and motion. Past, present and future are interlocked here to create a recurrent pattern. At the sunset hour, just before leaving the sea beach, Afa recalls his lost partners whom the sea has swallowed up- Annells, Bolo, Hounakinand also broods over the uncertainties and insecurities of the island natives. Gacia reminds his friends "Tomorrow again" and Afa sets the time at four o clock – the final interaction, seemingly routinal has a deep resonance. It is not indicative of end of the day's expedition but opens out into an uncertain future. And their final action "They furl the sail" points forward to the daily chore of fishing to be continued on the next day. Afa has also mockingly reminded Augustin, saying that they will return on the next day only if he does not go to church. It shows pain and suffering can work as a stimulant rather than foiling it. Thus, this death-saturated atmosphere does not undermine the life full of drive, forces and energies. Their final promise and commitment amply suggest how they have recognized that each passing moment is an echo for eternity rather than one brief episode in the pointless succession of events. What the playwright himself calls "fatal adaptability" of the race of the fishermen seems the ability to arrive at a state of reconciliation with fate. To put it in Nietzschean terms:

> "it is shown to my satisfaction that pain contributes to the nurturing of the human species as much as pleasure does, I shall say 'yea' to pain" (*Thus Spake Zarathrusta* iii).

Their ethical imperative is to lead life by tearing off the shackle of the past and to persist in their struggle – a decisive life-affirming gesture concerned with the living moment and future so that they can become what they are. This recognition of the inescapability of struggle endows upon them a positive mode of being. Since time is cyclical and each time returns in exact repetition, they appear ready to live and re-live it over and over again. In the course of their conversation and action, what surfaces is the consciousness of the future that already was and the past that will return with eternal inevitability. We find at the end Afa and Garcia are not merely resenting the injuries of the past but hoping for a return of the same. They will continue to negotiate with the phenomenal world of ceaseless striving and pain. The chaos and confusion of the daily life will be overcome in their willingness to relive such life over and over again. Afa does not only mourn the death of his mates but knows the grim insecurity that they will undergo the very next time they sail out to sea.

Thus, the motif of Afa, in course of the plot may be said to straddle between "dying consciousnesses" and "awakening consciousnesses" which Nietzsche believed to be constitutive of a continuum of a human life. The ending of the plot is underlined by this different stratum of consciousness, recalling the lost lives, yet also looking forward to the early morning departure to sea. Each passing moment of life is an echo for eternity, rather than a fleeting moment of life, since time is cyclical, and each time returns in exact repetition. While Hounakin has ended life prematurely, others have opted for life to repeat eternally; it is such a life-affirming gesture that may stave off suicidal nihilism. Reconciliation with fate asks us to tolerate the eternal recurrence – a counterpoint to a meaningful and ordered world of religious life. Notwithstanding Afa's sustained attack on value or belief system, the narrative affirms an existence, though without a promise of material change. The grim experiences of the fishing community have induced in this community a complete will lessness or indifferences to goals and purposes. Without standards and values to anchor their lives, the only ethical imperative that drives them still is the present life engulfed by "dirt" and "dismal poverty". In accepting its unchanging futility, a new existential confidence is infused in them. As old challenges will return on a new day, it is pointless to regret or deplore his fate. In his seminal essay "What the Twilight Says", Walcott had also observed that: "in the new Aegean the race, of which these fishermen were the stories, had grown a fatal adaptability" (17). The restless, ceaseless movement, constant striving and endless suffering, girded by the sea, endow upon their wretched lives a new meaning: "No possible satisfaction in the world can suffice to still the cravings of the will, to set a goal of its infinite aspirations and to fill the bottomless abyss of his heart" (Beer 31). Leading life in its painful and horrible aspects displaces life- denying skepticism. In the cold, inhuman world of Dauphin, in the world of its death and degradation a great amount of energy is expended in their grim battle for survival. Above death and change, the fishermen pose the challenge to become what they are. Their ethical imperative is in the willing of "eternal recurrence", to welcome the return of all aspects. Nietzsche believed that the strong individual can always embrace the inevitable and eternal return of all his past experiences- both good and evil. The Dauphin fishing community, by pledging return to daily toil, begins a process of self-realization. What becomes apparent here is that man's fate and freedom are inextricably linked with the totality of the cosmic fate. If evil and wretchedness are everywhere, the future is as dark as the past and the way to redemption does not lie in complete willless inaction. The ideal type of Nietzschean "strong" man, truly worthy of consideration is one who fights even harder when fate is hostile. Dauphin fishermen have learnt to live without hope, without illusion and endured buffets of misfortune. Notwithstanding certain cruelty and ruthlessness, Afa has startled us with complete self- assertion. He has advised Houkain against complete recoil from the chaotic and the disenchanted world. To tolerate the meaninglessness of the world, the response must be one of strength and not weakness. Their understanding of the chaos and confusion is corroborated by their undaunted confrontation with the world and experiencing it at its most threatening. In the process of "becoming", they free themselves from the chains of the past and manage to bridge the past with the future. In the end, the young boy Jule is asked to accompany them in their next sailing. Here we find their attempt to bridge the past and future. When past and future are recognized to be knotted together, any individual can cast off all ill will towards the past. The sea stands as the dominant symbol of a never-ending cycle of life and death. By evading the horrors, one cannot expect to cope with life; so, in embracing the unalterable pattern of creation and destruction, we must relive the past and go on with the expectation of nothing. Thus, the play attests to the process of creating values, and the need to create a new, alternate vision of being.

In *Thus Spake Zarasturshta*, Nietzsche claimed that an individual life is a continuum of creation, and need to be constructed and reconstructed.[26] Here the fishermen, a deeply marginalized community, demonstrate life to be an ongoing process of "becoming". The despairing resignation in the face of weariness and exhaustion, of the valueless world, produces a sort of "passive nihilism"; Hounakin succumbed to this form by ending his life. But what truly affirmed here is the strength which allows others to love it in the moments of hatefulness, accept the meaninglessness. Getting immersed in the organized flux of life, they have complied with "law of life" and willingly submitted to its decrees and thereby evincing what Nietzsche calls "formula for greatness in a human being" (12). He fervently argues that the experience of eternal recurrence gives life meaning and makes suffering meaningful. As demanded by Nietzsche, we can contend that Afa and his mates have no inkling in accepting certain meaninglessness, muteness, instead of divine faith in "God". By releasing drives and passions, they can liberate themselves from the moral constraints. Walcott in his analysis of the West Indian psyche has emphasized this quality in his 1980 essay "Meanings": "Our most tragic folk songs and our most self-critical calypsos have a driving, life-asserting force" (50). This healthful affirmation is a kind of Nietzschean "Yes-saying"- where life is affirmed as beautiful in spite of everything" (Kaufman 507). By strong articulation of a desire for eternal repetition one affirms love and life.

---

[26] Nietzsche was scathingly critical of pity and humility cultivated by the weak which was a form of conspiracy against the strong and noble nature—as it only preserves, Spink argues, a degenerate form of life (Spinks 90).

Without gilding their bleak life with metaphysical hopes or submitting to the dogma of a belief system or determinism, the Dauphin fishermen have conceived life differently to attain an Olympian detachment. They move beyond their determinant position and surpass the limitations of temporal life. Their life is a testimony to the Nietzschean process of overthrowing the old values and restoring to new meanings. By the time they leave the beach behind, they have created their own values in a process which thinker like Foucault has described as care for the self. Though they are thrown into a web of the network of constraints they progress towards self-making which corroborates the usefulness of alternative morality. Without banishing suffering, without pre-appointed end, the sailors exemplify how to risk life and happiness while remaining absorbed in the interest of the moment. And here lies the significance of Walcott's artistic alternative; Nietzsche also believed in every art work's probing to the realities of suffering and mortality as they make human life both understandable and bearable.

Chapter 2

Native "difference" and Elemental Man in *Dream on Monkey Mountain*

"I am not a prisoner of history. I must not look for the meaning of my destiny in that direction; I must constantly remind myself that the real leap consists of introducing invention into life. In the world I am heading for I am endlessly creating myself"

-Fanon

"Because it is a systemic negation of the other person and furious determination to deny the other person all other attributes of humanity, colonialism forces the people it dominates to ask themselves the question constantly: "In reality, who am I"?

-Fanon

I am talking of men who have been skillfully infected with fear, inferiority complexes, trepidation, servility, despair, abasement.

-Aime Cesaire

Walcott's fascination for folk memories and local cultural models finds the most consummate expression in *Dream on Monkey Mountain*. In 1967 he had described the play to be "an attempt to cohere various elements of folklore" and weave these elements into the fantasy of an old charcoal-selling hero, Makak. First produced in 1969 and recipient of much-coveted Obie Award (in 1971) as the best "foreign" play, it marked a watershed in Walcott's dramatic career. Within a rich symbolic texture, it unleashes a profound commentary on political and cultural deformation wrought upon by colonialism and the traumatic episode of Middle Passage. The psycho—pathologies of Afro-Caribbean self-perception, denial of identity and cultural over- determination had left serious scars on the Caribbean consciousness. Walcott stages it with an experimental theatrical architecture, seldom attempted by his predecessors. In an interview he had pointed out the cultural mission of his hero and the West-Indians of his generation, "Makak and his people he meets… are all working out the meaning of their culture; they are going through upheaval, shaking off concepts that have been imposed on them for centuries" (17). Unequal power binary, according to Hegelian postulate, always divides independent and dependent consciousness and Walcott was optimistic that the creole performance can liberate the Caribbeans from "dependency complex" and from experiencing what Aime Cesaire describes as "abasement" and "servility". Historically torn between colonial Europe and colonized Africa, the Caribbean society struggled for a balance of representational politics and find a negotiation between conflicting identity claims.

Walcott's famous contemporaries like Lamming and Naipaul were no less preoccupied with the crippling effects of memories of violent travel like Middle Passage and the huge migration of the indentured work force. Wrestling with self-doubt and self-abasing dependency Lamming admitted that the urgent task for the writers in respect to colonialism was the reparation of a damaged consciousness and subjectivity. They firmly believed that only the artist as a cultivator and carrier of cultural dignity could return the subject people to their rightful sense of identity in the early days of nation-building.[1] In an introduction to a new edition of *The Castle of My Skin* Lamming wrote: "Indeed, the colonial experience of my generation was almost without violence. No torture, no concentration camp, no mysterious disappearance of hostile natives, no army encamped with orders to kill. The Caribbean ordered a different kind of subjection. It was terror of the mind, a daily exercise in self- mutilation…The result was a fractured consciousness, a deep split in its sensibility which now raised difficult problems of language and values; the whole issue of a cultural allegiance between imposed norms of White Power, between white instruction and black imagination" (XXXIX, XXXVII). This split consciousness could enable the West Indian artists to reimagine the questions of identity, subjectivity, homeland, and nativism. This distortion of collective consciousness and deformation of subjectivity have been effectively borne out in the experimental dream narrative in *Dream on Monkey Mountain*. As Walcott's muse was always Caribbean, his plays, no wonder, strove to perform the native place as an independent image and without imperial inscriptions. In his essay "Society and the Artist" (1957), Walcott has also enunciated the urge for self-definition: "To see ourselves, not as others see us, but with all the possibilities of the new country we are making" (15).[2] In his recollection of childhood, Naipaul wrote: "We were a small part of somebody else 'overview', we were part first of the

---

[1] Dabydeen and Wilson-Tagoe in a chapter "The Treatment of Race" underscore how the psychology of race and colour and deep- seated inferiority inhibited the self- definition of the characters in Lamming, V.S. Reid.

[2] In this essay (1957) Walcott castigates the political achievement and political independence and asserts in the process of "thinking" a prospect of history-making.

Spanish story, then of the British story".[3] In order to forge a "narrative of their own", to reclaim their personhood, Walcott suggested that Caribbean artists should not wallow in self-pity or complain about lack of opportunities or state-patronage. Instead, they should find an affirmative cultural form and organize it to realize the potential of elemental man. About Makak, he has written "This was a degraded man, but he had some elemental force in him that is still terrifying; in another society he would have been a warrior" (*Critical Perspectives* 49).

Structured by oppressive institutions of colonialism and slavery the West Indian society, has identified the blacks with a lack of being; in a colonial society, "skin" has remained the key signifier of cultural and racial hierarchy. The natives, for their skin colour and other physical traits, had become a phobic object of extreme vulnerability. With his radical insight, Fanon described the challenge that a black man faces every day: "I had to meet the white man's eyes. An unfamiliar weight burdened me. In the white world, the man of colour encounters difficulties in the development of his bodily schema" (Fanon xxv). In this confrontation, as Fanon recognized, the colonized person, in some sense, actively takes part in white-scripted history and feels doubly alienated. This racialized subjectivity and the prevalent logic of colonial order came to permeate the West Indian society; the psychic tug-of-war of Europe and Africa came to stunt the cultural growth of his countrymen. As the blacks are locked in blackness and the whites in whiteness, both the subjectivities are defined by their respective racial categories. Imposition of white cultural norms and prevalent dyadic hierarchies between animality and humanity left them with low self-esteem and a sense of rootlessness. Trapped in this "contradiction of being white in mind and black in body" ("Twilight" 12) the Caribbeans would hanker after Western cultural standards, on the one hand, and suffer deep disregard for local traditions and value systems, on the other. From the beginning, Walcott was averse to Manichean binaries and hierarchization of cultures. The structure and values of a colonial society have always stereotyped and essentialised the identity of both the black and the white race. As racial discourses were dominant in the New World society what prodded the artists was to renarrativize the subject position of Caribbean "everyman", to chart a way for liberation from the world of structural violence. The privileged white subject alienated not only the black body but also the black psyche. The experience of subjection had alienated the blacks from their own people and forced them to descend into the "zone of non-being". The identity of the

---

[3] See, V. S. Naipaul *"Prologue to an Autobiography" in finding the Centre: Two Narratives"* 58-9.

native was construed in terms of inadequacy and impotence. In *Black Skin, White Mask*, Fanon examines how the "white narratives" had inculcated an inferiority complex or what he termed "epidermalization" or interiorisation of inferiority in the soul of all colonized people. In the colour-structured society of the Caribbean what was consensually accepted was the unequivocal inferiority of 'negro-ness'- as described by David Dabydeen and Nana Wilson-Tagoe, as a "sense of inferiority and self-abasement in his innermost consciousness" (58). Naipaul in his major non-fiction, *The Loss of El Dorado* discussed the futility and moral callousness of his "half-made" societies to its consensual acceptance of inferiority and debasement of negro-ness. Walcott's charcoal-burner hero, Makak is also a study in the internalization of "an overwhelming awe of everything white" and a West Indian "everyman" who fell victim to the neurotic condition- the condition of being awed by everything white. Such awe not only impaired the positive sense of the self but forced to regard the self as abjected and contaminated. "The colonial values" as Oliver Kelly observes, "deny the black man not just the individuality but also humanity... he is not allowed to make himself a lack of being to become self-conscious. Rather, he is chained to being, to his body and more particularly to his skin, by colonial values" (39). Walcott's early plays are premised upon the aggressive hold of the old colonial institution of the plantation economy and a deep psychic damage to the average West-Indians. The creole texture of his plays pays special attention to the struggle- fleshed out in Makak's fantasy, surreal journey to escape the prison house of race and colour. The irrational and disorderly progress of the narrative is committed to the task of emptying the mind of his native countrymen of incapacitating Western values. In the narrative of Makak, the oppressed, dehumanized charcoal burner, Makak is evolves "into a positive, collective one" (qtd. in Bhabha 329). Like Harris, Walcott's ostentatious purpose was to illuminate the Caribbean psyche and extend its sensibility in order to overcome psychic violence. His play texts were instrumental in overcoming all complexities and attempting a re-definition of selfhood. As racial pride and its claim of superiority would have encouraged only cultural parochialism, Walcott's syncretic texts aimed at articulating the resistance of the "elemental man" in the figure of Makak who is introduced as one divested of the ancestral memory, original name, tribal association and all cultural baggage. The figures like a woodcutter or charcoal burner were an integral part of west Indian mythology and captivated the dramatist's imagination - because "this figure represented the most isolated, the most reduced, race- containing symbols" (*Critical* 8). In Walcott's dramatic narrative, the knowledge-power dynamics of the colonial system comes under erasure and the oppositional agenda of nativist discourses is continually displaced. The stranglehold of the colonial imaginary on the Caribbean personhood is eased by affirming identity as fluid and in flux. Joseph Brodsky contends in his essay "The Sound of the Tide" in a glowing tribute to his friend Walcott's artistic genius that such creole artworks will prove to be "superior to the confines of class, race or ego" (36). It sums up the essence of a dramatic vision borne out by *Dream on Monkey Mountain*.

In a foreword to the 2008 edition of *Black Skin, White Mask*, Ziauddin Sardar mentions that the ostensible purpose of Fanon's investigation of the psychology of colonialism is the elimination of "the dynamic of inferiority". The present chapter seeks to study how the dream sequences and surreal situations here de-mystify "white" and "black" values and eliminate the racist assumption that *black is not a man*. It charts how the charcoal burner hero, Makak, undertakes a journey to discover dignity, relinquishes the dream of African chieftainship, and finally returns after all dream journeys to his mountain home. Through hallucinatory spells and dreams its non-linear narrative relocates the elemental man to his true Caribbean "home". From the smashing of Alcinador café to his return home on the Monkey Mountain is charted a process of how the consciousness is mutated and utter degradation and humiliation are replaced by self-knowledge. It is often admitted that Walcott is one of the earliest Anglophone Caribbean writers to have staged the problem of racism, identity and dignity. The challenges of poverty, race and lingering oppressive effects of slavery and colonialism have suffused the fiction and non-fiction of other noted artists of the later generation like Jamaica Kincaid and John Rhys. The crux of Kincaid's masterpiece *A Small Place* (1988) is the internalization of colonial values and distortion of the consciousness of the Antiguans in the context of a litany of power abuses; it probes the lingering effects of colonialism and slavery on those who descended from the slaves and the once-colonised Caribbean natives. Fanon's seminal work, *The Wretched of the Earth* does provide the epigraph to *Dream on Monkey Mountain* (Part 1) and the plot acts out many Fanonian postulates through Makak's encounters with his fellow natives and white masters. Makak's obsessive desire for whiteness is embodied in the irresistible psychosexual hold of the white beauty who inspires and reminds him of his royal ancestry. When old Makak says that all that he has is his "dreams", Tigre castigates him; "I can imagine your dreams. Masturbating in the moonlight. Dreaming of women, cause you so damn ugly" (225). His neurotic condition is induced by the delirium of chieftainship and the assurance of the White Goddess that he has descended from royal blood. This split of the West-Indians to be black in body and white in mind (as already mentioned) has resulted in a damaging appropriation of the oppressor's racist values. It manifests the fantasy of the native to occupy two exclusive positions, on the one hand, to occupy the master's place and nurture avenging anger of a slave (64-65). For this "psychic tug-of-war" playing on their consciousness, they were more defined than self-defining.

Race, ethnicity, religion or economic classes are some of the dominant external categories which not only produced hierarchies but also afflicted the blacks with an "inferiority complex". The racist narrative of white scripts and black chauvinism of the political system deepened their cultural alienation; they were construed as a population of degenerate types like primitives and savages. The individuals, by a racial phantasm, are forced to occupy the ontological status of the primitive. Like Chantal, the tiger of *Malchochon*, the major characters of Walcott's early masterpiece are identified as ugly beasts. If not directly by association, names like Makak, Moustique and Tigre clearly resemble monkey, mouse and tiger. In the colonies, the imperial power flaunted the control to name or change the original name- a practice that is described by Bhabha as "a specifically postcolonial performance of reinscription" (231). This Eurocentric hegemony of naming and un-naming, the manoeuvring of original identity only serves to affirm the sub-human status of Makak and the two felons with whom he shares the cell. The oppressive forces of culture, history and language have deprived them of subjecthood. Described by a racial epithet, the protagonist Makak has forgotten the legal name and is introduced everywhere with a derogatory name- Makak, the *patios* form for monkey. As Corporal Lestrade explains that his rightful name is unknown, alias Makak, a charcoal seller was arrested for unruly smashing of a café (224). A dweller in the forest in the Monkey Mountain, he is the obverse of the face of civilization.

> MAKAK I live on Monkey Mountain, Corporal.
> CORPORAL What is your name?
> MAKAK I forget.
>
> (Prologue, 219)

Colm Patrick Hogan has provided an instructive endnote in his essay "Mimeticism, Reactionary Nativism in Derek Walcott's *Dream on Monkey Mountain*" to the name Makak. The name, he contends, is very much suggestive of denigration and it undermines African values as well. Among the Yoruba communities, Monkey was considered sacred and such naming evoked a derogatory image and re-enforced their sub-human status. It did also distort and devalue a culture which considers monkeys to be sacred. The idea of naming, imposing identity has been integral to hegemonic practices; Walcott elucidates this practice of strategic naming in an interview with Rebekah Presson in 1992: "… in adjusting names […] You have to go through a whole process of becoming a name that you have been given. It's the process and technique of removing identity and altering identity so you can rule or dominate" (192). Lestrade charges Makak that with two felons as companions has turned the cell into "a stinking zoo". This public display of a human zoo was extremely popular in the nineteenth-century European society. Stigmatised with savagery, barbarism, and bestiality, they render service condescendingly – as Elleke Bohemer explains: "[T]he Other is cast as corporeal, carnal, untamed, instinctual, raw, and therefore open to mastery, available for use, for husbandry, for numbering, branding, cataloging, description or possession" (269). In the Prologue, the prejudiced and discriminatory structures of governance, maintains its hold on objectifying the "black body" - "black skin splits under the racist gaze, displaced into signs of bestiality, genitalia, grotesquerie which reveal the phobic myth of the undifferentiated whole white body" (Bhabha 131). Contrasted to the prisoners, Lestrade bears his real name; he appears to be a model of propriety, order and civilization. In the early scenes, Lestrade's constant reminder of the dichotomy between "civilization" and "jungle" underscores how race thinking and colonisation anchor upon a line of hierarchy among human types. The corporal sees this behaviour as a trait of human race and vents his opinion of the origin of the species, with the apes. Tigre and Souris are identified with animal howling, unable to articulate any meaningful sentence or phrase. The view at the heart of the colonial logic maintains that the black man is determined in advance by history as "subhuman" and ripe for domination. Their blackness has dehumanized them, impaired their individuality and also mobilized the colonizer's ambition to civilize or modernize the native" (Bhabha 62). The way Lestrade introduces Makak, it underscores their fractured subjectivity, caught between the "otherisation" of the Western discourse and own negated traditions. In Prologue, Makak stands before the judge, described by Lestrade as one without a mind, a will, a name, a tribe of its own. He appears to be a tamed and obedient animal (9-13.222). A champion of racist- colonialist ideology, the stage-direction confirms further his role as animal tamer cracking out his "order". The stage is reconfigured into a circus show where animals are brought for display under the severe commands of the ring leader. The ideological insistence that the dominated are necessarily inferior is further suggested in the observation of the chorus that Makak sits like a monkey and follows the order obsequiously (Prologue, 10-13.223).

Having lived under soul-killing domination, the native appears to be a mere puppet; his only re-action is submission to the coercive mechanism.[4] Bound to their assigned role, the prison inmates here demonstrate colonial mimicry which not only suggests a complete lack of confidence but also the normalization procedure of colonial administration. Fanon also noted that

---

[4] This "objectification" is described by Bhabha as "the Black is both savage [cannibal] perceived and fixated as the other, they are reduced to mere "objects".

the oppressed native, enduring dehumanization, ceases to become an "actional" person and thereby aggrandizes the self-esteem of a white man. As William. S. Haney describes, "They are often at the risk of becoming mimics of one or more cultures instead of genuine hybrids capable of rising above prescribed boundaries of re-discovering the self" (112). The setting of the cell with two prison cages on either side of the stage (212), is no doubt, a classic example of authoritarian governmentality and ideological manipulation. "The prologue" has been described as a ritual, presided over by Lestrade by Breslin. Here, the apparatus of colonialism creates a hierarchy of values and turns the colonized into supine and cultureless object against which the European culture defined itself. Lestrade's adulation of the white race and assumption of an attitude whiter than white themselves are evident in the early section of the play. He vaunts the ideological Mission of colonial governance in the far-flung colonies, to have borne the high torch of justice among the primeval people (1.3 3-5.256). He is unslackened in devotion to white law, language and religion and obsequious to "Her Majesty's Government" (217). Noticing the behaviour of the convicts, like the howling from the cell, he calls them inferior to "ape", a "nigger" who has failed to evolve. "Ape or, "monkey man, as Diana Lynn observes, "is one of the most crude and hurtful epithets thrust at the black men by white racists or their mimics" (49). With inordinate pride, he continues to proclaim himself as an instrument of the law (1, 279) or little later, "You can do what you want with your life, you can hardly call this liberty" (1.10-15,279). All his bombasts are balanced against Makak's introvert, almost inarticulate responses. In the Prologue, he is the *de facto* authority to force Makak to drill. He offers protection to all the villagers and promises to wrench them out of frustration. When in Sc-iii, Corporal in wig and gown stands in the spotlight, his rhetoric reveals the guise or the mask of the conqueror. In outright repudiation of the jungle law, he expresses thankfulness for the British law (13-16. 280). Here in the figure of reforming Corporal is given "a comic turn from the high ideals of the colonizing mission" (Bhabha 122). "The objective of the colonial discourse" as Bhabha contends, "is to construe the colonized as a population of degenerate type on the basis of racial origin, in order to justify conquest and to establish administration and instruction" (101). The cultural authority of the West embodied in reformist zeal and sermons for moral improvement is as absurdly extravagant as the figure of the "mimic men" who crowd the pages of Kipling, Forster and Naipaul.

Inside the cell, racist identification and devaluation have driven Makak to put on the white mask, hidden in his bag. In the year when the play was written, it was a commonplace among the black children to carry a white mask, an ostentatious sign of Fanonian "inferiority complex". To train the village crowd, Moustique also points to this practice of keeping white masks. With racist interpellation, Makak has not only lost himself as a subject but identified with racist myth and fantasy. The crisis that induces such mimic action is revealed in a monologue by Makak. He broods over complete cultural alienation. Without a wife and family, he turns to self-loathing and self-contempt:

> "is thirty years now, I have looked in no mirror, Not a pool of cold water, when I must drink".
>
> (1.13-16.226)

His frank disclosure of ugliness resonates with the words of Fanon's speaker in *Black Skin, White Masks*: "I took myself far off from my own being, very far, making myself an object" (112). He inhabits what Fanon calls the "zones of non-being" where stripped of culture and history the black subject, stripped of culture and history, becomes an abject. It is described by Fanon as a movement towards self-effacement, having failed to confront his own ugliness, Makak ceases to be a man in his own eyes. As Dazial R. Samad observes: "the speech indicates that Makak refuses to confront the nature of his human image not only because he is Black and thinks himself ugly, but also because he cannot confront what he really is - fragmented and eclipsed" (231). This manner of conceiving own black body makes him a sort of "anti-Narcissus" (Breslin 150) whose gesture of self- recoiling is induced from extreme self-loathing. Casting oneself off in violent disgust is somewhat akin to Kristeva's trope of "abject" which is disruptive of one's identity and conception of order. He seeks to propel away the bodily ugliness on the other side of the imaginary, to separate the self from what is threatening to it. To put it in Kriestevan terms, "The abject has the only one quality of the object and that is being opposed to I".[5] To construct a self-image, he must expel what is so revolting in him "I expel myself; I split myself within the same motion through which "I" claim to establish myself" (Kristeva 3). What Elizabeth Grosz has described as "a sickness at one's own body", may account for the self-revulsion of Makak. His body violates social propriety, disrupts codes of discipline and order. His ugliness threatens the integration of self-image and thus severs self from other. The black man's body is overdetermined by history and culture in such a way that for the black man it is not the body that he wants or recognizes. As Moustique bitterly reminds him as black, ugly, poor, nothing. "Small, ugly, with a foot like a 'S'. Man together two of us is a minus one" (237). This induces a hysteric condition of getting sunk in the Fanonian

---

[5] The breakdown of the border between self and the other is the crux of Kriesteva's analysis of "corporeal reality"; see, *Powers of Horror: An Essay of Abjection 1980.*

"zone of non-being".[6] In a long lyrical speech, Makak's somatised hysterical symptoms and psychic tensions are eloquently expressed as he describes how his blood is quickened after his encounter with the beautiful white apparition.

Fanon had also insisted that the white values, ideals enter into the very being of the colonized through their skin like foreign bodies to native culture. Having been subject to the mechanism of inferiorization, the colonized eagerly craves recognition and love: "I wish to be acknowledged not as *black* but as *white* ... I marry white culture, white beauty, white whiteness" (*Black* 45). In a hypnotic state, he faces her like the shining moon; her desire to possess the white woman, urge to be a part of white culture and sublimation into the white values is symptomatic of schizophrenic identity. The demand for recognition becomes a symptom of the pathology of colonization. Octave Manoni's *Prospero and Caliban: The Psychology of Decolonization* describes how the indigenous Malagasy of Madagascar, a group of "backward people" began to revere the French as colonizer as they once revered their ancestors.[7] As white values and racist ideology have penetrated so deeply into his being, Makak surrenders to the white Muse, craving acknowledgement and recognition. She reminds him of his royal lineage to restore him to a position of pride. In a trance-like spell, he tells Moustique that she has infused a new confidence in him and advised to shed the self- abnegating attitude (1.13-14, 236). Makak's words attest to a chronic complex of self-devaluation which propels him to crave recognition from the moon goddess. Addressing the judge, Corporal observes that the niggers are driven to insanity in making the impossible longing for whiteness (228). As Oliver Kelly succinctly puts it: "The success of colonization of psychic space can be measured by the extent to which the colonized internalize- or become inflicted by- the cruel superego that abjects them and substitutes anger against their oppressors with an obsessive need to gain their approval" (10). The woman who holds him in thrall is "the loveliest thing"; her singing drives him to frenzy. She is a saviour like figure helping him recover "identity and strength" and redeem from "inferiority" (Crow and Banefield 38). Recognition from the Whites can only elevate him from the damaging limitations which is also precisely the choice Miss Aggy makes in *Old Story Time*. When she reaches oldhood, she projects this desire onto her son Len who must climb up in his social and cultural

---

[6] Fanon describes in *Wretched of the Earth*: "In the colonial world, the emotional sensitivity of the world is kept on the surface of the skin like an open sore which flinches from the caustic agent; and the psyche shrinks back, obliterates itself and finds outlet in muscular demonstration which have caused certain very wise man to say that the native is a hysterical type" (56).

[7] Manoni's book (1950) is an early classic on the inferiority and dependence complex and he is now widely known for his influence on Lacan.

position - first through education and hopefully through marriage to a long-haired white girl Margaret. Aggy and Makak have a consuming desire, a longing to lose themselves in a mist of whiteness or desire whiteness as it is most desirable. Having no emotional reciprocation, Makak has a fixation for the white Goddess. Long trapped in the nightmare of his skin colour, he desires to break out of the prison; association with white culture has triggered hallucinations. It is the very image of the loveliest thing on earth. The apparition of the white beauty sends him into frenzied rapture and is swept off his feet as she sings. Transfixed, he feels:

> "A million silver
> needles prickle my blood,
> Like a rain of small fishes."
>
> (Prologue, 16-24, 227).

This is the way "that the native converts emotions and psychic tensions into somatic symptoms" (Kelly 74). Only by his association with the white woman, he can whiten himself and proclaim his manhood. White values have percolated in his soul in a way so as to develop into an obsessional neurosis; in looking up to everything "white", he further admits his own inferiority. In the opening pages of her autobiography, I KNOW WHY THE CAGED BIRD SINGS, Maya Angelou recounts her fervent wish to emulate white beauty having been brought to the South to live with her Momma: "I was going to look like one of the sweet little white girls who were everybody's dream of what was right with the world" (2). As "white" came to stand for everything right or just, she deluded herself into believing that her long, blond hair would compel the new neighbours in the South to recognize and appreciate "... I was really white and because a cruel stepmother, who was understandably jealous of my beauty, had turned me into a too- big Negro girl, with nappy black hair, broad feet and a space between her teeth that would hold a number two pencil" (3). Such fantasy, dream and delirium attest to the mental colonisation that persisted also in the West-Indians in the post- independence days. In the mock court of the prologue, Lestrade has already presented Makak as "a being without a mind, a will, a name, a tribe of its own", a mere mute animal, though "tamed and obedient" (Prologue, 9-11.222). Inside the cell, what is "Willfully created and spread by the colonizer, this mythical and degrading portrait ends up being accepted and lived with to an extent by the colonized. It thus acquires a certain amount of reality and contributes to the portrait of the colonized" (Memmi 87).

As the action leaves the setting of the jail, it retreats to his Mountain Home, where at the beginning of the day, Makak was knocked out of sleep by

Moustique. Stretched out into a hallucinatory fit, he feels possessed. As a matter-of-fact interruption/reminder, Moustique advises him to go "mad tomorrow" since it was a "market day" (1.6-7, 232). In a long speech, he reveals how he has been gripped by the vision of impeccable beauty, how the "loveliest thing" transfixes him. Her song induces a sense of manliness in him and he kneels before her in a gesture of chivalry. His hyper-aroused state makes him a visionary to such a degree that he felt a god-self in him. By colonial logic, whiteness is the ultimate ethical good and perfection and therefore, the natives struggle to live up to the ideal of whiteness. In a state of feverish excitement, he only sees the white while to others it remains invisible. It is the White Goddess who has loved him and restored him to his ethnic and racial lineage. She tells him that he should live no longer alone as the black man but crave for what Fanon terms "a white destiny". As Lestrade describes her as lime, snow, marble, moon light, lilies (2.3.9-11, 319). This split between the black body and the desire for the ideal of whiteness, the attraction for two mutually exclusive cultures- African and Western - defines the problem of mental disorder of the natives. He straddles between "colonial valourization of whiteness and culture" and the assumed glory of African royal lineage. All that he craves now are little love and understanding. Since the white man is a measure of all things, black man must define himself in relation to its "Other". It is in such circumstances when his self-esteem has completely evaporated, he becomes desperate to "emulate the white man, to become like him and thus hope to be accepted as a man" (Sardar). In a classic strategy of Afrocentric counter-discourse, Makak compensates his non-beingness with another identity, equally fabricated or constructed. In the court scene everyone on the stage exults Makak as an African king, greets him with noise, slogans and parades to be enthroned. This parodic ritual provides an important rejoinder to the process of hierarchization (307).[8]

In the post-independence years, West-Indian self-consciousness evolved within the wider context of movements like American Black Power, Transatlantic Negritude, and African independence. In 1970, when the play made its debut in American stage, it triggered fervent appreciation for its parallel between Black America and Black Caribbean. The discovery of "Africa" was a strong cultural imperative in the 1960s; in the West Indian context, Laurence Breiner has called Africa and its nostalgic longing as "a second parent-culture, alternative to Europe" (142). The continuity of African cultural heritage was also a major creative imperative for the writers like C.L.R. James,

---

[8] Lloyd Brown has drawn a parallel of the slave performance of the enthroning in a carnivalesque way with Leroi Jones's *The Slave* in his essay "DREAMERS AND SLAVES – The Ethos of Revolution in Walcott and Leroi Jones".

Edward Brathwaite. For these writers, the spiritual and cultural home was Africa, a mother's lap from which Middle Passage had ruptured the Caribbeans. Post-colonial subjectivity – guided by the politics of "return", had exerted appeal to the common islanders. Radhakrishnan in his essay "Postcoloniality and The Boundaries of Identity" contends: "The very necessity of the "return" is posited on a priori premise; the realization to be a post-colonial is to live in a state of alienation, alienation from one's true being, history and heritage. The "return" takes the form of a cure, or remedy, f or the present ills of post-coloniality" (755). When Makak is reminded of the royal African lineage or promises his cell-mates a return to the promised motherland, Tigre gloats over the land to be blessed and its earth as sacred mother (18- 20/289-290). Makak in a dream sequence plans with his cell mates a visit back to Africa- the land of "lions", "birds", "sound of flutes". He imaginatively soars beyond his material existence to claim majesty and kingship as he sees himself as The King of Ashanti, Dahomey, Guinea. Lestrade also flatteringly addresses him as "the king of Africa". The vaunting claims of the European cultural and legal system are counter-balanced by the triumphalist rhetoric of nativist politics. Broodingly, Makak romanticises the idyll of Africa the longing to return to its golden sand, the rivers and its lions, flutes and birds (9-13, 291). This diametrically opposed cultural disposition reflects the growing trend of what P.C. Hogan describes "reactionary nativism". Such adversarial politics, Walcott always reminded, was nothing but colonialism "in reverse" and this intense longing for African past or idealizing Edenic myth was not repudiation of whiteness, but rather re-affirmation of it. Within a few years of production of this drama, the West-Indian islands witnessed violent Black Power uprisings as it swept through America. Facing strong criticism, he persisted in his belief that such essentialist paradigms are dissonant with the complex cultural reality of the Caribbean. He had no interest in lightening the burden of Eurocentric literary tradition or abandon either of these two major cultural heritages.

In Part 1, Sc. III, in a crowded market, Makak appears in the role of shaman, a "Jesus-like healer" healing a sick man and acquires a reputation as a messianic deliverer. Josephus, a villager, a victim of snake bite, is healed not by herb or bush medicines but by putting coals under his body to make him sweat. Like a folk hero, he saves the life of Josephus with a home-spun remedy. Appearing before the folks as "Master", he asks all to "kneel" in prayer for the recovery of the sick man. His healing power is not derived from Africa, but burning coal becomes an instrument of his vocation. By opening his haversack, he asks his people to further his cause by dropping coins (14-17.251).

After the fit of miracle has been performed, he assumes a Messianic role as a son of the soil, one among god's chosen race. Makak also exhorts the villager to believe in themselves; it endows upon the petty and humble coal trader a new aura. After the healing is over, he shows promises to be a potential leader of a people. Long condemned to be irredeemably black and inferior, Makak infuses new vigour to the dispirited people as he likens them with the formation of diamond from the intense pressure of coal (2. 6-9. 249). Coal trading was the cheapest of all trades in Makak's society. In order to transcend the racial consciousness or racial identity what is affirmed here is that the diamond, one of the most precious gems, is formed from the pressure of coals over a great stretch of geological times. In this episode, not only the berated lives find their voice, but indigenous practices, the meanest of livelihood of gathering coal is restored to a position of dignity. In coming down from Monkey Mountain with good tidings, he replicates the role of the Moses. He attributes his success to some divine authority and describes "his own power as the instrument of a higher one" (Breslin 141). With two felons - Tigre and Souris by his side, his role has been equated with the role of Saviour. Beyond his quotidian life, material existence, the various layers of Makak's split personality are explored. As Paula Burnett notes, "When Walcott's drama enacts such rites as healing, a quasi-resurrection, as in *Dream On Monkey Mountain*, a miracle performed by the least respected person of a hierarchical racialized community, it does so as part of a strategy to mark the social deprivation but spiritual strength of a real, historic group" (103). The dispossessed hero receives adulation when his role is misused by Moustique through play-acting as a local healer; but a fake healer's spurious practice is, here, counterpointed against spiritual guidance of Makak. He exploits his master's gift for personal gain and thus reveals narrow political opportunism. Walcott knew well that borrowed power and fake healing was a corrupt version of shamanism and the darker side of ethnocentrism. Makak himself points to the rivalry and factionalism that existed among the tribes of his generation after independence: "The tribes will wrangle among themselves, splitting, writhing, hissing" (2.2, 3-4, 305). Such sectarian nativism, Africans fighting Africans could only occlude the harmony and peace of peaceful solidarity. Such romantic nativism narrows down the scope of identification by promulgating racist ideology.

In his seminal essay "What the Twilight Says: An Overture" Walcott fervently expressed abiding distrust of revenge: "the West-Indian mind historically hung over, exhausted, prefers to take its revenge in nostalgia" (18). He compared the pre-exilic return to the dream of an Eden. Once the tribe assumed control of power, he knew they would plunge into factionalism and relentlessly pursue uncompromising "revenge". This play within the play in the trial scene with Makak enthroned and in royal robe underscores Walcott's dig at revenge aesthetics. As Tejumala sums up the episode: "History is dragged out from the deepest recesses and accused of having trumpeted blackness underfoot" (107). Ethics of revenge reaches its apex in this trial episode; the lust for "black" revenge indicts all those celebrated in European history. Corporal claims the justice to be "hawk-swift" and "impetuous". Basil reads out the catalogue of white offenders which includes Shakespeare, Marlowe, Dante, Galileo, Copernicus, Aristotle and Plato – prominent champions of white values. The list includes navigators, explorers and naval commanders who paved the ways for colonizers and empire-builders. Lestrade eloquently states the rationale of the mock-trial that their serious crime is only their "whiteness" (11-15.312). They all are sentenced to gallows for being only "indubitably white", formidable promulgators of the power structure. Reactionary nativists upheld recrimination to subvert the power structure. Makak's fantasy is counter-balanced by the absurd Trial conceived in fantasy; the two being the outcomes of internalized racism. Lestrade, who has already changed sides already, voices the effectivity of tribal laws and swift system of justice which will be meted out to all offenders. In order to assert differences from the colonizer's influence, the colonised replicates the role of the colonizer. When Moustique, who is accused of selling the dream of freedom, is brought to the stand and he comments on the judgment of the tribes for revenge. The strong Manichean division informs the scene and offers an excoriating critique of adversarial politics. Walcott's narrative was in complete disagreement with and resistant to ideological and historical functioning of such binaries. He castigated Africanism in cultural practice/performance to be utterly futile and barren. By accepting the reactionary Nativism as an alternative to racist ideology will never help overcome the Manicheanism and he wondered about the utility of travelling in search "authentic" African experience with an imaginative association and illusory return.

In another dream sequence of the Apotheosis scene, the exaltation of the white values is excoriated; it is the firmest of all decisive actions. In Sc.3, Part ii, where Lestrade goads Makak to eliminate the vision of the white Muse by chopping off her head to discover beautiful blackness (10-11.319). If she is beheaded, he will be divested of the constraints of the Western value, obsession of many West-Indian blacks- an obsession for whiteness and abandon the image of a dependent nigger forever.[9] By chopping off her head Makak proclaims to be "free" and his psychic space is cleared of what Fanon calls "arsenal of complexes". If the myth of white supremacy is busted and its deception exposed, it will pave the way for de-subjugation. His exalted claim

---

[9] Fanon draws this from Germaine Guex's book *La Névrosed'abandon* (1950) and expresses it directly when writing, in the voice of Guex's Black man, "When my restless hands caress those white breasts, they grasp white civilization and dignity and make them mine" (1952 [2008: 45]).

of being "free" has been subject to political allegorisation. In America, the scene was lauded by the Black Power enthusiast when the movement was at its height and violence was recognized as a Fanonian "cleansing force".

Walcott himself pointed out that the American audience may have taken the violence as too eagerly, the act of reprisal as a clear sign of the freedom from white value systems. But Walcott was at pains to remind at the beginning of his *A Note on Production* that the play is only a dream and most of the things happen in the "minds of the characters". To find in the killing an affirmation of violent revolutionary politics in a manner of Dessalines is to miss the whole point of psychic emancipation –a prior condition for the revolutionary consciousness to be born. Critics like Hogan felt in the act of execution an agreement with Fanon's claim of violence as a "cleansing force" or cathartic. Fanon strongly argued that only through violence could colonized societies slough off their oppressors and their colonially constructed identities. As Fanon set forth his view, violence is a possible form of communication in the forces of colonialism. The act of beheading and disrobing of the royal robe are the signs of gaining self-knowledge: "He is a man, his independent self, free to begin anew" (Hamner 52). Instead of leading life as "blackman", he finds the freedom in living as a man. Getting rid of the awe-inducing vision of whiteness and by overcoming race-inflicted identity, the narrative repudiates black-white essentialised cultural politics, as Tejumola Olaniyan succinctly contends, "The challenge of resistance is no longer simply to invert the hegemonic discourse, but to radically alter the terrain of production of discourse and the relations of the subordinated to it. With Makak's final act—a rejection of black-white essentializing narratives—the dominant discourse's main supporting pillar, Manichaeism, becomes obsolete." Without resorting to political allegory, the plot allows the hero to gain self- knowledge, liberated from the prison of his dependent consciousness. It is the decisive moment for every West Indian to recognize the "green beginning" - the Adamic elation and discovery. This is the desired end of articulating the alternative among competing discourses.

The apparition scene has elicited an array of reviews and comments. John Thieme in his study *Derek Walcott* has interpreted the act of Makak as exorcising the stranglehold of European heritage and Afrocentric link before the narrative slides toward "post-colonial consciousness" (76). Walcott always believed that psychic liberation is a true enabler to the condition of post-coloniality. The act of killing as Daizal. R. Samad describes is symbolic of "polarized and static romanticized vision of his ancestral past" (242). Both the studies proffer the idea of identity as static, overdetermined. As Lestrade whips up frenzied Makak's passion for violent retribution Makak's final blow may have been fuelled by racist propaganda: "It is you who created her, so kill her!"(319) Walcott knew well that denunciation of "whiteness" is as reactionary as objectivization of the "black". In 1967 when the play was first produced, the consequences of revolutionary politics was not so obvious as it erupted a few years later in the early 70s. Stressing on the symbolic aspect of the scene, Makak is exonerated from what Robert. E. Fox calls "The bondage of kingship as well as that of the dream and all externally-imposed definitions of selfhood" (209). Progressive violence not only thwarts domination and oppression but as Sartre in his famous introduction to *Wretched of the Earth* put it is an expression of "self-creation".[10] Colonialism, Fanon argued in *Wretched of the Earth*, "is violence in its natural state, and will only yield when confronted with greater violence" (48). It may initiate a process of cure to the pathologies of colonialism. Unburdened by heritage or tradition, or possessed by some spirit, Makak rounds up his journey for finding his lost identity and original name, Felix Hobain. Throughout the play, the semantic stability of the categories like "black" and "white" are destabilized and various racially defined stereotypes are displaced. It alters, as Tejumola observes, "the terrain of production of discourse and the relations subordinated to it" (108). In Earl Lovelace's complex allegorical play, *Jestina's Calypso*, Jestina emerges as a denier of internalization of self- defeating identity ascribed to her. She sounds self- convinced despite her black, ugly face: "long after the echo of your laughter dies, I shall be walking still, striding still, with my head up against the winds of the world, battling to become myself" (25). With all the racial tensions within and without played out, Walcott's hero also regains his native identity. His dream is a possibility, possibility of the new identity that Lloyd Brown calls "the existential beginning of a new black self-definition" (201). Such possibility of "green beginnings" is enunciated in Lamming's novels like *Water with Berries or Natives of My Person* as they explore individual rebellion in resisting the tyranny of history. With such a beginning, a native will find liberation possible from any intrinsic racial identity and their hierarchization. And it will call into question the validity of race-based radical politics. Thus, Walcott's theatre aesthetic has taken to task the despotism of monoculture and political economy of identity.

Following sutures of all historical linkages, the Caribbean archipelago suffered a chronic homelessness or what Bhabha phrases "minus-in-the-origin". The interstices of alienation and intimacy, stasis and motion define

---

[10] Though such reviews failed to win the approval of the playwright. In an interview with J. P. White, Walcott offers a further explanation: "What he does is that he sheds an image of himself that has been degraded. When he thought he was Black, he did what he thought the black man should do. Both errors. So that the moment of cutting off the head is not a moment of beheading a white woman. It is a matter of saying there is some act, some final illusion to be shed. And it is only a metaphorical anyway it's only a dream" (166).

Walcott's "writing home"; he finds splintered but potent home of the Caribbean without its obvious association of belonging or origin. The Epilogue here brings to the fore the need to exorcise the "demon of alienation and homelessness" (Samad 228).

> "We left
> Somewhere a life we never found,
> Customs and gods that are not born
> again, Some crib, some grill of light
> Changed shut on us in a bondage, and withheld
> Us from that world below us and beyond,
> And in its swaddling cerements we're still bound".
>
> (*The Castaway* 35)

Having suffered exile, displacement and genocide down the centuries, "home" has been a problematic notion for the Caribbeans. Since the disappearance of an indigenous population in the fifteenth century, the islands were populated by those who flocked, forcibly and voluntarily, here from Africa, Asia or Europe; in Brathwaitean phrase all are "Arrivants" here: "the most significant feature of West Indian life and imagination since Emancipation has been its sense of rootlessness, of not belonging to the landscape" (Tejumola 94). For all its extra-regional population, geo-cultural dispersion, homelessness and uprooting from the ancestral homeland have been an inalienable cultural condition, as Makak describes his people - "like a twisted forest, like trees without names, a forest with no roots" (1:2, 16-19248). Violently torn from their distant home of Africa, they desired to locate them in Europe or America- the cultural, artistic or intellectual metropolitan centre. Or they looked to Africa for a reaffirmation of their identity, and as a means of dealing with their persistent sense of exile and displacement. In the words of Rajeev S. Pathke, "The sense of displacement found expression in a compulsion to set off in a real and symbolic journeying, in a constant and restless search for home that might appease displacement" (89).

But Walcott vehemently confronted this popular perception of the West Indians of home as spatially far-off, a locus of melancholic longing. By his own admission, all his artistic endeavours engage with "adamic" naming of the Caribbean as "home". This wrestling to articulate "home" has engaged several contemporary artists, like Harris or Glissant. Conditioned to dispersal and fragmentation, the West-Indian man tries to reassemble the fragments of his cultural past. In his noble lecture, Walcott himself said: "This gathering of the broken pieces is the care and pain of the Antilles. Antillean art is the restoration of our shattered histories, our shards of vocabulary" (54). The meandering and convoluted plot of *Dream on Monkey Mountain* charts a return to mountain "home" as its hero Makak appealed to the Corporal to be allowed the return only to his mountain home at the outset. He set out on his daily choir from the home with his follower, Moutique. As Daizal R. Samad observes, "In *Dream on Monkey Mountain*, the central character Makak attempts to re-discover the discontinuous links between the multiplicities of archetypes that reside in the oceanic layers of West-Indian culture" (18). After a dream-tossed, vision- ridden night passed in the prison cell, he walks back home. It appears that his home is isolated from political repression, a space seemingly outside the influence of the larger society. The in-placeness of Caribbean persona is a resistance to the colonial trauma of dislocation. After returning to the Monkey Mountain, he will resume his humble trade of charcoal selling. In *Prodigal*, Walcott's another masterpiece, the Caribbean home becomes a place of final rest; though here all wanderings and errantry are mental rather than physical. Towards the end, Makak has described himself as a mere drifter- one swept by sea-waves, uprooted and unmoored "washed form shore to shore". He exclaims that he has found the ground after all his wanderings to plant his feet (Epilogue, 5-7.326). Chorus with the refrain of "I going home" rounds up the action and what remains only is the movement of walking back to Monkey Mountain for Makak and Moustique from where they left at the outset of the action.

A quest motif underlies the non-linear, "contradictory" plot in *Dream on a Monkey Mountain*. Having undergone an utterly degraded life and after all the turmoil of soul, the home to which he returns is his hallowed mountain home. Notwithstanding his unchanged material position, he proclaims to have lived in the dreams of his people (Epilogue. 11-12, 326); thus, he has attained to the status of the prophet- leader of his community. It is not the vision and delirium of a deranged mind, merely. In the Epilogue, he is again asked and he confidently answers Lestrade:

> Makak: Hobain... My name is Felix Hobain.
>
> (5-6. 321)

In order to regain confidence, he shed the pejorative title, his name of abuse, Makak. By re-claiming his name Felix, meaning "happy" he also liberates himself from the degrading name of "Monkey". This recovery is described by Breslin as a stage of decisive transformation: "The main sign of his freedom is that, for the first time in the play, he remembers his real name- neither the derisive "Makak" nor the secret name given by the apparition, but simply "Felix Hobain" (153). Walcott was always aware of forced and artificial re-naming which needed to be cast aside before one can proclaim his/her personhood. Or the imposed name must be exploded before the lost identity is reclaimed. This recovery of the original name confirms the reclaiming of human identity; "The name, beginning as stigmata spell, turns into a panoply, a disguise, a protection to finally become the flag and emblem of a rebuilt community" (Loichot 12). In a more decisive gesture, he now rejects the white mask he used to carry in his bag. Both the illusions of White Goddess and African kingship are cast off as things of the past and he can claim the cultural mulatto in himself and recognize the mixed heritage in his personality. When he leaves behind the prison, he is no longer monkey-like individual but a human being. As a true West-Indian man, he can now assert where his genuine roots are. Deep in the heart of the forest, Makak recovers his humanity; he has fully reconciled to the fact of being one of Afro-Caribbean ancestry. Finding a new self- image, reconciliation with all incompatibilities dissolved, he is endowed with "a complex sense of the plural individual which contests the Freudian notion of schizophrenia as pathology" (Burnett 22). For Makak, Sunday morning is the morning to awaken from what Edward Baugh has called "dark night of the soul, his harrowing of hell" (85). To resume the charcoal burner's life, he must return to Monkey Mountain- to his profession at the lowest rung of society. This is a beginning with newness or "green beginning" as these lines from "Winding Up" makes clear:

> I live on the water,
> Alone. Without wife and children,
> I have circled every possibility
> To come to this
> a low house by great water
> with windows always
> to the stale sea.
>
> (*Collected Poems* 336)

This intermeshing of the realm of dream and practical reality has been a feature of Walcott's consummate artistry. In an interview with the New Yorker in 1971: "you forget Makak is a charcoal burner, he has to face a reality too. He has to come down to the market every Saturday to make a living" (18). Despite Walcott's exhortation to the contrary Makak's home-coming and claim of freedom have been opened up to an array of political, religious interpretations. Apparently, the episode can be studied as an affirmation of a life of dignified simplicity, without either shame or sentimentality. Makak is West Indian Everyman and by outdoing the demons of subjugation, he has assumed, what Crow and Banefield observe as "mythic dimension accorded to certain characters in folktales and folklore" (40). It may be inferred here that Makak has arrived into independent consciousness and overcome the "bewitching" of cultures. This emergence as a folkloric hero, this native West-Indian experience liberates Makak as he appears as "a solitary avatar of Walcott's Caribbean Adam" (Breslin 154). He not only found his home but also his dignity and confidence or what Soyinka calls his "cultural certitude". To put in James Baldwin's memorable words: "This past, this endless struggle to achieve and reveal and confirm a human identity, human authority, yet contains for all its horror, something very beautiful" (84). From the earliest days of his artistic career, Walcott was aware of the need to produce counter-narratives of self-definition and re-create and re-present the Afro-Caribbean histories that will enable them to see themselves anew. He has delved deep into himself to discover his innate contradictions and complexes. His journey has carried him from the illusory past to the solid materiality of the present. Like him, Lestrade also attains self-discovery and self- knowledge: "I was what I am, but now I am myself..." (2.2.299).

Moustique's advice "Go back, go back to Monkey Mountain, Go back" comes full circle with the refrain of the Chorus: "I going home".

This climax of "return" to West-India home counterpoints the "departure syndrome" of the West-Indian intellectuals and artists, stricken with undiminished sense of the rootlessness. The Windrush generation writers like Naipaul, Selvon left for the metropolitan centre from the place of birth or origin after disillusionment with living on the periphery of black colonial culture. At a critical juncture in the history of the region, Walcott's play articulated anew Caribbean ethos. Monkey Mountain is more than a physical home, a sign of cultural in-placeness. As Makak and Moustique walk back home, the memory of both the sun of Empire and African moon begin to fade away. Makak's homeward retreat is much more complex than the return to the lost home of Africa advocated by the political nationalists and its fruitless nostalgia. "For Walcott", as Daizal. R. Samad observes: "home is the Caribbean, fragmented but potent. We live there and strangely the Caribbean lives in a manifestly splintered presence within the oceanic layers of our psyche: a presence which will arise in us and address us in rainbow ways which we may not always comprehend, but which we must always put to creative use as we attempt to grapple with tortured existence" (21). In the first scene, Makak was woken up by Moustique for daily chores of selling coal. He returns to hut that Makak must return with small signal of smoke. For he is going "back to the beginning, to the green beginning of the world" (Epilogue 326). Makak has not only recovered his home and name in the Epilogue, when Lestrade asks him, Makak replies that he now believes in God. Though his is not the Catholic god of those who introduced Catholicism to the island, nor any African deity which has been re-introduced to replace the Catholic God.

Now he can clearly spell out his name or religion, his occupation of selling charcoal (12-13.322). No longer a king, prophet or shamanic healer, he has returned to his original identity of a down- to-earth, a poor charcoal seller. This is what may be called an exhilarating possibility of a New World man where he can proclaim "In the end is my beginning". Cultural independence beyond mimicry or derivativeness may have been an aesthetic mission of the programme of decolonization. Contrasted to the mutation of consciousness that takes place in Makak is contrasted another kind of transformation in the character of Lestrade, a real "straddler" between two cultural locations. At the end of the plot, he appears in a new guise; almost in a *volte face*, he claims to be a champion of the tribal leadership and holding up the mask he advises him to keep with him like others of his community. Unlike Makak, his is not a transformation of consciousness but a mere position changing which underscores political opportunism. His racial or cultural identification is motivated by cheap self-interest, positional advantage. Patricia Ismond puts it very succinctly: "The externals change but ethic remains the same: he looks to black code to regulate an order obliterating all native contradictions" (257). In the turbulent days in the 70s when the movements like "nativism" was surging up, Walcott's play fore-fronted the pluralism as a potent counter to exclusionary politics.

Throughout his career, Walcott believed that building a Caribbean self-image requires its artists un-construct the myth of white superiority and black inferiority. Like Makak, he considered a Caribbean artist to be an Adamic man in need of naming the objects and enunciating the cultural vision of his people. Makak in his final speech, describes himself only as an "old hermit" very different from prophets: "Other men will come, other prophets will come and they will be stoned, and mocked, and betrayed, but now this old hermit is going back home, back to the green beginning of this world" (Epilogue, 12-15, 326). The ending, as Paul Breslin has also noted, leaves open the question whether he has lost his heroic size in the resumption of his old trade. The charcoal seller's re-grounding of himself on the native soil embodies a kind of New World heroism, heroism of unaccommodated man. It is the heroism of Walcottian "nobody". In the absence of "king", "tribal chief" as model of story, his humble charcoal burner is re-coded as dignified fictional "hero". From extreme self-abasement Makak switches to exultant proclamation of his God-self after his transcendental encounter with the Apparition: "I feel I was a God self, walking through cloud/In the heaven of my mind". As Walcott asserts in his essay "Meanings": "This was a degraded man, but he had some elemental force in him that is still terrifying; in another society he would have been a warrior" (49). This terrifying energy of this elemental man reaffirms how the conflicted identity can help the Caribbean people relocate themselves. Old perceptions and beliefs, here, give way to powerful influence of hybrid reality in Makak's story and it issues out a challenge to the boundaries erected in the discursive arguments of the colonizer. The definitive closure as it is commonly assumed, does not leave us without some ambiguity. In returning to Mountain "home", Makak will return to the old, hierarchized society of material deprivation, the same place where he has chosen to live like a "wild beast" and feels most rooted like the Lebanese cedars (SC: 2, 8-11, 248). In making this journey, he has overcome his "big, big loneliness" (318). If there is "edenic promise", his fresh beginning is only a "hermit" like withdrawal and it will not matter if he is forgotten "like a mist". And it may be affirmative of Walcott's unwavering faith in a vernal space, a world apart from the twin pulls of Africa and Europe from where one may have contemplated fresh beginning. Lloyd Brown has found in the ending a beginning – "the existential beginnings of a new Black self- definition" (201). But it appears to be the beginning of unlearning the "native", "home" and above all, after divesting the Caribbean personhood of all baggage. Race may persist as a classificatory sign in the Caribbean, but Walcott's assertion of personhood grows beyond the shadow of primordial binaries. As racializing discourse of difference dislodged the fixed ontology of "native" and it ceased to become an inferior other and Makak's degraded life affirms this alternate representation of a rooted West Indian native. In an interview, Walcott has clarified the point most succinctly: "I say, he goes back to his mountain. It belongs to him. He has another name and now he can say it… I'm talking about the sense of ownership that allows him to feel that when he walks on that road, it belongs to him" (167).

A Dramaturgic Venture

In *Caribbean Discourse*, Glissant had already observed "experiment is for us [in the Caribbean] the only alternative; the organization of a process of representation that allows the community to reflect, to criticize, and to take shape" (209). *Dream on Monkey Mountain* fulfilled the need for an experimental alternative, a stage-product that encompassed the folk lives in myth, hopes and dream. Here, his stagecraft parts with the realism of some earlier St. Lucian plays and deploys more expressionistic technique-more syncretic, self-reflexive, and metatheatrical dimension. Walcott's instructive note on Production involves the audiences and actors alike in the performance: "The play is a dream, one that exists as much in the given minds of principal characters as in that of its writer, and as such, it is illogical, derivative, and contradictory. Its source is a metaphor and it is best treated as a physical poem with all the subconscious borrowings of poetry. Its style should be spare, essential as the details of a dream". Walcott has himself stressed that the play is a scripted dream. Much of its narrative is a dramatized subconscious. In this intricately structured text, the contrary impulses of the subconscious can best be explored in dream devices. The treatment of psychological complexity and rich symbolic design make the play a divided structure. Unfolding through dream sequences — through visions, delirium and hallucinations — its non-linear narrative is planted in the disordered and deranged psyche of the old charcoal seller. It fuses incommensurable realities of prose, poetry, reality and fantasy, sanity and madness. By a creative fusion of disparate artistic traditions, by crafting into "Coherent deformation" (in Allan Weiss's vocabulary), it appears as formless as the plays of Buchner or Strindberg. The plot probes into private areas of experience, inner idea or vision to shatter the facticity of the world and linearity of the plot. The masque, mimicry and mirroring as effective devises challenge the boundary between real and the fictive, role and role-playing of Makak or Moustique. Like any expressionistic drama, most of the episodes issue out of the mind of the dreamer. Though Walcott here adds the visions and dreams not of his protagonist alone but of the other characters that inhabit the dream atmosphere. In the Prologue, Makak relates how he catches feat and how he becomes possessed in the full-moon night. His words provoke the judges into laughter and while Corporal seeks to claim his notice by the mention of charges, he gets rapt in his speech. The apparition, like Banquo's ghost, appears before him and to none else as the Corporal mentions that he cannot see anything. The dream has implicated the entire community rather than remaining as individual derangement/delirium. As Lloyd Brown points out: "[O]ur revolutionary dreams are not a form of escape. They are also, paradoxically, psycho-existential affirmations of self, Black selfhood. However overly idealistic his revolutionary cause may be, and despite the romanticism of his "royal" African heritage, Makak affirms his human identity precisely because the capacity to dream has survived within him" (59). Hence, the focus must be shifted from Makak's hallucination and delirium to the dream of the community- long held under the thrall of colonial rule. As a Francophone writer Glissant stressed, "individual delirium and collective theatralization, as forms of cultural resistance are the first "catalysts" of this consciousness" (*Discourse* 195). Makak's dream utterances and gestures embody the emerging consciousness that leaves behind the baggage of history completely forever.

A quick overview of the plot will enable us to understand why Walcott's play structurally is called "illogical, derivative". The two parts (basic units) are connected by three scenes and separated by Prologue and Epilogue. Though Walcott has denied any such demarcation between reality and dream. On the realistic plane, most of the actions take place inside the cell where Lestrade is keeping surveillance on Makak and his two fellow felons, Souris and Tigre. Sometimes the cage vanishes out of sight, to add an air of unreality. The three scenes of the first act focus on Makak's vision of white beauty and the next three scenes shift to the pursuit of dream and kingship in Africa and his treatment of a sick man. The contradictory dream world extends in part 2 as

Makak escapes to Monkey Mountain after murdering the corporal with his cell-mates and subsequent jailbreak. The series of fantasy situations reach the climax in an elaborate and mock trial for indicting the crimes of the "Whites" against the civilization. The Epilogue returns to the cell and with the daybreak and as the night is over, Makak gets ready to walk back home. Walcott's reminder about the structure of the whole play blurs the line between the "realistic" plane and "surreal" situations; it straddles between a workday world and the dream world, the mundane and the visionary world. Though a non-linear narrative, it is markedly different from the psycho-expressionistic treatment of Eugene O'Neill's play *Emperor Jones*. The opening and ending are marked off from the six scenes of breathless suspense. There the action moves along the fleeing of the hero through the meandering forest path, in the course of a night, chased by the natives. He encounters spirits and gets dazed by hallucinatory spells. Jones's visions and hallucinations plunge him in complete alienation; all his past victims confront him and the ancestral memory erupts to strip him of his towering vanity. While Jones's is a personal tragedy, Walcott's play is rooted in the fractured psyche of a native West-Indian "everyman". Its spatial and temporal belonging is not fixed in the way it is with Jones. As when Lestrade accuses the resurrected Moustique of betrayal and some other characters jeer at the vision of Makak and offer their own comments on it. It is Moustique who has sought to exploit the visionary gift of his comrade by his impersonation and spurious performance of a prophetic healer. He also knocks Makak down from his dreamy state, reminding him of the market day and their trade responsibilities. By pitting practical reason, against madness, Walcott denies the plot of structural coherence. To liberate drama from the straitjacket of convention, the plot abandons order, clarity and the disjointed scenes capture the truth hidden in the recess of a mind. Each dream episode is not technical novelty but a part of his quest for claiming an independent identity. Almost in a carnivalesque reversal, the poor charcoal seller appears in a royal robe. Thus, the dream becomes an agency for imaginative reversal. Robert E. Fox illustrates the episode through historical facts, citing from Naipaul's *The Loss of El Dorado*. Naipaul in his famous travelogue mentions a widely popular cultural practice among the slave society in the nocturnal ceremonies and revelries in which slaves play-acted as kings and queens.[11] And in their masquerade, they would mock and jeer at their masters. This revelry allowed them to topple down the hierarchy of master-slave. It was a palliative against the bitter, oppressive realities. By allowing Makak a royal title, Walcott opened up possibilities of reclaiming

---

[11] Robert. E. Fox's critical study is intended to place the dream at the centre of revolutionary consciousness and he completely agrees with Lloyd W. Brown that the capacity to dream is a sign of human identity.

identity and offers an alternative to the bounded space of realities of lived experiences. As Makak confesses that though he has dreams they do not disturb his others' soul (225). In the Apothesis scene, the fantasy trial suggests an alternative to crude, physicality of racial reprisal. Very significantly, the act of beheading is rather "symbolic" and such an act could cleanse the oppressive mentality of the ruler and redeem the downtrodden. It is what also enables Makak's return from the realities of everyday world. Here, Walcott's surrealistic renderings become purgative of the revenge-politics and racial tussle. Walcott never ceased to lash out at the process of identity formation grounded on Black Power politics.

In using a dream structure strategically, the Canadian playwright, Thomson Highway's significant play *Dry Lips Ought a Move to Kapuskasing* resembles Walcott's masterpiece. In both of them, what is required is a heavily physical form of acting to be embodied through a trickster figure. Walcott's famous contemporary, Wilson Harris, also in his masterpiece, *The Palace of Peacock* deploys the narrative strategy which blurs the dividing line between historical and mythic strata. It wrenches the readers free from the gravity of history and prepare for a psychic journey. The amalgamation of poetic and realistic experience, lyrical and picong ensured a novel stage experience for his audience. Walcott had always stressed the proximity of the poem and drama and he defined drama as a form of enacted verse. In his note, Walcott lays stress on the role of the "unconscious" in structuring a play that negotiates between lyrically inspired moment and prosaic, official rhetoric or continuous oscillation between realistic and poetic realms. The play is a series of dream within a dream, play within a play and justifies its "contradictory", illogical nature. It is a dream that transforms Makak and Walcott's artistic vision. Walcott was always sceptic of teleological history as the linearity of the narrative perpetuates the hegemony of the colonial culture. His hero, Makak, in his recital of dreams, overcomes the dictum of history and the limits of racism lift him to the plane of sublime realization (5-7, 227).

Walcott reposed strong faith in poetry as an integral component of drama but also fused the native materials, the street language with lyrical exuberance. Readers have often found the play "difficult" for its complex ways to combine "modern drama of consciousness of the modern western dream play with the convention of West Indian folk story, the world of Frantz Fanon with the firelit face of the storyteller in the village compound" (Crow and Banefield 40). If the Epilogue finds the hero speaking for himself, proclaiming his "difference", the play still compels our attention by refusing to escape the "divisions between sanity and madness, reality and dream" (Baker 16). Veering between alternate realms, the plot leaves the audience in a precarious position between dream and reality and they experience the stage acts very differently from a straightforward liberatory narrative. The major characters mutate and transform and the consciousness is disburdened from any hegemonic control. In the process, "native" ceases to become a fixed, deterministic category. From painful negation, the Caribbean home becomes a sign of promise and possibility. This "incoherent play", as Errol Hill describes it, forefronts the multiple layers of personality, a mixed composition of the cultural selves and in so doing, theatre emerges as an alter/"native" sign of transversal dynamism of Caribbean cultural patterns.

Chapter 3

Staging Classics at the Interface of Creation and Criticism

"Re-writers", as Lefebvre observes, "have always been with us".[1] From the anthologies of Greek classics to the twentieth-century rewritings from the ex-colony, the originals have been "borne across" and transposed in a new cultural milieu. The distant centre and its canon have been instrumental in inculcating the Humanistic values in the colonial classroom. The artists who were the beneficiaries of this education have reworked "the European 'classics' in order to invest them with more local relevance and to divest them of their assumed authority/authenticity" (Gilbert 15). In the colonies, the theatre at its nascent stage—both as text and performance took classics as the point of departure; in reinterpreting the classics, they conflate the temporal, spatial and cultural distance. Though he was consistently drawn to classics, Walcott knew that they cannot "console enough" (*Arkansas Testament*); in his plays and poems, he has reworked, translated and reinterpreted their time-honored values and standards. Though the European canon was a foundation of the West Indian writers, Lamming and Brathwaite were capable of rejecting the colonial ideology and at the same time fostering a national consciousness. It was through the family's interest and "sound colonial education" that he was exposed to the classics and in his creative works, he set out to structure a comparison between Aegean narratives of the *Iliad* and the *Odyssey* and black diasporic experiences in the West Indies. His creative journey into the ancient world opened up new questions and trajectories in regard to the theater aesthetics and practice. It entailed the exigencies of local context and hybrid cultural practice, largely ignored in the canonical texts. As a colonial subject, he was prompted into an ambivalent dialogue with the classics while recasting the masterpieces of Homer, Joyce, and Defoe into dramas. Mounting an imaginative challenge to the hegemony of the colonial institutions and practices, his plays initiated a cross-cultural dialogue and the cross-pollination of different performance styles, which proved compatible with

---

[1] Lefebvre has described rewriting "as the motor behind literary evolution" in the opening chapter "Prewrite" of his Translation Classic (*Translation, Rewriting, and the Manipulation of Literary Fame*) to stress how it influences the reception and canonization of works of literature.

creolizing theatre and de-Westernization of Trinidadian drama. In Walcott's imaginative vision, Joyce was a contemporary of Homer and Homeric characters; for him, Homer could be reinvented in the twentieth-century Caribbean archipelago. For the New World artists as Walcott believed what mattered more was the fluidity of myth rather than historicist time: "These writes reject the idea of history as time for its original concept as myth, the partial recall of the race (*Essays* 37).[2] History, for them was mere "fiction"; New World artists believed more in simultaneity with the old time – a negotiation between different dimensions of temporality which provided the necessary underpinning of creole aesthetics. By infusing postcolonial energy into the classical texts and translating the values and ideological signs of the classics into the semiotics of theatre. The material culture and plural lifeworlds of his native place had offered Walcott an "in-between" space of enunciation - between the present and the past, local and global, centre and periphery. The authoritative discourses of the pre-texts could be strategically reversed through alternative, non-canonical narratives of "becoming". The multi-faceted colonial rule and their legacies underscored Walcott's "anxiety" and "desire", the contrary pulls between attraction and repulsion, the politics of his land and the aesthetics of Western literary tradition. This chapter is divided into two sections/parts as it engages with three major rewrites-*Pantomime and Odyssey-A Stage Version, A Branch of Blue Nile*. The first section discusses the "rewrites" as trans-genric manipulation and reworking of the master narratives and the second section focuses on how the staging of the classic benefits from the framework of metatheatre, a creative self- reflexive way to comment on the theatre-making in the Caribbean archipelagoes.

Walcott's literary project, like Soyinka's, has sometimes been castigated for its underlying Eurocentric universalism and proffering elitist European sensibility. Such reductive criticism has overlooked the complexity and ambivalence of his canonical rewritings or the fraught and problematic relationship to the masterworks. Tejumola Olaniyan observes, "Wole Soyinka and Derek Walcott engage in interesting ways the spectral insinuation of the dependence of their cultural practice on props from an "alien, imperializing culture" (485). Walcott had remarked in an interview. "But my generation was not schizophrenic about the heritage of the Empire and the heritage of the Caribbean. It was a double rather than a split thing ... there was no tension in the recitation of a passage from Henry V and going outside and making jokes

---

[2] In a collection of his essays, *Black Moods in the Caribbean,* "The Muse of History" was first published in 1974; it underscores Walcott's passionate dismissal of artificial rupture between Old and the New World, Past and Present.

in patois or relaxing in a kind of combination patois of English and French".³ Like Wilson Harris, Walcott had engaged with the ambivalent relationship between colonial past and postcolonial present. His passionate eulogy of Marlowe, Milton or Joyce and ostensible resolve to "prolong the mighty line of Milton and Marlowe" never amounted to mere Westphilia. In countering the European representation, he sought to translate the colonial legacy and all its borrowed influences to open up an alternate cultural space in which the past must be seen not in isolation but in a continuum. In making revisionary swerves from his artistic father figures, his narratives progress along the past-present continuum. Borrowing from the forbears and weaving a dense intertextual fabric, his plays have come to inhabit a liminal space between "adaptation" and "original". While remaining vigilantly critical of colonial legacies and affiliative identification, Walcott renovated the mega-texts of Europe to foreground the vision of post-national Caribbean society. A tug-of-war between his creative impulse and political orientation had refused him any settled position. This "schizophrenic" division became a major axis of his creole aesthetics; it proved his liminal cultural locations to be quite useful. Though woven out of the "already written" and "already read", all his major rewritings explore an imaginative space beyond the orbit of European definition. In Barthesian terms, his plays become a multi-dimensional space and opens out to innumerable centres of culture. In stage rendition, the performatives negotiate between incompatible traditions and incommensurable cultures. He always shunned the paradigm of "writing back" in the sense of wholesale repudiation; his stage adaptations of the ante-texts demonstrate how by "un-writing" and "re-writing" the cultural codes, the "other" may be transformed into an ambivalent, aporetic sign.

Almost all the major Caribbean and African artists have decoded many European classics and fought against the empire writers for their "representations of Africa and Africans atrophied" (Yousaf 17). Their adaptation constitutes a set of deliberate translative intervention which results in a "counter" text which cleaves to and from its source text. It corroborates the essential duality of its existence both inside and outside its culture. Rewriting, as a form of recreation, devises a strategy to achieve equivalence of situations while encountering cultural mismatches, misrepresentations and pejorative stereotypes. Through omission, expansion and other strategic manipulations, the adaptation violates an original while paying a tribute to it. The postcolonial artists, thus, were steered to the process of "learning to borrow selectively and

---

³ See, Charles H. Rowell, "An Interview with Derek Walcott, Part I," *Callaloo* 34 (1988): 81, 833.

unsupervised from Europe, those who had 'no culture' took the initiative in interpretation" (Boehemer 164). By challenging the contours of mainstream performance, these stage adaptations have rendered the anterior texts fragile and vulnerable. Walcott's plays attempt to explore the paradoxical relationship between the conditions that create West Indian rewritings and those that in their turn may subvert the effects. As effective strategies of de-colonizing the stage – voice, body, discourse, accents of speech – the whole semiotic network of theatre – disrupts the authority of the imperial canon and creates new resonances in them.

Without being burdened by his colonial inheritances or straddling between "native" and "foreign", Walcott concentrated only on the assimilation of his every ancestor. Distrustful of monolithic generalization of the classics, he had sought to "unwrite" and "rewrite" (Marx 89) the Western paradigms which were enablers of perpetuating cultural hegemony. His much-favoured mulatto aesthetics pave the way for the traffic between "mimicry" and "original", "oral" and "scribal". All his appropriations and revisionary swerve set aside relations as either complicitous or adversarial. This literary practice of Walcott "rejects the idea that a colonial education in English literature constituted an epistemic violence, since he understands literature to be much more than a mere reflection of the immediate world in which he lives" (Burns 74). Like Harris or Glissant he was suspicious of a linear ordering of the past and in searching for a "timeless" point his narrative oscillates between the past in the present. Every rewrite, as Walcott believed, is a product of a kinetic process, a mutation and transposition which cancels out linear genealogies. While reworking Homer, Synge or Defoe, he wrested away the narrative authority to subvert the imperial hegemony of the canon. Harold Bloom's well-known stricture against Walcott as a mere "composite voice" of post-Yeatsian modernists and totally lacking in "originality" has overlooked the deep ambivalence of his artistic make-up. In the aesthetico-political context of the nascent West- Indian federalism, his stage renderings displaced the codes of the dominant discourses and the stable temporal frames of the linear narratives. By the amalgam of custom and belief of distant temporal zones, the postcolonial artists could recode, radicalize the tradition that existed in a continuum with literary father figures. "Post-colonial writers", as Said observed, "bear their past within them... as potentially revised visions of the past tending towards a new future, urgently reinterpretable and re-deployable experiences, in which the formerly native speaks and acts on a territory taken back from empire" (31). The practice of "history seen as sequential time" ("Muse" 40), prompted by linear chronological trajectory, only encourages an aesthetics of recrimination and despair. For Walcott, the predecessor texts that fertilized his imagination were simultaneous and when appropriated in the Caribbean context, the past came to co-exist simultaneously in the present: Art, when conceived as simultaneity, will help us understand how Joyce appears to be a contemporary of Homer (*Essays* 62). Often described as a "magpie poet", Walcott conceived the politics of postcolonial mimesis to be a very fertile re-creative process which contravenes and traduces barren replication. His counter-discursive praxis offered a kind of "canonical counter discourse", a method by which "colonized cultures can refuse the seamless contiguity between a classical past and post-colonial present that the empire strives to preserve" (Tompkins 51). His stage adaptations of master texts and (ab)use of their metanarratives opened up serious questions about the nature and trajectories of cultural activity in the post- Independence days. In a very famous essay, "When We Dead Awaken: Rewriting as Re-vision", Adriene Rich has described revision to be an "act of survival which tends to enter an old text from a new critical direction" (18).[4] In contesting the monoliths of high imperialism, Walcott had manipulated his narratives to reflect from a critical angle. Initiating a cross-cultural dialogue with classical parents, these revisions maintain a median position between distance and proximity, adherence and rupture, fidelity and betrayal. Like his celebrated peers, Rhys and Harris, Walcott also repudiated the unidirectional link between the source and its "con-texts" to generate a continuum which may be described as "the disjunctive merging of the familiar and the strange, the present and the past, the repressed and the returned" (Cooppan 21).[5] This merging underscores the significance of forging an altered subject position and the alter/"native" cultural narratives refuses to lean either towards Eurocentricity or towards ethnocentricity.

A literary text allows us traverse a network of relations as it does not exist in a hermetically sealed universe. As "genes" of new text come from its ante-text, all literary text, inevitably, resists stable and objective interpretation. In Frederic Jameson's view, "each hermeneutical confrontation, between an interpreter and a 'text', between an interpreter of one culture and the text of another culture, always mobilizes, at each pole of interpretative encounter, a whole deployment of prejudice and ideology". Walcott's re-compositions were no doubt "interpretative encounter" and a process of mutation into several alternative discourses. In Barthes's famous trope every text is a form of "weaving" or "spinning" and as readers, we are launched into a wider,

---

[4] "Re-vision – the act of looking back, of seeing with fresh eyes, of entering an old text from a new critical direction – is for us more than a chapter in cultural history: it is an act of survival. Until we can understand the assumptions in which we are drenched we cannot know ourselves."

[5] In her essay "Ghosts in the Disciplinary Machine: The Uncanny Life of world Literature". Cooppan observes how the "temporality" haunts the texts with a spectrality and by such "ghosting" challenges the boundaries between "old" and "new" text.

transcultural horizons of experience besides meeting the classics' existing standards. In appropriating and abrogating the worldviews of the colonial masters, Walcott's theater "does not just "...select words from a language system, they select plots, generic features, aspects of character, images, new ways of narrating, even phrases and sentences from literary texts and from literary traditions" (Allen 11). These rewrites, in articulating difference', generate what Achille Mbembe calls borrowing a phrase from Du Bois "inner twoness" (12) - the difficulty of complete identification with native tradition or colonial modernity. Achebe's *Arrow of God*, while facilitating the hubristic tragic story of downfall so prevalent in the Western literary canon, foregrounds the local political struggle of the six villages of Umuaro. Like the Africans, the Caribbeans had also had the experience of co-habiting a concrete world of displacement, exile and living with the colonial legacies. In displacing the familiar narrative pattern to an unfamiliar locale posited Walcott's plays at the cusp between "the linear, fast time of modernity and the slower time of tradition" (Ven 12). The New World artists willfully turned away from the model of the literary forbears and repudiated direct link in transmission and reproduction of linguistic or cultural signs. In reconnecting drama to its "root", Walcott's creative confrontations were penetrated by different temporalities and fertilized by inseminations of voices. As in a radio interview, Walcott had affirmed "One's own voice is an anthology of all the sounds one has heard". The dynamic openness to all his masters —Homer, Joyce and Shakespeare— has infused Creole energy; for Walcott, staging classics in the Caribbean milieu and before a native audience was a challenge to his inventive dramaturgy. Moreover, the rewrite opened up a space for constellation of divergent worldviews, belief systems which pre-empts possibility of closure. Buttressed by trans-regional and trans-national theatre-aesthetic, they reconstruct their world "in the manner of a collage, made up of fragments and off-cuts of cultural myth and memory" (Boehemer 178).[6]

It is the "massively knotted and complex histories of special but nevertheless overlapping and interconnected experiences" (Said 32) of the Caribbean diaspora that yielded hybridizing and syncretizing influence on the artistic practices in the region. The Great tradition of the colonizer and the 'little tradition' of the subjugated people lay in such easy proximity that the "high" and "low" culture binary ceased to matter to the artists like Walcott, Harris and Brathwaite. Soyinka had also noted that European modernity had drawn

---

[6] Elleke Bohemer in the fifth chapter of *Colonial and Post-colonial Literature*, discusses Independence and the experiences of a new nation formation for the colonized and creole population which remained a major preoccupation with novelists like Raja Rao and Ngugi WaThiong'o.

Nigerians into constantly shifting pluralistic terrain and made the reduction of the nationalist contest into a bi-polar clash of cultures impossible. The discourses that locate the colonized as ontologically inferior, to be brought under the tutelage of the enlightening presence and influence of the "West", could be challenged and confronted by performative ruses and trans-cultural "(re) actions" to the Empire. The polyphonic structure of his new theatre emerged as a local alternative to the "purist" narratives of the Empire and their intrinsic hierarchical value system. Gilbert and Tompkins have contended that all performance texts which set out to violate the canon also proved to be a site of "an agonistic encounter between local and received traditions" (21). Such literary "take over" relieves cultural dependency and reclaims heterogeneity through all its semiotic signs — voice, body, discourses and accents of speech. In both these stage adaptations and revisions, the authority of the canon gets disrupted and supremacist Western ideology is demythified. They redefine the performance as expressive of affiliative impulse rather than filial acceptance and instrumental in reclaiming long-excluded cultural elements.

Classics, as Lucas has concluded, emanate from the settled cultures in which values are clear and identities stable. As cultural monuments, classics have enriched human mind and upheld the unequivocal moral truth. In Saint Beauve's view classic is not restricted to a particular age or author but implies a continuity of tradition as it is "open to endless intervention in successive acts of reading and interpretation" (Mukherjee 33).[7] Coetzee in calling classics 'radically new', has outlined its mobility and its potential for existing beyond its originary culture. In the seventies, his post-workshop productions as rewrites garnered serious international attention as the creole dramaturgy produced startling examples of an interweaving of Shakespeare and Calypso within the orbit of performance. At the interstice of alternate local and global performance styles, the translation of classics from "page" to "stage" involved cross-pollination between poetry and play—the two separate yet deeply connected creative realms. These two different dimensions are inventory; as Defoe's prose or Homeric poem were rich with the potential for drama. Walcott masterfully elicited and reinvented their essence in the postcolonial context of his native St. Lucia. The transgenric rendering of *Joker of Seville* or *Pantomime* testifies to Walcott's dynamic reworking "of the traditions using

---

[7] In an interview with Nancy Schoenberger, Walcott speaks in Beauvian cadences on the possibility of the modern classic: "What's new about a classic is that it stays new. You have your debts to your predecessors; your acknowledgement is a votive acknowledgement. Seamus Heaney recognized in a review that 'The Schooner Flight' opens like Piers Plowman. You put that there deliberately: 'as this reminded me of that, so let it remind you also.'" ("Interview" 17).

classical referents as the basis for new work which includes the idiom of the Caribbean" (Hardwick 239). As a rewriter and adapter Walcott had a firm conviction that the classics may be changed and perfected; through re-compositions they interpret and reinterpret metanarratives and grand themes of history. As a powerful cultural tool theatre's appropriation of the words, symbols and images helped him shift the power structure of the originary script. The creative confrontation that occurs in these plays bound "...performers and spectators together in a surreal journey of empowerment that carried the real potential for collective action" (Ampka 5). The theatricality of daily lives and the gifts of colonial education could generate a new theatrical experience for the dispossessed Caribbeans. The stage manipulation of these narratives proved the mega-texts to be inviolate whole and the reprisal to be a new thing which Bhabha defines as "neither one nor other".

Pantomime

Writing from the backwaters of the empire, Walcott's major rewrites held up to question the ideological bias of canon-formation. The very ontology of "universalism", the illusory fixity of the classics is confronted by rewritings and their counter-narratives; Achebe pointed out that it would be instrumental in redeeming the self-abasement of the colonized. After his several reworking of the Crusoe myth in poems, Walcott mounted a stage adaptation in 1978. After its first production, *Pantomime* was immediately recognised as a remarkably relevant and timely work; it unleashed a candid commentary on post-independence social and racial politics in West Indies. It is intended to be a comic skit of Defoe's classic – a rehearsal piece by Harry-the hotelier and his handyman, Jackson – to be presented before the tourist in the season of the Christmas. Within a framework of farce, it adds a critical edge to Crusoe- Friday relation and also interpolates the colonial stereotypes of the original. In parodying the story of the colonization through a rehearsal piece, Crusoe and Friday merge into "a composite identity". A stage reprisal of the Crusoe myth was not a mere upturning of the power hierarchy but a complex interplay of actor, director and performance. With a deft manipulation of the monocultural and monolingual source text, Walcott's stage version brought to the fore a jarring juxtaposition of popular, folk and European traveling theatre mode. He knew that the writers of his generation were "natural assimilators" (*Essays* 4). The benefit of reading the literature of empires, Greek, Roman, British, the language of the classroom and proximity to patois of the street led him to discover an alternative theatrical idiom. By a generic transposition, *Pantomime* has displaced its loci of signification because uncomplicated representation would have advanced the imperial agenda. In this comic two-hander the Crusoe myth gathers a transformative momentum and becomes an interpretative response. A Caribbean rendering of Defoe's classic and translating it into another culture involved the corruption of the text and interrogation of its seeming cultural "authenticity". Walcott resituates the story in a Tobago guest house and gives it a different political resonance by Carnivalesque teasing of the master script. The banter of the performers creatively disrupts the framework of a pantomime; their facial and gestural acting become the guiding force to the "inventive riff and reimagining of race relations between the modern-day protagonists, Jackson and Trewe" (Gilbert 129). Both the protagonists improvise through role-swapping, cross-gender play-acting which unsettles the centrist assumption of racial identification. A range of performative strategies adopted in the melding of performance idioms of English music hall and the Trinidadian calypso manages to make possible a "deconstructive assault on a vast array of cultural systems and codes which have defined the encounter of the colonizer and the colonized" (qtd. in Tompkins 38). This shifting strategy of creolizing through an effortless fusion of contrasting performance styles issues out (re) action to the classics. When Jackson mimics the axiom of colonial discourse, the enunciation appears "ambivalent", one that assumes a "new" different meaning in post-colonial times. His carnivalesque reversal of cultural hierarchy by assuming a different persona and de-sacralisation of the source text with *picong* effectively subdue the state power and official ideologies. The treatment of the Don Juan myth for his audience involved the incorporation of carnival elements, the musical form of *parang*, folk practice of stick-fight in Walcott's famous adaptation of a legendary Spaniard in *The Joker of Seville* (1978).[8] Here, in eliciting a comic skit out of colonial archetype in *Pantomime* Walcott manipulates the original with song, *picong*, carnivalesque acting for the entertainment and appreciation of his Caribbean audience, which together is often called the "creolizing" the stage rendition. When Harry's parrot initiates the name of the German owner "Herr Nigger" with a creole accent, the phrase sounds very much like "hey nigger" – it traces back to Fanon's encountering of a racist slur during a train journey.

"I know your explanation: that a old German called Herr Heinegger used to own this place, and that when that maquereau of a macaw keep cracking: "Heinegger, Heinegger," Language is ideas, Mr. Trewe" (A. 1, 133).[9]

---

[8] It was to be an adaptation of Torso de Molina's *El burlador de Sevilla y convidado de piedra* (*The Trickster of Seville and The Stone Guest*) who re-created from various legends the figure of Don Juan, a hero-villain- a seductive libertine who devotes his life in seducing women taking great pride in his ability. The original was a play set in the fourteenth century Spain. Walcott revises the legend, commissioned by the Royal Shakespeare Company and in the Caribbean milieu turns him into a "stickman".

[9] All the textual quotes are from *Postcolonial Plays: An Anthology*, edited by Helen Gilbert.

"Language for the individual consciousness", as Bakhtin says, "lies on the borderline between oneself and the other. The word in language is half someone else's (293). Walcott's creative manipulation of language not only destabilizes the relations of signifier and signified but also admitted the "Other" of the language within.

After its first production, *Pantomime* (1974) was immediately recognized as a remarkably relevant and timely work – a powerful critique against the racial politics and capitalist aggression in the West Indian islands. Walcott stages the archetype as an encounter between a white castaway and a local native, a hotel owner and his handyman, both coming from a performance background. The realist and linear narrative of Crusoe's solitary arrival on the island and subsequent stay with the savage boy Friday of the original undergoes role-swapping, masquerading to mutate into a "new" text. Instead of offering an oppositional reading to Crusoe- Friday dyad, Walcott has reworked them into protean figures who can act out their multiple selves by shedding the racially determined identity. Without giving vent to a recriminatory impulse, he exploited the subversive, performative potential of Defoe's original. While the master narrative of Defoe and its binary logic only bolstered the colonial logic of polarity and fixed category. Here, the multiple subject positions are played out in Jackson Philip's vibrant role-playing and masquerading. Such re-writings, not only metamorphose the unitary, rational, autonomous and self-sufficient agent of human history but also replace the characters with multiple subjectivities and split personalities. Through repeated theatrical strategies of improvisation, masquerading, mimicry, *Pantomime* re-codes the classic in the Caribbean postcolonial cultural context. In so doing, the Caribbean stage becomes a site of departure. The framework of Carnival adapted into British music hall style acting here lays bare the vulnerability of the dramatic paradigm. By dynamic infusion of cultural realities into the classical text, its canonical values are not only displaced, but the cultural, political complexity of postcolonial West Indies is forefronted. For the reverse rendition of the Crusoe myth from the outset, the two-men cast enters into a sort of carnivalesque rehearsal as Harry forges a panto script. Their creative experiments as actors initiate a process of theatre-making; it allows free rein to the emotions lurking behind the subject position of the employer and the employed. The process of "carnivalesque teasing of Defoe's and Western culture's assumption" (Gilbert 139) and disturbs the naturalness of the premises of the hierarchy. In re-enacting the myth of industry and progress, Walcott's play explores the continuum between the colonialist ideologies of mid-seventh century and late twentieth-century neo-colonial ethics of profit and loss. By the interplay of 'classical' and 'creole' acting, the performers disrupt the realism of play-acting- which Paula Burnett defines as 'non-mimetic method to raise political awareness" (159). When

Jackson takes a dig at the popular colonial axiom – "in the sun that never sets on your empire, I did what you did boss, bwana, effendi, bacra, sahib... that was my pantomime. Every movement you made, your shadow copied... (stops giggling) and you smiled as a child does smile at his shadow's obedience..." (A.1, 137), it corroborates how 'the same sign can be appropriated, translated and read anew' (Bhabha 55). When slapstick comedy and psycho-confessional drama intersect and jocular and serious acting collide, the host text becomes divested of its supposed "authenticity". In the interstitial space of performance, all figural binarism of its 'pre-text' like master-slave, black-white, colonizer and colonized, are dismantled. Here, the theatrical signs of voice, movement underline the text as more a 'citation' rather than "origin". Unlike very conventional theatrical communication in which gestures and series of bodily movements convey meaning between actors and audience, the Crusoe- panto becomes a "doing"; through the cross-cultural dialogue of the black servant and the white master appears to be a process riven with gaps, flaws and contradiction. Here performance signs do not merely represent a character but reflex back upon it to blur the divide between fiction and reality. Walcott underlined the confessional dimension of such acting - "The point is very simple. There are two types. The prototypical Englishman is not supposed to show his grief publicly. He keeps a stiff upper lip. Emotions and passion are supposed to be things that a troubled Englishman avoids. What the West-Indian character does is to try to wear him down into confessing that he is capable of such emotion and that there's nothing wrong in showing it" (*Critical* 214-215). Brecht had also found the driving of a dramatic wedge between the actor's role as "sign-vehicle" and his appearance as a social and physical presence to be very instructive. In the fluid space of performance, the apex of the hierarchy is no longer occupied by the actor and performers. In *Pantomime* performance event moves along freely and parts with the authorial intention to undermine the supposed finality of the script. In his seminal work *Postdramatic Theatre*, Hans-Thies Lehmann argued that drama and theatre exist in the popular imagination only as mutually supportive and interdependent; therefore, the audience's attempt to organize the cohesive ideas of the plot from the performance ends up in frustration. A very significant mutating effect of the rehearsal show is registered as both Harry and Jackson experience their subject position and confront freedom and history with race-swapping role and improvisation. The mutation of their subject position illustrates how "The human being is a node and a recursive loop in a complex system of interchanges and assemblages and flows" (Venn16). The rehearsal pantomime and its mimetic strategies of role-reversal engender an alternative form of agencies which undoes the mythic pattern through what Patrick Taylor calls "liberating narrative of the authentic Creole appropriation of the classical tradition" (296).[10] As mere structural opposition of colonial master narrative would have missed the negotiation and relationality, Walcott's retelling disturbs "the familiar alignment of colonial subjects- black/white, self- other' and disperse "the traditional grounds of racial identity" (Bhabha 58).

When carried over into the comic framework of the entertainment, the mythical narrative in both its British and African dimension exposes the dangers of fixity and fetish of identity and enunciates a possibility of "re-creation of the self" (Bhabha 12). By renaming the servant "Thursday" Walcott reverses naming as a right of the white Crusoe- a rejoinder of the "coercive right of Western noun" (Bhabha 334). In Defoe's original, Friday's learning of the Bible or dressing himself with the goat-skin proffers mimicry as unproblematic copying, producing an effect of resemblance; but, here, Jackson in making 'colonial mimicry' articulates what Bhabha calls, "the desire for a reformed, recognizable Other, as a subject of difference that is almost the same, but not the quite" (122). Serving breakfast for Harry, the owner of the guest house, Jackson places his service in the context of historical narratives of slavery. By pitting a daily choir against the macro-events of indenture and slavery, the modernist and segmented time of the source text is collapsed. Such self-reflection of Jackson provides a thoughtful lens upon the performative aspect of identity and what Bhabha terms as "performance of identity as iteration" (10). Jackson paddles his canoe, mimes a shipwreck and then proceeds to teach his white slaves in the African language. And his reminder of placing a time limit on piss-break and extorting more labour undermines "man to man" communication Jackson's mimic acts, be they verbal or gestural, no doubt produces their "excess" and "difference" and move towards further self-fashioning. Always distrustful of "originality", Walcott did never tire of pointing out mimicking as instrumental in displacing the structural equivalence and logic of superiority. Harry, too, in course of role-playing also reveals how this panto will relieve his past trauma and redeem him from seeming inferior complexity:

> "All right. I'll tell you what I'm going to do next, Ellen: you're such a big star, you're such a luminary, I'm going to leave you to shine by yourself. I'm giving up this bloody rat-race" (162, 4-7)

---

[10] In his essay "Myth and Reality in Caribbean Narrative: Derek Walcott's *Pantomime*", Patrick Taylor analyses the Crusoe myth as a translation and re- creation of a mythic narrative into a liberating narrative.

Staging Classics at the Interface of Creation and Criticism 79

This overlap of personal and political reanimates the mythic narrative of the mega-text. Advising him to regain self-confidence during his performance, Jackson brings Harry, his master, to self-knowledge. Showing greater purposiveness, Jackson embodies what Patricia Ismond describes as "the spirit of independence that has been gradually taking root in the region" (*Drama* 16). In Coetzee's *Foe*, Friday is denied any voice as he is rendered tongueless by a former slave trader and his enforced silence is suggestive of the failure of the centre to listen to its oppressed other. By contrast, Walcott's Jackson is verbally proficient, energetic and witty to actively confront the violence of the metropolitan centre. His creative improvisatory performance unfixes the signs of identity as determined and stable. Coming from different cultural backgrounds, Jackson and Harry here collaborate to forge a hybrid theatre practice which inscribes Defoe's text within the Caribbean context:

Jackson: "whether Robinson Crusoe was on a big boat or not, the idea is that he got ...(pause) shipwrecked. So I ... if I am supposed to play Robinson Crusoe my way, then I will choose the way in which I will get shipwrecked" (A.1, 139).

Before choosing to play Robinson Crusoe neither Harry nor Jackson could foresee how their performance will decode and recode the ideological signs and distort the perfect correspondence with the "original". It is through the collision and overlap of real and fictional realms that they overcome the *stasis* of their identity. Unlike the calcified role and fictive identity of the original, they have parted with scripted part and smoothly navigate between different selves- actor, persona and profession. By stripping away prejudice, they can claim different selves and leaving behind colonial yoke, they experience a new 'man to man' encounter. As Jackson's final calypso expresses:

> "Well, a limey name Trewe came to Tobago
> He was in a show business but he had no show
> So in desperation he turn to me
> And said: "Mr. Philip" is the two o"we,
> One classical actor and Creole,
> Let we act together with we heart and soul"
>
> (2 .36-45 151-152.)

The polarities of their relation in rehearsal performance are thus translated into "renegotiation of the roles in the post-independence period" (Thieme 130). The multipositionality of the actors, movements across different locations challenge the supposed cohesiveness of a character. In a comic rebuttal of the touristic representation and crude commercialization of the islandic beauty, this revisionist play invites comparison to Peter Carey's *Jack*

Maggs where the inherent contradiction of colonial discourse is exposed in representing Australia both as "convict hell and the site of Arcadian promise" (Letisier 14).[11] As the role-reversal of Crusoe- Friday is translated into linguistic and other codes of carnivalization, the performance text is emancipated from the subservience to the literary text. And the "text" to be a solid foundation or convincing authority is jeopardized. By tapping into ingrained cultural discourse of the host text, Walcott's Robinsonade offers vibrant, comedic commentary on the post-independence Anglophone Caribbean world. Performative border-crossing, for both the actors serves as a practical resistance in *Pantomime* and reinvents its canonical 'pre'-text in the territories of contested beliefs, manners and worldviews. Instead of an ordered, harmonious whole, the *Pantomime* produces marvelously dynamic and schizophrenic contradiction of creole theatre.

Odyssey- A Stage Version

The Western classics, according to Simon Gikandi, are the "pre-text (s) of/for Empire" (102); they have proved to be a major imaginative stimulus for the Caribbean artists. And Homer, long considered the fountainhead of Western literature happened to be the "Master", a commanding guide for St. Lucian poet- playwright Derek Walcott.[12] Homer, as Barbara Graziosi and Greenwood Emily describe, "is a good starting point for thinking about epic and its generic transmutations, for integrating challenges to and redefinitions of canonical literature and for reflecting on the politics of reading Homer" (5). Like Homeric poems, the Caribbean writers have reread many other classical texts strategically in an uncanonical way. Their rewrites were not enlisted as part of the West as they deployed colonial categories of knowledge to articulate resistance. The Anglophone artists, in particular, have often made re-interpretation and counter-interpretation of *The Odyssey* through its adaptation and revision- a venture to map a new territory of imagination which has been prompted by a desire "to undermine empire and to rewrite (perceptions of) the region's history" (Hardwick 145). While Oedipus and Antigone have been central to African adoptions, the figures like Odysseus, Helen and Penelope have been at the heart of Walcott's reprisals. The gulf of the New World and the antiquity of the Greek civilization has been obliterated by the denial of temporal and historical distance:

---

[11] Peter Carey's homage to Dickens involves manipulation and decentering of the Dickensian text which has been outlined as "re-righting" of Jack Magg after a lapse of twenty years' exile.

[12] Walcott has often been called Caribbean Homer. In *Omeros* he admits, "Master, I was the freshest of all your readers".

> ODYSSEUS: So you pick up various stories and you stitch them?
> DEMODOCUS: the sea speaks the same language around the world's shores.
>
> (2: 4, 9-12,122)

The radical imagination of the New World artist interwove St. Lucia and the ancient Mediterranean in the fabric of the creole stage. Discarding a mere "transcription" of the Homeric poem, Walcott was bent on doing something "theatrically exciting"; with his richly melodious verse, this play endowed fresh insights into the entanglements of race, colour which was a major component of the Caribbean culture.

Akin to the approach of Walcott, Wilson Harris had also strongly dismissed the idea of epic as a thing of the past and refused to endorse it as 'museum-text'. He had a strong conviction that texts of the past might be initiated in theatre and other performance arts. In his essay, "Creoleness: the Crosswords of a Civilization?" he has contended time past and future to be continuous which simultaneously exist in the artist's imagination. In both his poetry and drama, the temporal dimensions exist in easy proximity. Upholding the Caribbean basin as a gateway to the incessant dialogue of cultures, he writes (Harris 187):

> "To arrive in a tradition that appears to have died is complex renewal and revisionary momentum sprung from originality and the activation of primordial resources within a living language. We arrive backwards even as we voyage forwards. This is the phenomenon of simultaneity in the imagination of times past and future..." (qtd. in Greenwood 41)

Walcott also firmly believed in the imaginative kinship between Greece and Caribbean islands and returned, time and again to the Odyssey theme; he was keen on its episodic action and select scenes, and dramatic energy. In the Caribbean region, Homeric receptions have undergone a cultural make-over and enabled strategic (un) reading of the classical referents. "Homer", as Barbara Graziosi and Emily Greenwood describe, "is a good starting point for thinking about epic and its generic transmutations, for integrating challenges to and redefinitions of canonical literature and for reflecting on the politics of reading Homer" (5). In its Stage Version, Walcott has refigured a different travelling hero and the royal, Ithacan inmates to forge an "an essentially postcolonial representation of gender, race and power" (Burnett 282). The mega-text, no doubt, became the material for inscription of new ideas and ideals. By making a creative alteration through West Indian creole aesthetic, it endows upon the Homeric original a fresh insight. Translating the archetypes of Homeric narrative into Caribbean post-colonial condition entails "... webs of linkages and correspondences intimately and ultimately connecting across the wounds of history" (Bada 8). When Walcott undertook the staging of Homer at the behest of the Royal Shakespeare Company, he knew that it will not be another *Omeros*, as it came within a short spell of two years after and sprang from the same imaginative resource as his epic poem.[13] He was bent upon fashioning a stage product that would exploit "the possibility of the theatre of the piece" with "transformation or translation" (Burnett 282) as Walcott himself explained, "In a sense, my plays are large poems that are transformed before an audience".[14] He also argued that the modern dramatic poetry has raw, comic power and it does not merely seek an alliance to be an extension of the tragic tradition. *A Stage Version* (1993) as a creative metamorphosis of the Homeric original could proffer a dynamic model of reception of Greece in the New World and justify Walcott's plea for a reintroduction of poetry in modern drama.

For Walcott, translating the epic poem and its romance narrative into a theatrical text was no doubt, an exciting challenge– in fact, in the Western tradition classics have not been much deployed for drama. Finding the essence of the Homeric masterpiece in drama he agreed for stage adaptation- "I wouldn't have had any fun," he has said, "in doing simply a transformation, or transliteration, of the Odyssey—because who needs it? Just read the book. But to do something that is theatrically exciting—and not just for the effect but because I felt vitally excited by it, genuinely excited, by the possibility of the theatre of the piece. He himself described the assignment as "a technical challenge to construct a dramatic poem as close as possible to the original poem" – "a form of stage poem'. For the purpose of staging, Walcott compressed the poem into two acts of fifteen and six scenes, suitable for a three-hour performance narrative. And the verse form that he employed here is the alexandrine form of twelve syllables and the popular form of stichomythia or the continuous exchange of line and half lines. The young director of this production, Greg Doran, also underscored the use of flexible hexameter line divided in a way that everybody speaks only a line at once. A fruitful collaboration of Walcott and Doran has often been outlined by the play's early reviewers. In translating a creative Homeric poem into a stage event, separate episodes are threaded together to maintain a symmetrical structure. Instead of changing the original poem or finding the Caribbean

---

[13] It was Gregory Doran's approach to do the stage adaptation first but initially he was resistive to undertake this project.

[14] In Ronal Duncan lecture for 1990 delivered in London Walcott delivered his lecture on "The Poet in the Theatre". Here he passionately pleaded for remobilization of poetry in drama.

namesake of the epic/Homeric characters of the original, he re-invents it in the Caribbean. In emulating the Western master narrative, Walcott was not merely conferring glory or honor on his birthplace or "giving voice" to the native cultural lives but "acting out their own histories/identities in a complex replay that can never be finished or final." (Gilbert 23)

Walcott's adaption restructures the epic story into a three-hour-long theatrical experience that remains "faithful to the original to an extraordinary degree, yet it is also a wholly new work" (Burnett 281). It suggests how the cultural dialogue of the Old and the New World here maintains a balance between the epic spirit of Homer and the native "subjugated knowledges". And how different temporalities coexist to eliminate the synchronicity of realist narrative. As at the outset Billy Blue appears as initiator and calypso singer- a combination of part Greek chorus and part of Griot of the African tradition - connecting the poem with bardic tradition. This cross-pollination posits the narrative at the interstices of cultural, spatial and temporal to initiate a reactivation of a mythic homecoming of Odysseus and translocate the epic paradigm into the postcolonial present. Walcott never ceased to point out that every West Indian is essentially "rootless" but eager to return home after all restless wandering. A calypso singer, Billy Blue opens the play, claiming the story-telling as central to the oral tradition which is transmitted down the centuries in folk lives:

> "Gone sing, bout that man because his stories please us,
> Who saw trials and tempests for ten years after Troy,
> I'm blind Billy Blue, my man's sea-smart Odysseus,
> Who the God of the Sea drove crazy and tried to destroy."
>
> (1.4.1)

Billy Blue, sometimes identified as Caribbean "every-poet", delivers a prologue in West Indian dialect and *patois*. Eurycleia's use of vernacular connects her to tribal wisdom and the creole frame which "invades her conflation of African and Greek myth as well as decidedly West Indian *patois* of her speech" (Hamner 6):

EURYCLEIA
Nancy stories me tell you and Hodysseus.

TELEMACHUS
I believe them now. My faith has caught a fever.

EURYCLEIA
Launching your lickle cradles into dreaming seas.

TELEMACHUS
What were those stories? An old slave's superstition?

EURYCLEIA
People don't credit them now. Them too civilize.

She is somewhat like the West Indian Dadas and Nanas- a popular story-telling figure to Telemachus. In this Caribbean rendition, various cultural strands merge into the narrative as Walcott expands the closed Mediterranean world to the New World. The sea as a major component of the Caribbean landscape brings into a sharp focus the vision and revision of the antique world of the Greeks. Valerie Bada rightly points out, "Walcott's *Odyssey* appears as a palimpsestic 'tapestry' in which the Aegean and Atlantic texts are intricately interwoven" (13). Walcott's stage adaptation replaces the Homeric hero's irrepressible longing for Ithacan home – as he is utterly exhausted with wandering – with a migrant postcolonial subject condition – a median position between an impulse for home-coming and zestful wanderlust and love of adventure. After landing in Ithaca, we find, "the closer he gets to the physical place attached to the idea of home, the more this counter-idea of an internalized sense of home reasserts itself" (Friedman 467). Carrying the world on his back like a turtle he will take ten years to reach home after he has set out on a return voyage. The analogy of the turtle carrying home on its back is Walcott's major reinterpretation of the homecoming or *nostos* of the Homeric hero. Rather than being fixated on home, Odysseus veers between stasis and motion, enclosure and outdoor, security and hazard or risk and stability. This wisdom of dynamic relationship of root/route, voyage/home-coming is best summed up in the words of Seven Seas;

> "there are two journeys
> in every odyssey, one on worried water
> the other crouched and motionless, without noise.
> for both, the "I" is mast; a desk is a raft
> for one, foaming with paper, and dipping the beak
> of a pen in its foam, while n actual craft
> carries the others to cities where people speak
> a different language, or look at him differently".

(Book XI 295)

This Odyssean dilemma epitomizes the migrant condition of every West Indian, the dilemma that faced every artist in the 60s as Walcott states: "The migratory West Indian feels rootless on his own earth, chafing at its beaches" ("Twilight" 21). The voyage that the Homeric hero undertakes and all the adversities that he encounters become charged with political symbols. Foremost of them is the hero's confrontation with the Cyclops society where "thought is forbidden" and "history erased', the one-eyed monster is found to be a personification of spiritual blindness. This monologic, absolutist vision is repudiated by Odysseus "God gave us two eyes because we're human . . . One is for laughter, the other one cries." When society dismisses all contradiction and difference the impulse of revenge and recrimination are bolstered. And this regimented society, by blocking all passage to learning "There's no idea in this kingdom" (69) becomes a parallel to the modern-day totalitarian state, When Cyclops is outwitted by the stratagem of Odysseus' calling himself "nobody", it underlines how regional and cultural insignificance may be a privilege rather than a hindrance. The negation of personhood and place, often described with the epithets "nowhere", "nobody" was used by Walcott's other sailor-poet persona, Shabine. Autocracy and separatist political ideologies of his time received Walcott's imaginative opprobrium – as, here, symbolized by the Cyclops episode:

> CYCLOPS
> NOBODY HAS ESCAPED, NOBODY BLINDED
> ME!
> LOUDSPEAKER
> REPEAT, NO ONE HAS ESCAPED. KEEP
> LOOKING FOR HIM,
> NOBODY"S ESCAPED. NOBODY"S BLINDED THE
> EYE.
> CYCLOPS
> NOBODY YOU HEAR ME? NOBODY IS HIS
> NAME!
> ODYSSEUS (shouts back)
> SON OF POSEIDON. YOU OBSCENE OCTOPUS!
> YOU TON OF SQUID- SHIT WITH YOUR EYE
> POURING BLACK INK!
> MY NAME IS NOT NOBODY.! IT' S ODYSSEUS!
> AND LEARN, YOU BLOODY TYRANTS, THAT
> MEN CAN STILL THINK! (SC IX, 72)

It demonstrates how the wit of a "little man" can outmaneuver totalitarian politics. As Lorna Hardwick observes, "So, Walcott's redrawing of the otherness of the Cyclops in terms of political tyranny and lack of human feeling both dissolves the distance between Homer and twentieth-century Caribbean and denies that it is natural to exploit ethnic difference as a criterion for 'otherness'" (9). By transposing the Homeric hero into a contemporary Caribbean context Walcott demonstrates how the classic remains vigorous, fresh and how the theatre adaptation can resist the legacies of a hegemony in the newly independent Caribbean states. In re-making Cyclops as a native, a despot and Odysseus, a displaced and native colonizer Walcott suggests why settler-native binary is far from static. The contemporary resonance of the Homeric original proved the play to be a (re)action to the hegemony of all stripes. T.S. Eliot believed that such trans-historical consciousness and recoding of tradition will help the artist maintain an unconscious balance between past tradition and the originality of its contemporary moment. This complex, revisionary and renewal momentum of Walcott's play, also, sheds light upon the neo-colonial aggression of post-independence days.

The subjects identified as subservient and without agency in the master narrative are recuperated in Walcott's Stage Version. Despite their position as social subordinates, they occupy multiple subject positions and interrogate the privilege of the leading white characters. But Walcott's manipulation endows upon them resistive energy. Eurycleia, almost an absent figure in the Homeric original, is translated here into a repository of old culture and wisdom, appearing in a crucial moment of the reunion of the father and the son. Like Ma Kilman of *Omeros*, she is imbued with practical consciousness and described as "this house's foundation" (184). When she looks at the massacre of the suitors, she utters a cry like a sufferer and prays for the eternal rest of the departing soul. Like the old nurse, Eumaeus sees herself as a member in the royal household. She claims familiarity with both son and father; besides being a nurturer, she's been a teller of old nurse's tales as was popular in the West-Indian society. Another maid, Melantho, appears much more spirited and less servile to exhibit class resistance. In the end, when Odysseus threatens her with death, both Eurycleia and Penelope intervene to protect her. With this re-presentation of the black maids, Walcott, no doubt, "revolutionizes the elitist assumption of the Homeric treatment" (Burnett 303). In ruling out the revenge as a heroic code and its wanton cruelty as morally loathful, Walcott allows the agency to the female members in the Ithacan palace. The code of heroic triumphalism is taken to task by the women in the Ithacan palace. This episode – the denouement of the play– unfolding visceral slaughter and bloodbath testify to the presence of the 'other', the margin of the Homeric pre-text. The redoubtable presence of the black slave in Robert D. Hamner's view "symbolizes the possibility of the underdog emerging triumphantly…". But Peter Burian refuses to see it as reclaiming space of the marginalized; rather than dismantling hierarchy, he believes, a cultural commonality has been forged between the Ageans and the

Caribbeans, between the continents.[15] The serenity of homecoming is undermined by the gruesome acts of slaughter; the bloodbath revives the memory of Troy:

> "Troy' s mulch! Troy's rain! Wounds. Festering diseases".
> (2.6, 13.151)

Though Odysseus tries to convince Penelope that the slaughters were committed for the sake of her defense, ("To Kill your swine, Cierce"), her response is one of revulsion and vehemently categorical rejection of all forms of cruelties and bloodbath: "You had to wade this deep in the blood"? (2.6.7,153). She, "a fine, bright soul" (124), has unraveled tapestry night after night to counter the approach of the suitors- "My own bed is besieged by a hundred suitors" (130). Full of "milk of human kindness", she extends hospitality to the beggars. From the days of his Haitian Trilogy, Walcott's juvenile enthusiasm for rebel leaders began to ebb away and be replaced by the down-to-earth, spirited resistance. Walcott's rich and profound weaving of the stories of two archipelagoes–the Aegean and the Caribbean –yields a transformative impact on the monoliths of cultural identity and redraws homecoming with a different brush. Walcott's innovative response and radically new articulation outmaneuver the past to mould the present consciousness.

By paring down the ante-texts, shifting the gear of narrative progress and stepping across all conceivable borders both these plays have sustained the tension between "hypertexts" and "hypotexts". Within an intricate and intertextual fabric of these re-compositions, parody and pastiche, the metanarratives of colonial ideologues in *Robinson Crusoe* and the unquestioned, perennial value of *Odyssey* are rigorously questioned. In a way, by "Caribbeanising" the anterior texts, these re-appropriations infuse dynamic openness to the indigenous theatre: "A new reality emerges, which is not a mosaic of characters, but a new phenomenon, original and independent" (Latmore 19). This new reality comes to occupy a position between fidelity and betrayal which initiates a new cultural and existential awareness. This interactive and permutational reproduction of a text always dissolves the boundary between source and target to produce what Walter Benjamin famously phrases "continua of transformation". Repositioning the familiar narratives to an unfamiliar locale, they ask why both repudiation and acceptance are both problematic choices for the postcolonial artists. Walcott's adaptation generates thrill by following without being faithful, by regaining

---

[15] He makes them equal partners in a common culture that is complex and diverse, to be sure, but not describable in terms of center and margins, same and other ("Build" 80).

what is lost in translation and by adding a radical dimension to the postcolonial concerns. In such creative revisions, the Oedipal relationship does not hinder the rewriter from growing and expanding; rather, by surpassing its antecedent, it helps him claim freedom from parental bondage. The praxis of theatre issues out a political statement on the postcolonial present, a "now" moment carries the "traces" of the earlier texts or does a form of "ghosting". All the performative styles not only decentre and rupture, but also steer towards self-regulation and self-determination. And reveal the ways in which theatre-praxis becomes a political statement and performative space becomes a major site of cultural intervention. This proximity and alienness animate all rewrites. This performance style enables what Dipesh Chakraborty has found in all cases of postcolonial repetition to be a "creative expression", generating "a form of newness" (qtd. in Mukherjee 219).

II

Like every artist, Walcott's creative imagination was extremely self-conscious about language, literary form and the act of writing fictional narratives. He was obsessed with a tenuous and fragile bond between life and fiction; rather than easy correspondence or equivalence, their relation appeared to be problematic in *pastiche*, parody. It underlines how Walcott's late plays began to be unmoored from plot and character and the validity of realistic representation on the Caribbean stage was interrogated. Both *Pantomime and A Branch of Nile* draw our attention to their status as artefact and provisionality of a truly "native" performance to which their plots aspire. With continuous reflection on the creative process itself, here, mimesis gave way to self-analysis, and drama is subsumed in "metadrama" (Fly).

Locating the metatheatrical *moments* in the plot often helps us identify the dislocation of power. Refusing to be our theatre in Trinidad, and spearheading the Trinidad Theatre Workshop group, Walcott reflected upon theatre-making through the prism of his plays. A performative intervention proves instrumental; without being merely oppositional re-working, these two plays- *Pantomime* and *A Branch of Blue Nile* demonstrate what Gilbert and Tompkins describe "counter-discursive performance". As the fictionality and the lived reality brush against each other, these revisionist performances articulate "tension between Anglo script and its local enunciation" (Gilbert et al. 116). The plots are devised to comment and critique on the experiences and challenges of producing indigenous theatre at the interstices of race, sex and culture. Aware of their nature as a theatre they do not merely re-play the pre-texts but deploys a self-conscious method to exploit its own devices and conventions. These performance narratives, not only exploit their own fictionality and violate the formal blocks of realist productions but draw the audience to the contemporariness of the rendition in the cultural context of the Caribbean; "Metafiction, then, does not abandon 'the real world' for the narcissistic pleasures of the imagination. What it does is to re-examine the conventions of realism in order to discover – through its own self-reflection – a fictional form that is culturally relevant and comprehensible to contemporary readers" (Waugh 18).

When Harry has tossed up a plan for reverse rendition of *Robinson Crusoe* or a troupe of Trinidadian performers has planned to stage the Shakespearean classic, *Antony and Cleopatra*, they already knew that they were theatrical and the playwright has the obligation to acknowledge and accommodate that theatricality. In a very nuanced analysis of Metafiction, Patricia Waugh has described how an opposition between the constructions of a "fictional illusion" and "laying bare" of that illusion becomes a strategic pattern. Almost all the major characters, like Sheila, Chris, Harry or Jackson are exposed to this deconstructive experience of performance where playtext and performance text exist in metonymic tension. Both these plays exhibit how metatheatrical strategies can help the playwright comment, critique and interpret a society. What is decentred in the process is not only the clutch of the cultural hegemony but also the supposed authority of the dramatic text- its aporia, fissures and indeterminacy. "Reality" is not only constructed through literary fiction, but a jarring contact occurs between the world within the fiction and the world outside the fiction. In the framework of metatheatre, an alternate performance structure like "banana play", pantomime or comic skit, seeks to construct a new set of discourse by undermining the authoritative discourse (Fly). For Patricia Waugh the metafictional novel tends to be constructed on the principle of a fundamental and sustained opposition: the construction of a fictional illusion (as in traditional realism) and continuous undermining of that illusion ... it breaks down the distinction between "creation" and "criticism" and merges them into the concepts of "interpretation" and "deconstruction". It involves the oscillation of performance style between general and particular of Shakespearean plays. Or translating the classic of Defoe to the Caribbean context. In handling *the stage adaptation in both these plays*, Walcott was clearly aware of the multiple codes to be respected in the theatrical text: how to bring out different levels of cultural meaning, how to re-construct the identities of the characters, how to underline conflict, achieve emotional intensity, motivate the dramatic action. These adaptations were meant to issue a native "re (action)" to the way the originals disseminated the Western/European influence. By a flamboyant mixing or mash-up of acting styles, the canonical values get subverted.

Shakespeare has always loomed large into the popular life of the Caribbean colonies; his influence was mainly disseminated through curriculum and travelling theatre companies. Walcott had always admired the Caribbean style of acting and vocal quality of West Indian actors in performing Shakespeare. The theatre practice and performance in a native context could displace Shakespeare's theatre as a transcendental signifier. The issue of finding a performative alternative to the mainstream productions, he lets his directorial experience play out in the 1983 play *The Branch of Blue Nile*. It is not only theatrically self-consciousness; rather, its subject is "drama itself" (Hornby). A creative, political and critical work at once, it is a site of multiple intersections — between canonical and banana play, between theatre in First World and in the hinterland, between creole and classic acting. Deft use of a metatheatrical framework, here, not only decentres the 'universal' pattern of characterization and unequivocal authority of Shakespeare but makes performative translation appear provisional and contingent. Here, a troupe of actors, fledgling rather than established, has decided to put on a production of the Bard's *Antony and Cleopatra*; their ambitious project falters right from the outset of rehearsal. The challenge of handling the role of Cleopatra and Antony in performance is pitted against the reality of the dark and light-skinned body of the actors. The bare stage of a small theatre, where the action is set, is indicative of the dearth of material provisions of the performing group. In the opening scene of rehearsal, Sheila fails to satisfy the director in replaying the part of the Egyptian queen Cleopatra. She stands apart from the assigned role and refuses to be entangled in the fictional part:

SHEILA
I'm not her, Harvey. I can't play all that.

HARVEY
Play what you feel about Chris, not Antony.

SHEILA
Just leave my private life out of this, please.

(A: 1 Sc:1, Location 4525)

Reciting the famous speech of Cleopatra after Antony's death, Sheila attempts a modernization of the tense:

The soldier's pole is fallen: young boys and girls
Are level now with men; the odds are gone. (A: I Sc:1, Location 4635)

And receives a rebuff of the director who reminds her "the odds is gone. Singular, Marylin, please". The gaps between the classic and its rendition for the non-British, non-White actors begin to widen. What jeopardizes the prospect of playing Cleopatra further is the lack of sensuality in black-skinned

Sheila, as pointed out by Harvey, the director and then by Gavin, her co-actor in the company. She admits her limitation to play the "sensual serpent" and the public performance jostles against her propensity to act too "decently"; her sense of propriety is limited by the border of a black body's performative scope. These rehearsal episodes help the playwright show to his people the hold of the original Shakespeare and also the challenges in mounting an indigenous or native version of it. In the 1965 Ivory-Merchant film *Shakespeare Walla* the narrative engaged with the British-led Shakespearean troupe struggling to perform in post-independence India where their "acting" jostles with the real-life experience.[16] Here, in mounting a Shakespearean production in another far-flung colony, the more the rehearsal progresses, Sheila finds the identification with her role on the stage to be impossible: her coloured, sexed body or acting body occludes her from classical acting of Cleopatra's part.

"I'm not a fucking queen, I'm not a celebrity; when you turn my name into mud it stays mud, and no magic in any theatre in the world can turn that mud into gold" (A: 1 Sc: 1, Location 4614).

During a practice in the empty theatre, Sheila and Chris discuss why the subaltern body hinders in perfect recapturing of Shakespearean stage experience/performance tradition. She mentions "can't talk Shakespeare, though," and Chris responds, "Lips too big" (A:I, Sc: 2, Location 4854). The cultural taste of Sheila refuses the method acting recommended by Harvey. Thus diction, colour, bodily features, belief system immediately provide additional layers of signification that call the assumption of the canonical "pre-text" into question. It generates tension with the dominant cultural signs. Sheila's steadfast refusal to fuse professional with personal life, to divest herself of the stage-image and by relinquishing the stage to devote herself to more "sacred" life to join a branch of the Seventh Day Adventists. Muriel Spark's novel *The Public image*, Annabel's life came to be determined by the publicity image- "English Tiger Lady"- that has been constructed for her. Though eventually, she became aware of the fiction-making process and decides to step out of the image and resist the enslavement to her stage persona/image. Complete transmission from the source to target text or from the host to guest culture is suspended as Walcott's heroine finds herself trapped in a masculine, racial economy, in a "void" *vis-a-vis* the mainstream production.

Contrasted to Sheila, Marylin grows to identify with her image of a diva, the star or the queen of the stage. She, as Sheila believes, is "light-skinned" and

---

[16] Real life challenge for the troupe emanates from the spread of Bollywood Popular Hindi Movies.

more likely to qualify in the role of queen Cleopatra or to work abroad (A: I, Sc:3, Location 5423). Her mulatta, light skin- type places her in a more advantageous position in pursuing a higher professional goal. In the post-independent Caribbean society though the mulattas were vilified as the product of sexual promiscuity of the white master, yet in the show-business, they radiated more promise. The racial inscription on the actor's body has hindered the protean freedom of Gavin, too. He has come to realize the deep constraints by travelling back and forth between his native land and New York in pursuance of an acting career; the insuperable barrier between his skin colour and the American stage left him to perform the part of some fist-jerking revolutionary Afro- American protester. He's returned embittered not only by the racialized gaze of the American theatre world but has learned how the question of economy disrupts the seeming 'universality' of theatre in its praxis: "Don't dream like me about the universality of the theater. It's economics, and economics means race" (A: I, Sc: 2, Location 4739). Like him, Harvey is also a returnee, the director who has returned to Trinidad with a mission to develop a local theatre group of the highest standards. But as the plot unfolds, the vision begins to peter out. Within the ambit of postcolonial performance, Walcott offers theatre's inherently racialized frame and dearth of material resources as occlusive of egalitarianism in Caribbean theatre. Inserting play- within- a- play, Chris is seen to be writing a Trinidadian play on the staging experience of *Antony and Cleopatra*. The representational crisis is exacerbated by a clash of cultures, 'high' and 'low' dualism as a local reviewer finds the cut out of banana or figs placed behind Marylin/Cleopatra's speech as sacrilegious tampering of a classic. Hence his scathing and excoriating review of the fiasco in first the night's staging of the Bard's classic; the local troupe's staging of *Antony and Cleopatra* was a mere banana play, an abbreviated and abominable rendering "Certain things remain sacred, or else our civilization is threatened . . ." (A: II, Sc: 3, Location 5658).

The attempt to make *Antony and Cleopatra* is dismissed by Gavin as a "provincial shit". For Brother John, theatre is a desacralisation of life and must be removed from any chance of collision. As he advises Sheila to segregate the theatre persona from the congregation (A: II, Sc: 4, Location 6072). The dichotomy of real and theatrical continues when Chris manages to persuade Sheila to return to the stage life as she admits "I don't see the congregation. It's like the theatre. The difference is that it's day. No spotlight moon" (A: II, Sc: 4, Location 6120). Sheila's reflection upon life-theatre- church nexus adds another dimension to the criticism that this play consistently makes. These tensions, as described by Baugh, as "part of the postcolonial angst" (143), animate the play's commentary on the sustainability of developing a native theatre. And in the final moments it is Phil, who has taken the role of a madman or fool who imbues upon the state of theatre almost a prophetic vision: "I does summon brimstone and ashes on everybody head. On a government that don't give a fart – excuse me, miss – for its artists, on a people you have to remind to find some pride" (A: II, Sc: 6, Location 6354). To sum up, Walcott's counter-discursive enunciation takes on Shakespeare's masterpiece to demonstrate how... "the local reconstructions of Shakespeare disrupted the singularity of Shakespeare through claims about his universality and timeless transcendentalism and imported new meanings to India" (Bhatia 52).

In another late work, *Pantomime*, a rehearsal experience is punctuated with play- within-play, role and gender swapping. All the metatheatrical ruses offer a parodic postcolonial reprisal of Defoe's classic *Robinson Crusoe*; in mimicking the original the meaning is refracted, here. Leaving behind its "base play", the metatheatrical framework provides "further sites of reading".[17] In devising a pre-seasonal entertainment, Harry, the white hotelier and his black handyman, Jackson find the displacement of the base text and its mutation into an alternative script. In a reverse rendition of the classic tale, the comic skit assumes a serious, satiric dimension. Through self-referencing performative acts, the play here challenges the binaries like the stage-page, performer-actor, and original-copy.

Gilbert and Tomkins, in their nuanced study, have described the postcolonial metatheatre as "a spectacular resistance" that splits the action into multiple locations. The reverse role- playing of Crusoe-Friday is here unmoored from the mimetic responsibility and their improvisation slides into "play-within-the-play-within-the-play". It is exhibited in Jackson's playing the part of Helen, the ex-wife of Harry and this playing upon the character permeates the borders of 'fiction' and 'life', reality and illusion. As Harry bursts out in the middle of their play- within- the play recalling the old rivalry with his wife on the professional stage and how he recoiled from it: "all right, I'll tell you what I am going to do next, Ellen: you're such a big star, you're such a luminary, and I'm going to leave you to shine by yourself, I'm giving this bloody race and I'm going to take up mike's offer" (2, 4-7,150). Like Chris and Sheila, Harry too is entangled with personal relation and the personal issues of their performance background meddle as they play their part. His devising of the 'panto' is inspired by the real-life competitiveness with Helen who used to outplay him in the role of Friday in London. The protean skill of Jackson, his self-conscious reflection on role-playing sums it up:

---

[17] In her essay "'Spectacular Resistance': metatheatre in Post-colonial drama", Joanne Tompkins discusses Nowra, Soyinka, Walcott and Mojica's metatheatrical moments as a strategy of resistance in the postcolonial context.

> JACKSON: "I could play Robinson Crusoe, I could play Columbus, I could play Sir Francis Drake, I could play anybody discovering anywhere, but I don't you to tell me and where to draw the line" (140).

This playful self- reflexivity not only problematizes the real 'real', but contravenes the identity as stable or static. In the fluid, liminal space of theatre, the idea of hierarchical positioning is always decentred. His parodic acting with self- referential cultural views destabilizes the ontology of the colonized and coloniser or identification of race and nationhood as determinative of subjecthood. Like *Branch of a Blue Nile*, it is a rehearsal piece and lays bare the promises and pitfalls of representation. As they both bring into the Crusoe story their own interpretations, the realistic narrative of Crusoe-Friday undergoes various reconfigurations and a new rapport between the director, actor, character or performer is forged. They add refreshing and imaginative variations to the cultural identity formation and suspend uncomplicated theatrical representation. The cross-cultural encounters testify to the endeavour of Walcott towards making theatre a non-hierarchical, demotic cultural forum for his countrymen.

Chapter 4

The Vision of Plurality and Collaborative Politics in Walcott's Late Plays

In the newly-freed Caribbean islands, when the expansionist energy of colonialism was petering out and ethnic and other cultural nationalism were on the ascend, the desire for post-national solidarity became a major articulation of cultural essentialism and purism. In his famous intervention on "other question", Bhabha drew attention to what Fanon has called "the dangers of the fixity and fetishism of identities within the calcification of colonial culture to recommend that 'roots' be struck in the celebratory romance of the past or by homogenising the history of the present" (Bhabha 9). In the early seventies, the newly freed islands in the Caribbean witnessed the unconditional affirmation of African identity after replacing the violent logic of colonial rationality and a surge of Africanist/Nativist movement. This solidarity and affirmation of cultural identity were problematized by Walcott's new plays to generate "the possibility of a more generous and pluralistic vision of the world" (Said 277). They initiated a dialogic process and complex negotiation to reimagine the transactive process of colonialism. Infused with creole energy, these plays proved all cultural borders permeable. The portrayal of post-independence reality posed a challenge to Walcott, the dramatist, to mould his vision.[1] In what is sometimes also described as post-Trinidad Theatre Workshop years, Walcott's plays engaged more directly with volatile political reality. And his dramaturgy shaped itself to depict the new reality. In the aftermath of decolonization Walcott experimented with new content and form of his prose plays. In them, the cultural representation, the material injustice of post-independence society attempted to redefine the scope of postcolonial theatre. These plays trenchantly expose to what Paula Burnett calls "taking on capitalism principally in its imperialist manifestation" (210).[2]

---

[1] In his *Cambridge Introduction to Derek Walcott*, eminent West Indian critic and poet, Edward Baugh has drawn attention to Walcott's response to "challenge for change" which is a pointer to the "twilight" temporal zone/point in the Caribbean islands - the interstices of the passing of French and British rule and the political autonomy of all the major Caribbean islands., including Walcott's own island, St. Lucia (Feb. 22, 1979).

[2] In drawing analogy with Brecht, Burnett has noted in Walcott a trenchant critique in of the imperial manifestation in the island lives.

They are mostly concerned with middle-class, ordinary mass who were deeply impacted by the power politics and the individuals who grapple with the questions of identity amidst all political upheavals. In them, the encounter between the individual and community lives, irreconcilable tension between tradition and modernity often spells out a tragic ending. They also register how Walcott's deep distrust of the structures of power and political belonging grew more acute. In his novels and travelogues, Naipaul has held corruption and violence responsible for political barrenness in Trinidad. It was his conviction that plantation colonies lacked recognizable political convictions. The failure of political modernity reflected in Black Power, Negritude Movement or the fracture nationality and identity, also surface in these plays. All the commonplace paradigms of cultural kinship look fragile and at the same time, diverse representations and discourses coalesce in these plays to render the homogeneous formations invalid.

Remembrance

Walcott's *Remembrance* was first produced in Joseph Papp's New York Shakespeare festival in 1979. It marked his venture into composing prose-play and experimenting with dramaturgy. The aftereffects of British colonialism on West Indian society and inexorable changes are the axis of the narrative, here. It tells and retells the life of Albert Jordan, the protagonist, a black school teacher and a writer of modest reputation after the departure of the British rulers. His unflagging love of the Empire is pitted against the evolution of community and family living in independent Trinidad. His is a complex portrayal of a romantic idealist, though Walcott intended to be an act of homage to the schoolmasters (Baugh 128). He is so much attached to the past that he fell out with his next generation and their values. Though it is a prose-play, in *Remembrance*, Gray's masterpiece *Elegy* serves as the most important intertext. In fact, the play ends on a choric recitation of Gray's memorable lines as it also opens with Jordan's solo recitation. At the hour of dawn, the action opens and darkness envelops the retired school teacher protagonist Jordan who is crest-fallen over the passing of his heydays of the professional and creative career. There is another greater anguish- the loss of his elder son in the Revolutionary movement-which makes him more withdrawn, suffering a sense of futility. He has cocooned himself in the family to live in alienation from his community. As the interviewer describes, almost quoting the words of a radical critic that he is a man who has avoided the realities of our society and he has refused to heed to the voice of the suffering black people. His self-absorption has led him to avoid such unpalatable realities (Sc:1, Location 510) and he, also, reels under an emotional wound of losing a son in the February revolution. He finds the best self-image in Gray's memorable line: "Full many a flower born to blush unseen". In Trinidad, he, like many other idealist teachers, he has faced the same, sad lot as they go unrecognized, unadorned. In the opening scene, he introduces his frustration of having been denied the position of principal and remained in the position of a school teacher. But it is not the same Walcott of the early plays who was deeply engaged with the obscure, disempowered lives. Unlike those plebeian figures and their redeeming potential and survival instinct, in the Belmont village of Trinidad, Jordan stands out as an Ideological failure, a misfit, and an anachronistic idealist who remains immured in his past.[3] A divided and doubled personality, he bitterly realizes that he is no longer the same object of veneration and is sealed into inessentiality.:

> Gray is ofay, black is beautiful
> Gray is shit
> ....
> Jordan is honky,
> Jordan is a honky-donkey white nigger man!
>
> (A: 1, Prologue, Location 112).

Approached by his editor-friend to recount his life story, he discloses that he loves poetry still and will prefer to shun prose. Before the interviewer, he passionately recites a section of Grey's elegy which his mother used to recite in his early young days. The romantic streak of his nature is further underlined when the interviewer asks him whether his two stories "Barrley and the Roof" and "My War Effort" reflect his own life. Both the autobiographical tales were added a pinch of fiction as pepper sauce is added to meat (A1, Location 138). "Bored and Fed up" with his own life, he urges his son Frederick to leave Belmont for the United States with his white mistress Anna. His is a divided personality - split between his self- image and the reality of his position which results in his growing alienation in his own community. He continues to live under the illusion that he's burned away his talent in the domesticity. The lines in *In a Green Night* may well describe his predicament:

> "...Each spring, memories
> Of his own country where he could not die assaulted him.
> He watched the malarial light Shiver the canes.
> In the sea-coloured pool, tadpoles seemed happy in their element.
> Poor, black souls
> He shook himself. Must breed, drink, rot with motion."

---

[3] Judy Stone in her analysis of *Remembrance* has pointed out this new turn in Walcott to find a protagonist from the middle class.

In this vivid portrayal of Jordan, Walcott has also shed critical light on cultural anxieties experienced by old, local school masters in Trinidad; the play charts the individual life in its entanglements with the upheavals of emerging Black Nationalism, the growing trend of Americanisation of the indigenous society. The cultural identification with the nativist position for all disaporans appeared to be more problematic than ever. Jordan demonstrates the breaking apart of old certainties and the emergence of new, hybrid identities.

The work is meant to be an artistic tribute to Walcott's mother who was one such teacher of his generation.[4] As Edward Baugh has put it, "or whatever was admirable in the ideals and values, however contested, which they inculcated in their students these teachers have occupied the status of a legend" (129). Walcott knew that such figures, the local legends, were fast disappearing in the changing times; their subjective position was conditioned by a sense of displacement. They adhered to values and ideological conditions which faced the threats of erasure in the consumerist world. Here, Albert Jordan is discovered as a stripped, lonely figure; he is always at odds with the existing values whose self-contradiction makes him a figure of extra-ordinary psychological complexity. Moreover, the plot here "evinces nostalgia for some of the values it [colonialism] has instilled" (Thieme 223). *Remembrance* was commissioned and premiered by the courtyard Players in St. Croix in the US virgin Island and it appeared a year after Walcott had parted with Trinidad Theatre Workshop. The play's structure is often considered simple and naturalistic with too obvious political allegories. Of all the aspects, Walcott's dramaturgy triggers dispute among his scholars. Thieme has denied it any merit from the view point of performance, though he admits that as a monodrama it has been a successful stageproduction. The difference from the early St. Lucian plays has been attributed by Lowell Fiet in his essay "Mapping a New Nile" to the demands characteristic of US productions; "tightly-knit, one-set, small-cast "realistic" plays that concentrate on conflicts between characters in family, work..." (140). The Prologue opens with the interviewer meeting Jordan with a tape-recorder and a microphone which deeply annoys him. He asserts him to be self- fashioned and is dismissive about the aid of technology when his own utterances are recorded for the publication purpose and he goes onto recount the stories of his life, undertaking a journey through the time. Patricia Ismond in her essay "Walcott's Later Drama: from "Joker" to

---

[4] Walcott's own note to the 1979 Trinidad production states that the play was intended to pay respect and "honour of the great_teachers [he] had the privilege of knowing in [his] own boyhood...". It was meant to be a tribute "to the teachers in the colonial society". And Walcott's mother was one such great teacher who had abiding influence in the society.

"Remembrance" has described it as a brilliant stagecraft. Here, the plot intermeshes past with [42] present and the past comes live onstage and their intersection make it "imbued with the atmosphere of reverie and trance" (98). It is a lyrical and somewhat poignant celebration of the old colonial school masters who contributed to the society significantly and were gradually replaced by the well-informed civil servants. The multiple techniques of memorizing, telling, writing animate the "showing" of Jordan's past and present. In his interview, he discloses that the only machine he ever trusted was his old Raleigh bicycle. He even considers its use as a fad of the young people as somewhat irritatingly he tells the Interviewer that all young Trinidadians prefer to "handle a machine without reading a book" (1, Prologue, 3-4, Location 72). The devices of projector and tape-recorder and the microphone help to intermesh various time-sequences as he looks back to the days thirty years before - when he had written his story book, *My War Effort*. The devices add to the evocation of the good old days of empire through several flashback effects. The temporal border breaks down as Jordan relives the past youthful romance with Esther Hope. His published books are focused on the projector and the interviewer reading a snatch of it captures the mood of taking a trip down memory lane. While the interview goes on, he steps out of his present and begins re-enacting the life of the days of school teaching. Even before the Interviewer, he picks up a book, reciting his own favourite poem amidst the voices of the schoolchildren. Then he suddenly turns to the young Interviewer and, seizing a ruler, commands him to spread out his hand. But the books that recount his life-story is not unvarnished reality; he admits to have coloured with the hue of imagination. He lapses into play-acting to animate the past that he is recounting.

In these late plays, Walcott's concern with the fast-fading colonial values and the presence of the white families problematizes the notion of home and belonging; the spiralling political turmoil displaced "native" as a stable, fixed identity category. As Jordan reads an extract from his own story, he discloses that he was not English though considered himself to be such. The Anglophilia and adoration of England was prompted by his romance with a British lady, Miss Esther Hope. This two-act play, as its title indicates, revolves around the past and the nostalgia for olden times and the characters are mostly found in a poignant situation. In fact, the action opens on the Remembrance Day, the occasion of his deepest personal tragedy, a painful reminder of the loss of his son in the rebellion which Jordan considered to be vain. As a staunch defender of the traditional ways and values, the use of machine and apathy for books cause ire in him. He is only fiercely proud of the old Raleigh cycle even though he reveals that it's been dumped in the back-yard. He is so self- opinionated that he rejects the idea of his publisher friend that with ageing, his eye sight may have dimmed. But nothing upsets him as much as the din and noise of the rubble, observance of the 70s February revolution. As it claimed his son's life, he lives with a painful memory and has grown averse to the ideals of radicalism, ultra-revolutionary or oppositional ethics of Black Power movement. He is so rigid about that he has never visited his son's grave for seven years; he still believes that his son was only led by the "bush-headed niggers". He takes a dig at the attempts of making his son a martyr and he can never forgive the black niggers who claimed his body. He cannot forgive his editor friend also, for brainwashing his son with revolutionary political ideas. The clash of values and traditions forced him to live through the trauma generated through the Trinidadian Revolution. He is an adherent to old colonial values and a passionate lover of canonical literature. As he is found to be brooding over past glories, it runs counter to his advice to his wife that life marches on. The background voices describe him as "white nigger man". Towards the end, he encourages Fredrick to leave the small town for England and avail fresh opportunities with Anna. To remedy his own frustration, he longs for the success and fulfilment of his son's romance. His Anglophilia was gratified only when Esther praised his flawless English accent. His divided personality has elicited comments from the critics. His dividedness is reflected in his avowed rejection of creole registers, his staunch defense of Queen's English and at the same time speaking in "creole" with the young interviewer. He considers his own marriage to be "thirty odd years of total misunderstanding" but again compares his wife with great-souled fictional women. Though his favoured medium is poetry, both the books reveal his potential as a prose-writer. Though his wife and son have not uncritically supported him, they ultimately endorse his policies and views. During a conversation with his editor friend, he recalls how his disciplinarian habits used to vex his son who called him a "fascist" and accused him to have run the house like a classroom wielding discipline with severity. When he says that we are born alone and suffer alone (1:2.1, Location 613), it seems his loneliness is invented and a sheer sentimental gesture. On basis of his utterances on several occasions, Lowell Fiet has considered him to be suffering from self-aggrandizement and rhetorical posing. This seems to hold the key to his tragic image as a failed artist. Though Patricia Ismond credits him with overcoming of racial cowardice and exhibiting strength in accepting Anna, the American hippie. But as he mostly repudiates Americanism and disapproves American hippy culture for his son again, it shows how his dividedness may have turned him into a perpetual loner.

However, one single episode in the first act reveals Jordan as a more integrated personality and Frederick with clear personality traits. The father-son divide fleshes out the in the vogue of Americanism invading the local community life and eroding the hold of local culture and institution. His second son Frederick is a painter and looking for an opportunity to sell his work to a visiting American art collector. What he has painted on the roof is a travesty of art and invites jibe from Jordan as "the greatest thing since Picasso". He motivates strongly his artist son despite his modicum of success. Contrasted to Mabel's slight indifference, he bursts out in rapture to call Frederick's painting a masterpiece. His exultant mocking reaction is issued from a sense of deep hurt at the idea of American flag painted on his roof. He sharply retorts by calling it only "idiotic Yankee doddle" (Sc. 1, Location 304). He revolts at the idea of seeking aid from America and rules out any gesture of help from the American capitalist houses. He reprimands his son for painting the sign *Help us America!* Which is a symbol of distressful dependence which is third-worldish (Sc.1, Location. 323). As soon as Barrley appears to settle the deal, Frederick withdraws and he refuses to accept even a blank cheque. His steadfast refusal attests to the energy of resistance. Here Americanisation is very strongly pronounced when Barrley leaves the family with a card which has a message to sum up his own life's principle. It proclaims that the United States can render helpful support when the future gets rocky for such island (1:1L:5-8, Location 4). The sweep of neo-liberal economy all over Trinidad provokes an angry reaction Jordan: "You American think you can buy any blasted thing." (1:1L:1, Location 410). He is fiercely proud of owning his house and will never accept the proposal of selling the roof. His steadfastness anticipates Otto of *Beef, no chicken* who clings to his business property and refuses to be bribed into selling his possession to the Highway company. These are resistant voices to the global consumerism which defined the traditional Caribbean society. In *The Wine of Astonishment*, Earl Lovelace portrays a figure of champion stick fighter, Bolo from pre-war days who gets embittered when the cultural norms are fast disappearing, encouraged by Yankee-dollars.[5] Here, against the backdrop of American interventionist policy and crass materialism comes apparent that his two sons have denounced the father's ideals - one by Joining the rebel group and the other by refusing to flee from Trinidad. They manifest the twin side of Walcott's own position- Jordan vents much of Walcott's own antipathy against the bandwagon militancy and at the same time, he refuses any challenge to the values.[6] No observation sums up the character of Jordan as beautifully as does

---

[5] The major thematic focus is on the unity, integrity of the Shouter Baptists or Spiritual Baptists community and the power and authority of the ruling colonial system.

[6] In a long passage Patricia Ismond finds a semblance between the dramatist and Jordan "Walcott's own autobiography is inscribed in Jordan's story. Paying tribute to the kind of min d that helped to stimulate his work, he is acknowledging his own colonial origins. He affirms the contribution of that pioneering generation, and the need to conserve its values and gifts in the ongoing struggle for freedom, though the weapons have changed".

his editor friend, Pilgrim as he compares him to an old spider like an old spider chaining remembrance in his retired life (A.2, Sc. 1, Location 1097). The relatively static impression of the narrative is rooted in the dogmatic stance of the protagonist.

The vivid portrayal of Mabel testifies to Walcott's engagement with rounded, complex women-figures who assert their difference in a male-centred drama. Jordan's hopes, longing for success or failure cannot undermine Mabel's role in his life. She plays the part of a measuring-rod with full claim to dignity; she is never a mere echo of her husband's voice; she recalls with bitterness that she has burned his talent in domesticity and somewhat wasted his life. Both in appearance and speech she is ungainly and full of earthy vulgarity. To call her a mere nurturer and provider would be to undervalue her practical or worldly-wise dynamism. As a mother and wife, she articulates her strong, independent views. She does not appeal as a model of desire like Esther. Rather she is strong-willed and the mainstay of Jordan's life. She is in fact more realistic and less fragile than her husband. Edward Baugh observes "Mabel commands our respect and sympathy without any appeal to glamour or sentimentality" (132).

She is shrewd enough to brush aside the idea of selling off the roof. She forgives her husband's lapse of temper by advising her to eat and sleep in an orderly manner. She reminds Jordan of the fatherly duty of visiting the grave. But to no avail. She is dignified without being domineering; poised without being sentimental. Though she knows that her stories allude to his British beloved Esther Hope. Like Miller's Linda Loman, she is full of emotional sanity and as Linda can diagnose Willy Loman's rapid failure, Mabel has brought her extravagantly romantic husband to see clearly his own situation. As she confesses that he is a "small man". When Frederick is vexed and blames his father, she reminds him of the stature of the man. Despite affection and loving care, she is critical of his pride and she balances the excess of romance in the family circle. In her figure, Walcott finds a balance between emotion and reason; her personality has an aura of her own.

Compared to its companion piece, comic two-hander *Pantomime*, the plot of *Remembrance* ends in relative stasis. At the end, when Frederick withdraws from the journey and Jordan tires out from exhortation the action returns to the sombre, grave seriousness of the lines of Gray's *Elegy*. All the members of Jordan's family withdraw into deep isolation. It is unmistakable how the plot from the beginning promotes *stasis* as most of the actions are conducted through the reminiscences of Jordan. A lugubrious air hovers over the everyday life of the community, its desire for the unfulfillment. John Thieme also notes how the later section drifts into the "elegiac" and what comes to the fore is that the protagonist is suspended between an undesirable concrete reality and metaphysical plane of distant and unreachable possibilities. He is never lifted out of the ruling values or admits the changing order as valid. His motivation to Frederick for realizing his romance is rather an attempt to set right his own mistaken course of action. His schizoid personality remains suspended between [58] tangible reality and imaginary wanderings. In fact, the family remains fettered in "verbal prison"; much of their verbal energy restricts the action and lacks the momentum for change. The characters in Arthur Miller's *Price* or *Death of a Salesman* are found in the grip of illusion and undergo little or no change. Jordan and his family members, like Miller's characters stand at the impasse of actuality and possibility.

The Last Carnival

Often considered to be a more complex work of his mature period, *The Last Carnival* more directly engages with the Black Power movement and its pitfalls; unlike *Remembrance*, it comes to the fore of the plot.[7] The colonial society portrayed here is much more multi- faceted and the analysis of the colonial situation is very much subtle. The divided identity and complex inheritances and the accommodation of the legacies remains the hallmark of this work. The politico-cultural setting of Trinidad underlines collective identity as "a performative act rather than a static product" (Stevens 465). Unlike the elegiac ending and relative stasis of the action, the plot of *Remembrance* explores the interface of culture and politics and their jagged contradictions. Its lively narration explores the interfaces of the dwindling influence of the planter class and the rise of the black underclass, the fast-fading elite European culture, and emerging Black Power politics. The narrative is posited at the interstices of Trinidad's colonial past and revolutionary present. What makes the play particularly interesting is that it explores multiple subject positions and fuses old and new perspectives. Jean is representative of the new Black political class, Sydney, the Black rebel, Agatha the British colonialist, Victor, the French aesthete. Truly the play demonstrates what Stuart Hall described as "critical points of deep and significant difference" (394).

Walcott always upheld the idea that Caribbean culture represents a combination of mixed differences, culturally interdependent and interconnected spaces. As in the tumultuous days of the rise of Black Power what had preoccupied and inspired Walcott, was "the validity in the West Indies of European culture, and the rightful place there, if any, of the colonial descents" (Judith Stone qtd. in Burnett 245). Few of his contemporaries have

---

[7] This play was first performed in Trinidad in 1982 with Derek Walcott himself as the director. It was derived from an earlier play *The Wine of the Country*.

engaged with the predicament of white lives as Walcott did. He spent his curfew hours working on a play in which, by alternating his scenes the black and the white milieu, he contrasted the militant extremism of the Black Power movement with the gentle decadence of the French enclave.[8] Thus the plot moves beyond the naturalised conceptions of spatialized cultures and affirms that "cultural differences produced and maintained in a field of power relations in a world always already partially interconnected…" (Jameson and Gupta 17).

The opening scene unravels West Indies as a place of abiding serenity and sensuous natural beauty. And the French creole family has hired an English governess, Agatha Willet. Who upon reaching the coast of Trinidad is overwhelmed with the breath-taking elemental beauty of the shore (A.1, Sc:1, Location 106-107). Victor is a self-proclaimed impressionist, a devoted follower of Watteau, renowned for his mastery of bucolic painting. He is dedicated to colonial mimicry and scornful of the transformative political vision of the governess, Agatha. In his artistic preoccupation, he's indifferent to the plight of the down-trodden plantation labour. He is changeless and frozen as his picture frame itself. Locked into a stasis, his vision fails him and his accomplishment leaves him disillusioned, leads ultimately to self-immolation. His paintings are suggestive of paralyzing stillness. His Francophone pride makes him reject creolised forms of culture prevalent in the island society and he pours out his scorn in the shadow play he composes, recreating Watteau's "A Voyage to Cynthera". He proposes to offer high art as in the Carnival but when it is performed by Oswald and Agatha, the plays leap into the carnivalesque. His angry yell underscores binary pairing of high/low, civilised/vulgar; as a cockney bitch Agatha and her comrade Oswald only coarsen and vulgaris (1.4, Location 1089). Like Naipaulian "mimic man" Victor plays the part of the imitative colonial artist, resigned to mimicking European aesthetics, whereas Agatha and Oswald play out the process of creolization and enact the transformative possibilities of re-doing the metropolitan script. He is the head of the French-creole family, the De La Fontaine; his ancestors were forced exiles who fled the war-torn Haitian during the time of slave revolt to settle in Trinidad. The French cultural values are articulated through literature, music and theatre. Measuring himself against his icon Watteau, Victor has become deranged. He has shut himself off from the political and cultural realities of Trinidad and finds his art pieces only cheap and

---

[8] The festival Carnival itself is a part of mixed inheritance. Though it originated with the French planters, it was appropriated by the black slaves and becomes a celebration of the procession of celebration of emancipation through a canboulay procession (French cannesbratees, burning of the cane). In the 1950s it became a major tourist attraction.

uninspiring: he indicts himself as a mortician. When he paints all the pasture, the mango trees getting rusty, the church spire, his brushstrokes don't exude a liveliness (1.6, Location 1229). His maladapted vision, marginal artworks, as Camilia Stevens describes, makes him a "mimic" artist in a Naipaulian way, only capable of sterile mimicry and uncreative imitation. As the realities of the tropical island are at odds with the artistic vision, Victor gets mired in frustration. His madness and eventual death underscore the "predicament of the white colonial artists". Burnett attributes his sad tragedy to the lack of self-reconciliation to his exile while his earthier brother Oswald escapes by easy adaptation to Trinidadian life and culture. His view of art and experience, inertness to the changing social and artistic world, exhibits the predicament of the effete French-Creole family in the days of nation-making. He returns to the final moments of the play in the conversation of his children who reflects upon the artist's father's life. Clodia is less critical of him and believes his despair to have stemmed from his inability to express in colour his love for the place: "... may be my father was no great shake as an artist, but he was not damn so lizard to change when colours changed" (2.2, Location 2048). Here, Walcott has underlined the European heritage as inextricable in the cultural make-up of the West Indies and part of Trinidad history and the integrity of some figures like Victor in the midst of political opportunism. In Naipaul's *A Bend in the River*, the predicament of the trading family in Salem's story in the face of anti-colonial politics, their silence in the decolonizing politics, also underlines the two overlapping historical frames and the stranglehold of the two incompatible ways of acting in the world.

Agatha, the British governess is not only a formidable presence but a more complex character, more dynamic, who draws people around her in the alien land. She draws all the members of the estate around her reformist propaganda. She assumes a vital political role besides the professional duty of a governess, a distinctive position which has merited attention. She inspires all the natives to believe that they are equal. As a socialist English woman and with her liberal idea of social equity, she has exercised a strong political influence upon the servants. Very aptly, Patricia Ismond has described her as the "main conscience of the play" ("Race-containing" 143) but her sensibility and influence elicit mixed review from the multicultural society. After leading a life of privilege, she finds herself corrupted, at the end. Notwithstanding all dynamism for reform, Paula Burnett has called her "static and her politics is locked into "past, frozen order." But what seems more plausible is that she diverts her energy into new roles to gain ascendency in the De la Fontaine household. She is a social climber who uses her humble working-class background to become the mistress of the great house and then as the companion of Oswald. She is the agent to initiate a process of recognition and enable them how to "face the reality of their living, to extend themselves beyond their privilege and plantation". (Lovelace 372). Clodia estimates her as the essence of aristocracy compared to whom they are a "bunch of rich, dumb and stupid people" (2.1.5, Location 1829).

Soon after her arrival, her fervour over the island's beauty is resonant with captivated tourists' reaction to the exotic place. Her appreciation of the ambience is sensuous as she stands before the cocoa valley, Agatha recalls the good hot tea prepared from the cocoa powder and wonders whether they were exported from these islands. Her observation corroborates "the workings of empire and of international capitalism are emblematically exposed through the reminder of the third world countries' role as agricultural primary producers, laid down by imperialism but sustained by the post-independence neo-colonial system" (Burnet 250). Later on Brown the journalist dismisses her as "neo-colonialist". Her wonder at learning that Malaria exists still in this part seems a little naïve. Soon after her arrival, Victor also sees her with the eyes of a captivated painter to be resembling a Watteau shepherdess. Apart from the captivating views what seizes her notice also is the state of plantation workers whom she finds singing at their work. She, with her Marxist ideological leaning, asks if they get their bonus; her concern is pitted against Victor's naive belief that the workers are "perfectly happy". A cockney and graduate from the London School of Economics, she raises awareness of the labour force of the estate. Her serious political activism soon after her arrival triggers an agitated chain of events and gradually exposes the family to insecurity. Oswald repudiates her involvement in local politics and finds London School of Economics degree will not help her in gaining the knowledge of Trinidad where she has entered as an outsider; she finds herself changed in the island though she had the vision to change the islandic community life. She defends her involvement by saying that she loves the place not for the privileges it offered to her but for the challenges it offered. Her Marxist zeal is obvious at the moment when the federation is about to come into being: she is concerned about the labourers and conditions of their work in the estate (1.2.17-18, Location 1055).

Under the rhetoric of equality, Agatha inscribes Jean with colonialist ideologies. She initiated a school-teaching programme with Jean and Sydney to spread more political awareness. However, Oswald draws the attention of the Interviewer Brown, that the part of Agatha is not above doubts as she made the "damn black people" her comrades and never relented from supporting Jean and her manipulative skill in making the leader and controlling colonies like a remote control (2.2.19-22, Location 1848). The short-sighted appreciation of art and politics in the heydays of Black nationalism is laid bare by the passionate protest of Oswald. Though Jean has not wholeheartedly accepted the idea of reading books for the village council elections because she prefers "Carnival to politics". Towards the end, when the volatility of the Trinidadian society is at its height and the military crackdown is about to start, she even accuses Agatha of encouraging this political course:

> Life was so uncomplicated at Santa Rosa Girl, this could be the last Carnival for years. (2.1.7, Location 1644).

Immediately after the Independence, reclaiming the "black" and "African" elements became a fraught question in Trinidad since here the larger population was formed by the indentured workers from India. But throughout the West-indies, the sweeping influence of Black Power movements in U.S. Trinidad protest, also dubbed as February Revolution, and Rodney Riots in Jamaica were two key challenges to the governance of the Anglophone Caribbean. Though Walcott's play does not offer any immediate solution to the post-independence problems of Trinidad, this play probes into the entanglement of new cultural nationalisms and issues of chauvinism, the network of power. The play covers a time-span passing through important political events; it begins in 1948 and then jumps into 1962 and then onto 1970. The first date represents the post- war phase of new immigration. These two dates are politically very significant: as 1962 being the year of failures of the newly formed West Indian federation and the 1970 is of the tumultuous uprising of the militant Black nationalism and its eventual squashing. The second part is centred on the 1970 moment and investigates the moment from a critical angle. This section undermines the claim that the Caribbean is a timeless zone of an unspoilt beauty- as soon after her arrival Agatha throws out her watch into the sea, deluding herself that and she is stepping out of the linear temporal course. In the changing social world, the younger generation of the de La Fontaine is more drawn to "bacchanal" culture of Carnival, its change and new value system; it lies in tension with the pictorial and artistic stasis and the image of timeless, exotic world. The romanticism associated with the Black Power and demagogic assertions about the past provoked Walcott's scepticism: "Walcott spent his curfew hours working on a play in which, by alternating the scenes between the black and the white milleux, he contrasted the militant extremism of the black Power movement with the gentle decadence of the of a French enclave" (Stone 115).

As the plot unfolds to investigate volatile times, culture appears to be a highly contested site where ideologies criss-cross. Multiple legacies of colonialism, complex cultural confrontations are enacted through the episodes of Brown's interview with the De la Fontaine family and the aggressive episode of burning down of Santa Rosa, which prompts the departure of Clodia from the estate. In the later part of the play, the younger generation is found to be more rooted in heterogenous society and culturally prefers creole to standard French. Two of Victor's children, Clodia and Tony, play-act, parodically, the role of Victor and Agatha. They mock their father's self- doubt and Agatha's manipulation before Brown, the journalist, who seeks to celebrate the artist's life and work in his column. Clodia, though educated in England, is in a deep attachment to Trinidad and it is an impulse that she shares with her father. She interrogates the compatibility of the race with the love of the country; she belongs to the country though her ancestral home was far away in France:

> "I don't read no poetry, my head is pure sawdust, but I know one thing. I know I stupid." ((A.2, Sc:2, Location 2054).

Even if stupid he will be proud to be attached passionately to flowers, mountains and black people like a true 'native' son. She is free of illusions; by birth and culture she is Trinidadian and without futile longing for the home of the forefathers. Such self-awareness saves her from the cultural dilemma that so much tormented her artist father. As Brown meets her for the interview, she sharply retorts that he owes his two children some other apology Apart from his artistic despair.

> People don't die for art.
>
> (A.2, Sc:1, Location 1355)

Clodia accuses Victor of self-consuming despair which has left Santa Rosa haunted. She has internalised the multiculturalism of Trinidad by speaking mostly creole rather than standard French and dances with the Carnival band and taken Sydney the militant participant of the movement as her lover. The play closes upon her departure which is a clear parallel of Agatha's arrival from England; she is sent to Europe in the midst of the turmoil of the country. These two migrations, two exiles, one voluntary and the other forced, destabilize the fixed category of nation-making as an undifferentiated category. As Camilla Stevens succinctly puts it: "This arrival and departure bracket the historical period dramatized in the play and invites the audience to consider how the seemingly fixed and uniform past is, in reality, as unstable as the category of nation itself" (458).

Clodia's brother, Tony offers a remarkable change to become a designer of the local carnival; he illustrates interest in a local cultural event, quite unlike his father's sharp dismissal of them. Generational difference of values in art and life continues here, too. Like Clodia, here presents the transformative role of the indigenous culture. Other minor figures like Jean or Sydney compel our attention. Jean, Agatha's protégée, has been transformed from the maid to a minister of the new Government of Independent Trinidad. She can carry forward the ideals propagated by Agatha that Jean Beaux champs has a voice in the government. Though her rise offends Oswald as she calls him by first name and appropriates the colonial language when she takes it over and decentres it from the privilege of the white people. Brown strongly castigates the role of Jean as it is intended to advance the white values in the Govt. But she does not enjoy complete freedom in assuming a position of political privilege. The revolutionary hope of Sydney is dashed to the ground as he directly becomes a member of the movement. He refuses to accept Agatha as a well-intended socialist and her ideals only lead him in direct involvement with the frenzied Black Power movement. And as he grew up among the servants and developed a sense of inferiority and began to nurture a desire for revenge.

Even after finding *The Last Carnival* a "strong and textured play", Earl Lovelace faults Walcott for incomplete characterization and argues that the play fails to press home, those truths that are within the social fabric of the play. But much more interesting criticism is directed at the Black Power Movement and its exclusionary politics in the midst of the atmosphere of the Carnival. The burning down of Santa Rosa is the crudest manifestation of the politics of reprisal; as a violent and destructive phenomenon, their political ethics is questioned by Oswald as the "black" people want only "black government". The racialization of governance and homogenization to create a "Caribbeanness" was common to the conditions of many islands. As the old order began to crumble away and Black Nationalist Movement heightens Brown cautions against the feeling of arrogance and fast creeping intolerance. He believes the rebels to have adopted roles with specific costumes: it is "another carnival". It has become directionless and unresponsive to the local realities. Like Carnival, it has little to offer to Trinidad's political future. Clodia satirically dismisses it as some frivolous roleplaying, black power and its ideologue as vain (A.2. Sc: 2.17-20, Location 1311).

The final scenes very powerfully articulate the wrong-headed heroic ideal of black activism. The power structure and political control are effectively undermined as the backwater of empire undergoes radical cultural changes. Along with *Remembrance* this play is energised by Walcott's personal, autobiographical stance on the connection between race, culture and politics. They explore the interface of decaying white minority culture and militant extremism and also the possibility of reading the personal life along the line of history. Thus, Walcott's exploration of the colonial and the postcolonial reality and large cultural concerns help in redefining his people. They both attempt to yoke the world of politics and art- the stories of movement and stasis, arrival and departure are woven into the well-crafted plot. The ethos of racial and cultural superiority and the popular reactionary nativism drove Walcott to enunciate alternative "militancy"-that is the "militancy of art"- as he famously proclaimed in his seminal essay "What the Twilight Says".

Beef, no chicken

The Caribbean, as mapped in Walcott's drama, appears not only "as the receptacle of history's debris but also as a beginning point for a new and unpredictable connections between historical forces and current configurations of the global capital" (Bhattacharya 7).[9] Over the decades, Walcott's growth of stature as a playwright has run parallel to the changing political fortunes of the Caribbean. Robert. D. Hamner has noted: "the fact that Walcott's life coincides with the Caribbean independence movements makes his career significant for historic and aesthetic reasons" (121). In his poems and plays, Walcott has expressed his deep concern with the advance of global capitalism, the state's drive towards promoting tourism and commercialism of the "folk". In the two-act light comedy, *Beef, No Chicken* (first produced in 1981) the small Trinidadian town, Couva is the focus of the main action where the proposed event of building/constructing an express highway threatens to displace the popular roadside roti shop and garage of Otto. Such construction projects thrive on demolishing the existing structure and replacing it with technologically advanced, faster communication system. The growing appeal of Televisual shows in the popular mind symptomatizes this changing time in provincial places. What Walcott is primarily concerned with here is the tussle between modernization and tradition and the clash between new and old ways of life. The small-town community is extremely divided over the project. Comic, light wit permeates through the plot, as in *Pantomime*, where serious intervention is made into performing the reversal of colonial logic of dualism and futility of local resistance.

Here the protagonist, Otto Hogan, owner of Auto Repair and Authentic Roti Shop, is a stringent status quoist like the retired school teacher, Jordan. Despite all persuasion of the borough council, he stands defiantly opposed. The young generation whizzes past him, leaving him a "wreck"; the promise of employment cannot dash his spirited fight for stopping the project. He hopelessly waits for the demolition of his shop and is bound to provide the food for the workers in the project whom he calls "enemy". Like him, Deacon expresses a strong dislike of the Highway project. He bemoans how the countryside settings are eroding fast and replaced by the spread of

---

[9] In the sub-section, titled "Two Maps" in the *Introduction of Postcolonial writing in the era of World Literature* this observation occurs.

Americanism, the introduction of neon, television and urban amenities "It's about McDonaldizing everything, it's Kentucky frying everything, it's about going modern with a vengeance and televising everything" (A: 2 Sc: 2 Location 4387). Amid the cheers, Cedric is in a celebrant mood and he believes that it signals the entry of Trinidad in the twenty-first century. This progressivist notion clashes with an unyielding spirit and integrity of Otto. He has the daring to tear up the contract of Mongroo construction because he prefers "sound sleep" to a "fat deal". Corruption and corporate projects go hand in hand - as Joe calls it, a "moral poison". Cardiff, who travels back to the country, cherishes the difference and variety in the natural setting of the place. He regrets that the fervour for development and urbanization will turn the place into a dull uniform pattern "like everywhere else" with the shopping malls and plazas (Location 3909). A returnee to his native place, he cherishes the natural ways to be continued. In the face of sweeping changes, he feels to be an outcast and outsider. Even in the days of his stay abroad, he fondly recalled "larks", "grazing sheep", "hills". Otto feels irreconciled to the changing disposition of his customers for mall and plaza and finds his country shop is becoming outmoded and on the verge of disappearance. The rapid changes do not cow down his spirit as the abiding beauty of Couva will be blurred by projects like this. And Otto believes that an honest man is so rare that if an angel runs through the town with a lantern, it won't find any. Corruption issuing from development projects faces the local resistance commanded attention. Another sign of modernity in such a small town is the television and it brings glamour to the provincial life and the opening of the highway is broadcast zestfully. This hold of televisual media on the popular minds is broached by Deacon, "a vagabond preacher":

"we believe in our images
instead of ourselves until everything that lives
ain't holy no longer but fully photographed,
and the rest of our creed is: 'I saw it on TV' (A: II Sc:2, Location 4299).

He finds the faster mode of life empty and inconsequential. Such fissures and disruptions to the traditional ways of life are the underbellies of development in the periphery or "third world"- as Cardiff Joe interrogates whether the government bothers about the living conditions of the locals when holding out promises of progress.

If they want the kind that destroys the people, be it a new highway or a new bomb?" (A: 2 Sc: 2 Location 6643).

Mr. Mongroo insults Franco, the schoolmaster, by harshly reminding him that only money 'talks' (Location: 3736). This crass materialism was no doubt an affront to the traditional values of provincial society. It exposes the vulnerability of the old values. His scornful dismissal of Otto as the old-fashioned roti seller and passionate upholding of highways point to the clash of generational values. The view of the local Mayor is antithetical; a passionate advocate of progress in terms of infrastructure, he charges Otto why they should stick to the old ways as when cows would lie down and the cars wait for them to get up. He repudiates the natural simplicity of Otto and calls him a "simpleton". The rhetoric of politicians and policy makers is borne out when he claims to make the town one of the great cities in the world, to have the views of traffic jam and industrial smoke.

Walcott was tirelessly critical of the politicians who planned artificial structure on the natural beauty of the islands. In Couva town, rapid commercialization has involved the country girl in posing for sell of products, lured by Yankee fashion. In every way, the synthetic progress invades the quiet, serenity of a small Trinidadian town. Mongroo also fails to convince Otto about the prospective benefit by citing the instance of McDonald's in America in comparison with Chrysler. He refuses the money offered to persevere in his opposition. A story of a ghost treading the road in midnight from the silk cotton tree is circulated to ward off the construction team, which is a part of the local superstition. But the workers of the town are not cowed town by this superstitious tale. Euphony believes "mystery" to be the spirit of such a town and resist any attempt to rob the place of its spirit. This play, often considered a minor work of Walcott, trenchantly critiques the neo-colonial economic and political policy.[10] Beneath the farcical and humorous texture, we are startled by the tragedy of the country people and the sad undertone of the abrupt change to the rhythm and harmony of country life. In the post-independence days, neo-liberal economics moved into the phase of new empire in the Caribbean archipelagos. In probing the pitfalls of the promise of development and ongoing inequity, Walcott's play interrogates cultural hegemony sustained by metropolitan capital. As Robert Young elucidates: "Historically most empires give way to further empires. The end of the European empires, by contrast, produced a new global and political formation that distinguishes them from all empires that preceded them: the world of nation-states. It was in that environment that the postcolonial

---

[10] "These popular artists are trapped in the state's concept of folk form, for they preserve the colonial demeanour and threaten nothing. The folk arts have become the symbol of a carefree, accommodating culture, an adjunct to tourism, since the state is impatient with anything which it cannot trade" (*What the Twilight Says* 7).

emerged as a specific way of addressing the inequities and injustices of both imperial rule and its global aftermath" (6).

Chapter 5

"Creole-Continuum" and Radical Disruption in Theatre

"The new cultural and creative consciousness lives in an entirely polyglot world. The world becomes polyglot, once for all and irreversibly. The period of national languages, coexisting but closed and deaf to each other, comes to an end. Languages throw light on each other: one language can after all see itself only in the light of another language"

-Mikhail Bakhtin

"There is no language in itself, nor any universality of language, but a discourse of dialects, patois and slangs and special languages. There exists no ideal competent speaker- hearer of language, any more than there exists a homogeneous linguistic community"

-Delueze and Guattari

In the face of several conflicting linguistic inheritances and their aesthetic claims, Walcott had found it a quite formidable challenge to fashion a new theatrical language. Finding a new theatrical idiom and vocabulary in the face of conflicting linguistic in the face of conflicting linguistic inheritances and their aesthetic claims was, no doubt, a formidable challenge for Walcott. The islands, unmoored from any originary culture and having undergone historical displacement were left with fragile linguistic bonding. In such a situation, finding a language authentically native to the place and people, was only a futile pursuit. Without a common linguistic foundation, the island artists were compelled to pass beyond the "mimicry" of "High Culture". The plurality of culture underpinned the decolonizing narratives to write the West Indian subjects into a history and sought to rebut and renounce the monolingual register as only valid literary expression. Walcott turned the English language into a hybridized, Antillean *patois* that successfully captured regional accents and idiosyncrasies of the St. Lucian people. The Anglophone writers have used the Western tradition to the advantage for self-representation and stretched the possibilities of the English language into a creole expression to suit new speech patterns of different vernacular and dialect. Achebe's fiction has also demonstrated how the English language may be manipulated to recreate the Igbo language structure. Without assuming the radical position of Thiong'o, vis-a-vis English language, he reappropriated and extended its frontiers to hybridized, Igbo-English. In his inimitable way, Walcott also described his unflagging appropriation of the imperial tongue as an act if theft into the "master's house"; in place of steadfast adherence to its vocabulary, he formed a new register with different creole speech patterns. This linguistic expansion and enrichment contributed towards making (an) another language- one that can carry the weight of indigenized egalitarian aesthetics.[1] All these major non-Western writers like Achebe, Soyinka, Naipaul and Walcott were credited with belting new energy to the English tongue while forging alternative literary traditions.

The language situation in the Caribbean has always been both complex and fascinating. The variety of colonial languages and cultural involvement with the colonial powers have reshaped the syntax and lexicon of the vernacular and led to the emergence of many non- standard forms. The choice of an expressive language for dramatic art was itself "political" for writers like Thiong'o, Walcott, Achebe; it sought to thwart the dominance of imperial language and its practice of scribality. Though English was their dominant medium, the infiltration of indigenous words had made the question of 'authenticity' "more vexed". Walcott's "mad" love for English and uncompromising hate towards the colonial policy had made him "divided to the vein".[2] As a St. Lucian, he was an heir to the triple linguistic heritage—French Creole, English creole and English. Besides, he knew that the Creole or dialect was diversified from one region to another in the West Indies: "Every island in the Caribbean has its own syntactical structure," explains Walcott, "a Trinidadian is not going to understand a Jamaican the first time off". When adopted and inserted into English—the language of education and administration— the popular *patois* vocabulary had altered the English speech patterns. What it resulted in was a refusal of the privilege of the authority of the imperial language (Tompkins and Gilbert 165-166) and the formation of a syncretic language, enriched with syntax and grammar of different islands. Language with centralising power, like French and English, Walcott knew, will only maintain hegemony and

---

[1] "[W]hen we borrow an alien language to sculpt or paint in, we must begin by co-opting the entire properties in our matrix of thought and expression. We must stress such a language, stretch it, impact and compact, fragment and reassemble it with no apology, as required to bear the burden of experiencing and of experiences, be such experiences formulated or not in the conceptual idioms of that language." – Soyinka "Aesthetic Illusions: Prescriptions for the Suicide of Poetry", "Art, Dialogue and Outrage: Essays on Literature and Culture".

[2] "How choose/Between this Africa and the English tongue I love?"- *A Far Cry From Africa*.

authority. This melding of standard and non-standard variants, incorporation of a range of possible speech variants proclaimed the alterity of theatrical idioms and endowed postcolonial stage with what is commonly called "creole-continuum" (Tompkins 185). This choice leaves upon his stagecraft a seal of humanist voices – differently directed towards disparate cultures and traditions; it entailed the oral language like *picong* with rich poetic diction to resist linguistic hegemony. In the 70s, the polemical question - Creole or English? triggered a debate within the islands which Walcott had found futile and brushed off as either/or choice; it only contravened the cultural hybridity of the Caribbean and disseminated the notion of "authenticity" to play into the hands of exclusionary politics. As one of the earliest Caribbean dramatists to attract the global audience, he imbued the creole variants with a new prestige, turning them into a vehicle for the complexity of regional representation. Seamus Heaney, his friend and, Irish Nobel laureate, in an essay "The Language of Exile" has eloquently lauded his rare gift: "I imagine he has done for the Caribbean what Synge did for Ireland, found a language woven out of dialect, neither folksy nor condescending, a singular idiom evolved out of one man's inherited divisions that allows an older life to exult in itself yet at the same time keeps the "cool of the new" (*Critical* 304) literature. In the same way, he draws attention to his fidelity to West Indian speech. No doubt, his new linguistic register was rooted in his own earth.

> The smell of our own speech,
> The smell of baking bread
> Of drizzled asphalt, this
> Oderous cedar… (*Another Life* 185).

In 1956, George Lamming's essay "The Negro and His World", posited language as instrumental in deterritorialising the colonial subject and shared the dialectical view that language could be a tool of domination and resistance.

At the outset of his career, Walcott found that "French-creole or patois, the vernacular of most of the St. Lucians, was yet to be fully mined in Caribbean writing" (Breiner 8). All pidgin and creole variations were kept under the rubric of marginal languages. They were often identified as "baby language" or "unnatural language". In the opening chapter of *Black Skin, White Mask* Fanon draws attention to how the language situation for the Antillean subjected him to condemnation for not knowing French. The middle class in the Antilles never spoke Creole except to their servants. In school, the children of Martinique are taught to scorn the dialect. One avoids Creolisms. Some families completely forbid the use of Creole, and mothers ridicule their children for speaking it.

> My mother wanting a son to keep in mind
> if you do not know your history lesson
> you will not go to mass on Sunday in
> your Sunday clothes
> that child will be a disgrace to the family
> that child will be our curse shut up
> I told you must speak French
> the French of France
> the Frenchman's French (10).

On the other hand, resorting to Standard English was a signifier of colonial mental residue. To overcome this dilemma, Walcott's early plays deployed "vast linguistic variations, declining gradually in the later plays only Creole inflexions of syntax within a more or less standard English" (Tejumola 488). The never-ending cross-cultural encounter of his plays underscore the corrupt and deformed versions of a different linguistic register which can explore new ways of imaginative representations. Walcott made a practical solution between the actual speech sounds and the grapholect of Standard English. The Caribbean writers were always aware of the differences with which they lived and found a communicative corridor between languages to negotiate their outgoing fascinations and innate/inward choices – that is, to forge a set of registers, a grapholect where cultural translation could be made possible.[3] It could enable what Sam Selvon has called "the welding of our polyglot community... the weddings of our culture" (*A Brighter Sun*). As Cuban poet Nicolás Guillén (2003) puts it:

> We have been together from long ago
> young and old,
> blacks and whites, all mixed,
> one commanding and the other commanded,
> all mixed;
> San Berenito and another commanded,
> all mixed...
> Santa Maria and another commanded,
> all mixed
> all mixed

The emergent intra-regional creole speech habits were the strong indicators of modern West Indian performance tradition. Walcott was keen to borrow

---

[3] Judy Stone was one of the earliest critics to describe the exploration of Walcott's "lifelong concern between the classic and the creole. See, *Theatre*, 136.

from Asian, African and European traditions rather than Africanist cultural practices. For him, the indigenisation of performances was tangential to transculturation rather than seeking to identify "the concerns and obsessions of a self-cocooned Western canonical enclave".[4] In the postcolonial stage, language does not appear to be "confined to the substitution of another language for English" (Tompkins) but with creating alternate "tone", "rhythm" and "lexicon" which will generate resistance. Eminent Jamaican writer Victor Reid had infused English with lexical and idiomatic Jamaicans, which acted as a catalyst for activating West Indian consciousness. The end impression for Reid was in listening to a quintessential Jamaican voice and experience. Walcott's attachment to *patois* or French Creole as a literary medium enabled a condition of verisimilitude of St. Lucian folk lives. In such local languages, his culture's stories and concerns are powerfully retold. His manipulation of linguistic practices of this stage is succinctly expressed by Ned Thomas: "In the first place, it must reflect a commitment to the salted vigour of the ordinary speech. However, compared to many West-Indian poets, Walcott achieves this effect by a very few touches drawn from West-Indian syntax and verb-forms, devices that in no way lose Walcott his international audience" (88). With an array of innovative linguistic strategies, the polyglossic register of his plays has found a new habitation- a home away from home. Superseding colonial mimicry, these forms rejoice over the collision and collusion of speech habits and marks theatre as a site of unfamiliarity and unpredictability. A diverse web of connections and complex intercultural relationship also helped the stage language overcome fixed system, tradition and their overdeterminism. Creole in its variants was under active consideration of Walcott and his early play *Ti-Jean* originated in a folk tale. It expands into a web of connections between standard, poetic and mundane, oral and scribal. Considered to be a landmark of West Indian theatre, *Henri Cristophe* (1949) brought to the fore Walcott's artistic representation of the society in which he himself grew. Here the influence of Jacobean tradition outweighed the vernacular of the low-life characters and Walcott seemed far from ready to endorse creole as an apt medium for literary expression and particularly for the portrayal of historical figures. These early writings carefully eschewed the binaries of standard, non-standard, scribal and oral.

Walcott once described Caribbean people "ashamed of their speech" like actors, they "awaited a language". No doubt, it was the centrist scorn that had forced them to feel ashamed of the secondariness of linguistic position.

---

[4] In his much- cited article W. J. T. Michell "The Chronicle of Higher Education", April 9, 1989 points out that the cultural transfer has been a two-way traffic especially between the declining power of the imperialism and the former colonies.

Domestic language, though multiple, was felt to be unworthy and inappropriate for serious study.[5] Pidgins and creoles were scorned as mere corruption of metropolitan languages. The Jamaican poet Mutabarku's observation is so apposite "the Language we talk we cannot write; and the language we write we can't talk" (qtd. in Breiner). The leading poets and the playwrights were found making adjustments between the two touchstones, "seriousness" and "society in general". Soon after parting with the rebel histories, Walcott resorted to the whole language continuum and explored the strength of vernacular speech. The dichotomy between standard English and the creoles, the balance between the high tradition, formal English and salty, raw speech of the folks had to be restored in an alternative register:

> Language and the experience of illiteracy among the poor is a profound problem that divides the West Indian writer. The more sophisticated he becomes, the more alienated is his mental state. It is not his business to lower the standards to insult the poor. When one is confronted with his problem of language, two situations occur: wanting to reach one's people; and realizing the harsh realities of the society and the economic exploitation. At the same time that one's intellect becomes more refined, and one learns more about the society, there is a movement away from the society (*Conversations* 39-40).

Through constant manipulation of language, a playwright can wrest the power from the top-down monolithic imposition. Walcott always considered the limited access of the creole for the international audience to be a hindrance though the French-based creole was the dominant language in the rural areas. His early heroes like Makak, Afa and Chantal were hailed from folk lives and legends and their common everyday speech bristled with French-creole. Though keen on adhering to West Indian syntax and idioms, he was not ready to sacrifice his international audience. Walcott's experimentation was one of the markers of assertive claims of creole as a literary medium which was not yet regarded for prestigious literary production in London or Paris. Many Anglophone writers judged the creole as unaesthetic and inaccessible and discarded it as an expression of indigeneity. But in the multicultural setting of his society, considering the unique situation of his homeland, Walcott had to make his adjustments among the rich resources of

---

[5] See, Jefiyo "On Euro-centric Critical Theory: Some Paradigms from the texts and Sub-texts of Post-colonial Writing". https://ro.uow.edu.au/kunapipi/vol11/iss1/13.

several metropolitan languages and creole languages.[6] First staged in 1954, *The Sea at Dauphin* depicts a day in the life of Dauphin, a remote fishing village. Like its canonical "pre-text" *Riders to the Sea*, it aims to reproduce the language of the people. Set in the cultural milieu among St. Lucian fishermen, Walcott knew the magnitude of translating the vernacular speech into a lyric and yet accessible language. It marks a decisive departure from the emulation of great Elizabethan and Jacobean dramatists. Walcott's note on the translative energy of the Irish idioms deserves to be mentioned in full:

> When I read Synge's *Riders to the Sea*, I realized what he had attempted to do with the language of the Irish. He had taken a fishing port type of language and gotten beauty out of it, a beat, something lyrical… If you know very clearly that you are mutating such and such work, it isn't that you are adding another man's genius, it is that he has done an experiment that he has worked and will be useful to all writers afterwards. When I tried to translate the speech of the St. Lucian fishermen into English inflected Creole, and that was a totally new experience for me, even it did come out of Synge. (*Interview*, 188-89)

After the first publication in 1960, Walcott revised it for the Farrar Straus edition of 1970 and removed some French-creole idioms and gave it closeness to English. As the play and its immediate intertexts issue out of different cultural milieu, the lexicon and syntax are also very different and it helps the narrative to be relocated to a different cultural location. Walcott's devising "a medium that could communicate features of spoken Creole while remaining readily comprehensible for any Anglophone reader" (Breiner 6) underlines the writer as a "translated man". In the 1970 edition, the two fishermen Garcia and Afa start their conversation by greeting each other with "*bon matin*" which is considered less appropriate than "*bon jour*" as French formal way of saying good morning. Though this phrase may be an informal greeting between the workers as it also denotes "bright and early", as the fishermen have met at very early hours in the morning. There is also exclamation like *Bondieu* (Good God) or phrase like *Eh bien* (well then) or creole expression like "fairenasse" for fish with an etoras Hounakin calls the fellow fishermen "*Mes enfants*", meaning "my children". Directly related to fishing expedition a few *patois* words are denied this glossing: *call abase, cooyon, grace* (meaning

---

[6] … "the lively and inventive Trinidad dialect, which has won West Indian writing many friends and many enemies abroad, is disliked by some West Indians. They do not object to its use locally; the most popular column in Trinidad is a dialect column in the Evening News by the talented and witty person known as Macaw. But they object to its use in books which are read abroad" (*Middle Passage*, 68).

calabash, fool and beach). The name of the sailor protagonist, Afa is an African name that Walcott heard mistakenly from a group of fishermen and thought it to be a creole version of Arthur. Walcott's treatment of creole and sublimation of it into poignant lyricism was a strong alternative to the "nation language "model proffered by Brathwaite. When the dialect or folk speech entered into literature as a linguistic device, it could "present and preserve striking rhythms and locutions" (Breiner 165).

Grounded in folk lives Walcott's early one-act plays uphold the creole speech which was often considered sub-literary. Because Louis Bennet had observed "People are as accustomed to reading the dialect as they are to listening it".[7] Another play *Ti Jean and His Brothers*, under this rubric, demonstrates his inventive approach to St. Lucian vernacular speech. With the purpose of performing before a non-native/foreign audience he glossed the creole speeches of the devil and demon:

> DEVIL: "Bai diable- "la mnger un "timamaille"
> (Give the devil a child for dinner)
>
> (8.69)

The African story-telling practice through Cricket, Frog and Firefly was akin to the practices of the Greek dramatists. And Walcott's glossing was a useful manipulation in these performance texts in view of his foreign audience. Though in Sc. 3, the off-stage utterances of the Devil remain untranslated and suggests the centrality of the French creole in the St. Lucian life. This hybrid form is more strongly present in the English translation of Ngugi's novel *Devil in the Cross* (1982) where the Africanization of English is marked by replete with borrowings from Gikuyu and Kiswahili and it proved more commensurable with oral tradition. The legend of Chantal in *Malchochon* or *Six in the Rain* is introduced with this kind of glossing as French creole and English are juxtaposed (11-15.17). The musicians and the Conteur here easily shuttle between English and Creole. The plurilingual register corroborates how the colonized subject could restructure and reinvent their own language. Because Walcott knew that in his society language had already had "a protean vitality" but it had not formalized its own "syntax and variety" (Poetry 3) he was creatively impelled to use the whole range of dialects.

Walcott's deployment of the full range of language repertory in *Dream on Monkey Mountain* deserves a careful scrutiny. In this early masterpiece, the narrative traverses official English, *patois*, creole- English; as a consequence,

---

[7] See, Dennis Scott, "Bennet on Bennet", *Caribbean Quarterly* 14:1&2 (1968), 98.

the language continuum here sums up the quest for identity, displacement and search for the lost home. The court life, the jail and the market, the legal register and secular register exist in tension and the contrastive language registers testify to the "an encounter, within the area of an utterance, between different linguistic consciousnesses, separated from one another by an epoch, by social differentiation or by some other factor" (*Dialogic* 359). The Prologue of the play is animated with this cross-cultural dialogue. In the opening scene, the conversations that take place inside the jail between Corporal Lestrade and the two felons, Tigre and Souris, is in vernacular or local English. Contrasted to him, Chorus and the Conteur use non-standard English with syntactical variation and depart from Standard English spelling with "de" and "dat" for "the", "that". But soon Lestrade assumes the official position and begins to deliver commands in standard English. So, the intersection of normative and non-normative English brings the fore the "decolonizing" of language as a major cultural concern for a Caribbean writer.[8] The legal records only validate the names of Makak, Moustique and Tigre and their association of bestiality with individuals. "The interpellative process of European languages", as Gilbert and Tompkins note, "frequently resulted in a reductive and simplistic construction of subjectivity as "other", here also these native peoples are stripped of their cultural being or personhood" (165). When Corporal Lestrade suggest that his place of residence must be Africa, Makak corrects him:

Makak: Sur morne macaque (Prologue, 218- 219).

Infuriated, Makak asks him to use English only in conducting the judiciary activities. His interrogation continues in official English and Makak replies in French- creole as he has no access to the language of power and authority. All the inmates cry in unison, "Let us hear English" which underscores acquiescence to the cultural supremacy of English. As Fanon argues, "[t]o speak means to be in a position to use a certain syntax, to grasp the morphology of this or that language, but it means above all to assume a culture, to support the weight of a civilisation" (*Black* 17-18). This monocentric view of human experience ran counter to the broad humanistic concern of postcolonial writings. In the polyglotic Caribbean society the privilege of French or English looked always vulnerable.

---

[8] Walcott attended University in Jamaica, the Anglophone Island which possesses the most distinctive form of Caribbean English, characterized by a true creole continuum and by very significant divergences from standard English in lexicon and syntax as well as in pronunciation.

The habit of code-switching in the West Indies forms an intrinsic part of the hybrid register of this play as his aesthetic principle never endorsed the centrist assumption of language. In an interview with Edward Hirsch, Walcott expressed his fervour for the languages and their polyphony in the Caribbean: "On every island there is a dialect, a *patois* which can become a world of fascination for someone who may want to write or use, or absorb into the whole West Indian idea of language" (286). In the market scene, the commonplace vendors talk to each other in creole English and allow us to glimpse into a non-hierarchical and a demotic way of communication. During a quarrel between husband and wife regarding the healing power of Makak, no single set of arguments prevails over another. Only when Lestrade appears on the scene and advises the vendor to call "melon" a "pawpaw", he yields to the dominant, authoritative discourse. In the face of repressive law, speech habits are framed for the natives (1.3:15-18.260-261). Language and skin colour as the very basis of identity in the West Indian society is further enunciated by the fake-healer Moustique when he says:

> Moustique: All I have this is this shows the mask, black faces, white masks!"
>
> (1.3.271)

As Lestrade gradually divests himself of the hold of the white racial part of the identity he leans towards the "other" part of black self. He ceases to uphold only Roman law and dismiss the tribal law. As a mulatto he equates Roman law and Tribal law, standard and vernacular English. The issue of linguistic hegemony is displaced and the monolith of culture appears vulnerable as towards the end Makak recalls his original name – Felix Hobain. This recovery of name and redemption from interpellation with his return to the Mountain home affirm the increasing significance of margin and minority in building a national culture.[9] As Paula Burnett describes it very succinctly: "It is once again, at the heart of language itself that the process of redemption is initiated" (147).

The comic two-hander of *Pantomime* seizes a carnivalesque atmosphere through inventive use of subversive strategies like parody, repartee and anti-poetry. The flip rendition of Defoe's classic *Robinson Crusoe* did not attempt a mere repudiation of Standard English within the framework of a comic skit; rather interconnected cultural lives converge and diverge at the site of

---

[9] In the subsection "Community Matters" of the chapter 8, in *Location of Culture*, Bhabha calls he Caribbean as a space possessed through the power of naming and recalling of the original name, according to him is a "sign of survival" (336).

performance. Full of wit and piquant humour, Jackson Philip code-switches, parodies and makes playful intonation to decode the ideological signs embedded in the monolingual script of Defoe's original. As the plot unfolds, language as a sign of racial and class hierarchy faces erasure. The nativization of the archetypal story of Crusoe in a dilapidated guest house corroborates how the alternative linguistic register can productively challenge the epistemology of race and unequal power relations.

The different social and economic context of both Harry and Jackson make the realistic representation of the pantomime or a light-hearted, straightforward reversal of Crusoe story impossible. The indigenous life and local speech patterns deauthorize Harry Trewe's directorial part in arranging a pre-season show for the guests. His factotum, Jackson reiterates colonial axiom to find in language an agency and turn the act of mimicry on its head to make his role-playing more productive. His background of calypsonian performance allows him to speak on the colonial dynamic, distancing himself from the British culture and establishing a culture of their own. In situating his chore of serving breakfast against the backdrop of historical master-slave narratives, Jackson demonstrates how his act of "colonial mimicry" is expressive of "the desire for a reformed, recognizable Other, as a subject of difference that is almost the same, but not quite" (Bhabha 122). In one of his brilliant mimicries, Jackson acts out the "history of imperialism"; by paddling his canoe, miming a shipwreck, he proceeds to teach his white slaves in the African language. Harry's reminder of placing a time limit on piss-break and of advising to use a personal toilet is a ploy for extorting more labour which undermines 'man-to-man' communication. Megan K. Ahern in a well-nuanced analysis in "Insubordinate Speech: Mimicry as Bourdieauian Heterodoxy" argues how Walcott distinguishes between language as expressive mode of identity and language as a disruptive and parodic medium. The more Jackson participates in pantomime, the more he overshadows his master. Megan has placed him in the latter category performer who by deft manipulation of language deforms the standarized accent and diction.

It is through his consummate performance that Jackson mounts a deconstructive attack on language as a fixed cultural system and code. A truly Caribbean performance, Walcott always insisted, would not be a mere rebuttal of its Western model: "Once the New World black had tried to prove that he was as good as his master, when he should have proven not his equality but his difference" (*Essays* 9). He steals the show with his verbal zest and communicational proficiency as he deploys the verbal strategies like innuendo, code-switching and many other improvisatory techniques. He spells out a rejoinder to Harry's version; in a long interpretation, which is a profanation of the sacred poetic utterance, he performs carnivalesque subversion. Unlettered

Jackson pronounces "marina" in alluding to Coleridge's Ancient Mariner and desacralizes its immediate classic intertext:

> JACKSON: And Robieent thinking 'bout his wife and son and O silent sea and wondrous sunset; no, Robie is the First True Creole, so he watching the goat with his narrow eyes, narrow, and he say blehhh,eh? (146).

The highly inventive, gleeful rhetoric and piquant humour of Jackson's interrogative and interruptive performance, as Edward Baugh has described, is a "hilarious send-up of the language being given to the black savage by the civilized white man" (134). Jackson's anti-poetry counterpoints Harry's lyricism, by creolizing both the vocabulary and the grammar in borrowing freely from Spanish and slang alike. He appropriates the language of his master when he impersonates Helen, the ex-wife of Harry, and in an impeccable British accent he scolds Harry:

> JACKSON: (weeping) I love you, Harold. I love you and I loved him too. Forgive me (151).

Unlettered Jackson pronounces "marina" when alluding to Coleridge's Ancient Mariner and desacralizes its immediate classic intertext:

> "He looks up and see the fucking beard watching him and smiling, the goat with its forked fucking beard and square yellow eye, just like the fucking devil standing up there..."

The highly inventive, gleeful rhetoric and piquant humour of Jackson, as Edward Baugh has described, is a "hilarious send-up of the language being given to the black savage by the civilized white man" (134). Such subversive strategy not only turns the gaze back upon the colonizer but also dismantles the hegemony of the imperial tongue; the exaggerated form of Creole diction and code-switching help him satirize the condescending tone of the servant and unsettle the directorial authority of Harry. The status quo of the stage experience is defied whenever verbal ploys of code-switching as well as piquant humour are adroitly maneuvered by Jackson (Ahern 5). Sarcastic phrases and diction foil the attempt to express a coherent identity through the normative, "standard" version of the metropolitan tongue and topples the hierarchy of identity categories. His verbal gifts of parodic, disruptive speeches and the adroit use of mixed register and code-switching render the "text" aporetic. In re-telling of all source texts and the reworking of received cultural systems, Walcott's mongrelized vocabulary generates a new power relation through which "... identities are tested, remodelled, played out – and played with" (Gilbert 130). In the tensile space of performance, such autonomous, expressive recreation destabilizes languages as a marker of identity and dismantles its own register. "This sort of speech", as Ahern explains, "both affiliates the speaker with a particular group and expresses an inhabitable identity" (4). This easeful switch problematizes the easy correspondence between race, language and cultural identity. Naipaul's narratives also fuse Standard English and Trinidadian dialect where the dialogues move along the 'creole continuum'; but another contemporary of Walcott, Sam Selvon, in his first novel, *A Brighter Sun* had dared to make a breakthrough in literary language by code-shifting from the standard English to creole as a vehicle for introspection. In Earl Lovelace's masterpiece *The Dragon Can't Dance*, the first-person narrator switches between standard and the vernacular to counter the structure of power. Moreover, Jackson veers between standard and non-standard accent to upset the uniform speech pattern in terms of accent when he presents before Trewe scramble egg (A: 1 11-14, 133). As a performer with calypso background, he can exaggerate the British accent as he refers to piss break in Alabama. This verbal playfulness imbues the text with alternate semiotic signs and throws language into constant mutation. As Katalin Trencsenzi describes it: "The actions of the actor's body, the expression of his face, the sound of his voice, all at the mercy of the winds of his emotions ... emotions possess him; it seizes upon his limbs, moving whither at will ... Art as we have said, can admit of no accidents. That, then, which the actor gives us, is not a work of art; it is a series of accidental confessions" (108). The uneasy juxtaposition of the Crusoe narrative and its creole counterpart, the intersection of standard and mongrel idioms corroborates how the different cultural sensibilities travel across time and space.

Walcott's sophisticated dramaturgy features new structures and is enriched with the sounds, rhythms, and wordplay of creoles, pidgins and local idioms. He has renewed the value of the local cultural resources with affiliations of distant cultures. In *Branch of a Blue Nile* the Shakespearean performance undergoes a nativization, a new creole staging – placed at the interstices of dialect and standard speech pattern. The linkages of cultures from the centre and periphery fleshes out in deft enweaving of various lects, poetic and picong.[10] The intentional artistic hybrid performance could only be commensurable with the West Indian hybrid identity; three major characters like Gavin, Harvey and Chris, speak English with American, British and Trinidadian accent to make English (ex) centric. The regional varieties of

---

[10] "English is not a pure language but a fascinating combination of tongues welded into a fresh unity". (Narasimhaiah *The Swan and the Eagle* 8)

English help the cross-cultural performance and doing alternative Shakespeare on stage. In the stage space English becomes "a continuum of 'intersections' in which the speaking habits in various communities have intervened to reconstruct the language" (Ashcroft et al. 39).

In a conversation with Baer, Walcott ardently mentioned the high-quality intonation of Shakespeare by the West Indian actors: "Some of the finest Shakespeare I have ever heard was spoken by West-Indian actors. The sound of Shakespeare is not the sound we hear in Shakespeare, that androgynous BBC-type, high-tone thing. It's a coarse thing – a great range between wonderful vulgarity, and a great refinement, and we have that here. We have that vulgarity and we also have the refinement in terms of diction" (110). This multi-faceted performance styles of the Caribbean actors already attempted a strong refusal to enter into the domain of "authentic". The complex weave of cultural experience is borne out in the moments when a Trinidadian troupe has attempted a native rendition of *Antony and Cleopatra*. When a canonical play text is performed in the far-flung colony or translocated in a non-western milieu it becomes a "new" text, a new way of "staging", endowed with polyvocality and syncreticity. While Chris has brought vernacular to speak the Shakespearean lines, his creole interjections cause laughter. And Harvey's repeated Americanism is laughed at by the fellow troupe members.

Sheila makes confusion over Bard's English and attempts to regularize the grammar when she recites the mourning speech of Cleopatra after Antony's death (in A: IV)

> "The soldier's pole is fallen: young boys and girls
> Are now level with man; the odds are gone.
>
> (1:1 3-4, Location 4640)

At this, the British director reminds her the "original" lines: "the odds is gone, singular, Marylin, please." Harvey, also, questions the supposed the "purity" of the Bard's English; he alludes to the clown's speech, dialect fused with the rhetoric of Jacobean verse (2.3 8-10, Location 5647).

Beside the main plot runs a parallel attempt to mount a dialect version of *Antony and Cleopatra*. Chris's back-yard comedy is suitable entertainment for the West Indian audience, which underscores the choices available from comprehensive creole. Chris is strongly arguing with Gavin that language and place are so much defining of one's identity that his Americanism is a severe case of displacement, which is a bane for any artist. The encounters between linguistic consciousness animates the plot and keeps the "migration" of the source-text in alien setting alive. In Bakhtin's observation: "…[a]nother's sacred word, uttered in a foreign language, is degraded by the accents of vulgar folk language, re-evaluated and reinterpreted against the background of these languages" (*Dialogic* 76). From a "non-English" context Walcott's *Branch of a Blue Nile* repudiates all essentialist stances and the universalist view of language as a transparent medium of representation.

Even though Jordan, the protagonist of *Remembrance* is a staunch defender of King's English, here collects his life and teaching career while preparing for an interview in the Trinidadian dialect. He was admired for his "British accent" by his ex-beloved Esther, but Here in this plot, effective communication and official protocol not only contend but also intersect. In *The Last Carnival* Victor's standard speeches are set in diametric opposition to the earthy, vulgar creole of his brother Oswald. The socio-cultural values of the Caribbean people could only be justified by deconstructing the assumption of the hegemonic system. Even when Walcott rewrote Homer onstage, his narrator, Billy Blue or Eurycleia, is marked out for his macaronic speeches. All the marginal figures in the Ithacan palace with their Jamaican or Trinidadian accents contribute towards creolising Homer. As in *O Babylon!* Walcott drew on Rastafarian cult and his use of different local vernaculars repudiate the charge that Walcott was hostile to the culture of orality prevalent in the region. Here, the vernacular is not a truthful representation of the French or English-based creole but a translation and a compromise which lays bare the inadequacies of the imposed discourses. The transformation of conventional syntax offers a new way of resistance to the dominant culture. By using "I" instead of "me" and "my" and the "I-and-I" symbolizes how the individual can entail the entire community in the phrase:

> I -and- I shall be poor
> but, in I- and – I pride,
> I -and- I rich with more
> Revealation inside
> Than who by the law
> Of Babylon abide,
> O Babylon! (*Joker* 224)[11]

In the aftermath of political independence, when linguistic insularity was quite prevalent, Walcott struck a compromise between creole speech, Jamaican creole and accessible medium of Anglophone audience. The lyric blend of English and *patois* is the defining quality of language register of the *Joker of Seville*, too. As the slaves sail across the Atlantic, they sing in English-

---

[11] This coinage offers an apt symbol of Walcott's practice, in its refusal to recognize a fixed boundary between self and other (Burnett 22).

based creole, the popular language of the mass. As Tiseba meets Juan for the first time, she switches from metaphorical language to bashful creole reply: "Me? Oh, ent nobody, Sir. Tisebe. A poor fisher girl" (1.4). The tension of literary and popular register, no doubt, disperses any claim to singular authority of a particular discourse.

Walcott's early English critics like Harold Bloom and Helen Vendler had found his aesthetics "macaronic" and jettisoned it as unpromising for any poet. But Walcott's lead was followed by other illustrious figures like Reid, Mc Kay, to make this polygonal register and its polyrhythm more viable medium. In his self-descriptive phrase, Walcott was "a mulatto of styles"; his linguistic legacies are successfully translated into a creole fabric of new theatre. His theatre not only addressed directly his people but reached out to the Western audience and his alternate register affirmed the linguistic identity to be in flux and articulate their shared sensibility. As Jean D'Costa, the Jamaican children's author, observes about the Caribbean authors in general:

"The [Caribbean] writer operates within a poly dialectical continuum with a creole base. His medium, written language, belongs to the sphere of standardised language which exerts a pressure within his own language community while embracing the wide audience of international standard English" (qtd. in *Empire* 44).

Conclusion

A prolific theorist and one of Walcott's eminent contemporaries, Edouard Glissant– a Francophone artist cum thinker believed stage product to be generative of new consciousness.[1] He asserted theatre to be an enabler of galvanizing collective consciousness. Because in the performative zones, theatre as a major form of representation fosters national consciousness and reconfigures a national imaginary. Because the playwrights and the performers took on their terms the relevance of the genuine communal theatre without shedding the influences of Western theatre. It has not been merely a bastion for consolidating tradition or re-imagining a native community. Rather it has explored the tryst between intercultural agendas, cosmopolitanism, and neo-colonial enterprises. The hybridized aesthetic vocabularies of the nascent federal states mobilized the desire for a change and finding agency. The post-independence theatre could be resistive to postcolonial state apparatus. In advancing the theatre as a valuable cultural tool, the day-to-day realities of colonized people have been encoded, which also added momentum to their collective consciousness. With Walcott's intervention, the practice of theatre in the Caribbean islands powerfully articulated the postcolonial reality, with its multi-layered subjectivity, it stimulated critical thinking for the audience both at home and abroad. The dramatic narrative has always posed the question of limits to our most sure ways of knowing–a new optic to see into what is every day and quotidian reality. Etymologically, the English word "theatre" derives from *theatron* which comes from *thea* ("to show") and the Caribbean theatre, for Walcott, could build a self-image and deliver or "show" it up to the world – an alternative dimension of reality. The "theatricality of lives" in the island societies, the pervasive informal entertainments paved the way for natural theatre, a truly popular form to appeal mass and the elite alike. Through myths and rituals, drama could provide an alternative social model and the society could promulgate and reaffirm its values; the superior, standard Western model of communication began to give way to the performative human transactions. Theatre, on the one hand, was an effective mode of understanding the reality of their situation and reshaping reality into a more satisfying form. Here, the overlap of the highbrow and popular sphere testified to "play"/theatre as a new transformative medium for constant mutation of identity. As an autonomous activity and meant for the home community first, theatre does

---

[1] See, *Acoma*, no. 2 July 1970, 42.

not merely refer to external reality but interprets, inquiries about, (de) forms it. And the audience gains a different perspective on reality- real as not empirical or objective. In the performative zone, his actors and "characters slip in and out of their roles", analyses, comments on their fictive part to uncover "the shifting truth which lie beneath colour, representation and truth" (Trivedi 266). Instead of perpetuating traditions, the Caribbean society was incredibly dynamic to find its performative practices always in flux. All of the plays discussed here demonstrate how politico-cultural life may be strategically transformed and theatrical ruses can negotiate different worldviews and belief systems. In so doing, they interrogate the deep structure of inequality and exploitation perpetrated by the colonial power. Their hybridized aesthetic vocabulary and mixed modes explore the legacy of colonial histories and postcolonial subjectivities or respond to the challenge of attending to the cultural imaginary of distinct national agendas at a time of intense cultural flux and repositioning. Walcott's artistic vision and theatrical apparatuses have significantly resisted ruling ideologies and dominant structures and also galvanized a cultural awareness to transcend the neat polarities between Eurocentric and nativist discourse. Like every postcolonial performance, the 'native' comes to exist in a complex representational matrix and occupies a firm speaking position for asserting cultural selfhood.

The critically conscious plays, through manipulation of narrative and conventions of drama, explore and explode the notions of subjectivity, ideologies of difference and monologies of mastery. Walcott's dramatic practice did not call for the portrayal of "authentic" Caribbean tradition, sealed off in its pristine purity. Rather it sought to touch upon indigenous consciousness and selfhood through a synthesis of contending cultural traditions that existed in different islands. Its creole performance sought to find common ground between indigenous Caribbean modes, ritual performance and European approaches – a lively coexistence with radical differences. By erasing master scripts, these plays claimed self-mastery. Caribbean self-representation could hinge upon theatre of creolity – a new, hybrid art form to bridge the fissures between conflicting traditions, customs and world views. His play texts consistently avoid contours of history and the common humanity remains his uppermost concern; in most of his plays the privilege of the white, European man is displaced by the script of lives of the "unaccommodated man". In theatre aesthetics and praxis, the "native" receives alternative cultural representation: the transmission of performance, its mobility, cross-cultural traffic disrupt the cultural hegemony of Western performance tradition. In speech rhythms, musical tonality, dialects and in its overlap with Western written tradition, the "new" theatre products could manifest the society's creative imagination best. Such performance proved radically transformative through extraordinary masterful technique and through the conviction and power of the message.

Conclusion

The new theatre and its creolized stage version could break down the *deshi-videshi* (native/foreign), folk/serious dichotomy. Drawing on the creole continuum and European literary tradition, Walcott forged alternate theatrical idiom and committed it to the cause of building the society. The interconnected lives of his plays underscore the values of "interdependence", rather than "independence". Its unending syncretic process through the contact of different affects, desires, energies and intensities challenges all the ruses of hegemonizing the performance space and its normative oneness. A community without any form of hierarchy formed the centre of his life-long dedication to theatre-making: "this earth is one/island in archipelago of stars" (*Star Apple Kingdom, 20*). Stage space, as we find in Walcott, navigates various subject positions and performance styles and through borrowing, retellings and adaptations it becomes liberatory from the grids of the nation, space or caste. Paula Burnett describes it as an attempt to "write alternative histories for his own people, reflecting different starting points, choices…". In imagining a changeable world, stage narrative coalesces sameness and difference, particularity and universality. Theatre, as moulded by Walcott, maintains kinship with other performance forms, by linking to other locations of culture and other social formations. What permeates these creative, plurivocal performances is an alternative reality which is at once a "copy and counterfeit".[2] It reconfigures the socio-economic reality through a symbolic mode; a change in the symbolic realm is strongly suggestive of the material change though Walcott always hated radical political agenda or the promise of power politics. "Like Brecht, Walcott typically gives trenchant exposure to the materialist causes of action, taking on capitalism principally in its imperialist manifestation" (Burnett 210). As his characters are drawn from a community (de) formed by conquest and slavery, they not only grapple with the subjugation in terms of geopolitical and sociocultural history; the theatre allows them room for articulating independent cultural affirmation. Without perpetuating the coloniser and colonised opposition, the native is remade into a polysemic sign- no longer a fixed object of institutional and ideological domination. By perpetuating the illusion of their victimhood, the New world artists could only produce "a literature of recrimination and despair, a literature of revenge…" ("The Muse" 37). But Caribbean subject position evaded the paradigm of victimhood and preference for either/or position of racial polarities. The forum of new drama and its new architecture of cultures (*History, Fable and Myth* 10) thereby redeemed them from the position of *stasis and* bondage.

---

[2] The appropriations of Coetzee and Walcott at once resembles and does not resemble the intertexts and maintains ambivalence of a creole text.

The chapters organised here around Walcott's major play texts underscore how the "alternative" theatricalities counter the dominant and official version of the Caribbean reality and monology of the Western master script. The subversive potential of the ritual and customs, carnival, in his major works like *Dream on Monkey Mountain* or *Pantomime*, debunks all forms of authority; performance of subaltern resistance and lower-class participation in these plays confront the norms of social hierarchy, master-slave distinction and other binarized relationship. Like his eminent predecessor C.L.R. James's shanty dwellers, peasants and maroons, Walcott's characters are Caribbean 'everyman' - those who are stereotyped in master narratives, yet refusing to be trapped in it and as part of the nationalizing communities can produce alternate heroism. In the heydays of Garveyism Walcott felt that true emancipation starts when the mulatto middle class and the dispossessed lower class can shed the yoke of colonialism and slavery and are reinscribed into an affirmative West Indian identity. The oral tradition, street festivals, *patois* become not only potential dissimulation of the misrepresentation of the Western master scripts but a "native" resistance to the process of dehumanization. This is also a counter to the reactionary nativism and its violent revolution of everything white and European. The growing expansion of neo-colonial and neo-liberal networks became a major thematic concern in late plays. The postcolonial selfhood here grows out of the multiple legacies of colonialism as well as postcolonial anxieties. For Harris and Walcott art remained the means of redemption in the face of a contemporary crisis and the catastrophe of history in the Caribbean region.

The effective design and dramaturgy of Walcott's plays, as discussed in this study, when read through the lens of alter/"native", no doubt, help us understand the formations like assemblage, network, ensemble – "which describes the interactive totality of subject and object, thought and thing, in any effective design" (Gandhi 178). This new form, throwing off all forms of subjection, becomes assertive of the history and identity of the Caribbean people. Against all forms of totalitarian misrule, Walcott's stage plays offer resistance but in a different way from the satirical plays of Soyinka, where the exposure is more trenchant and criticism more hard-hitting. It proves more effective against modern capitalist globalisation. Instead of being liberationist in a narrow political sense, they generate "mutual mutation" of all adversarial relations. When examined closely, the major plays of Walcott's *oeuvre* captures the continuity of cultural practices that affirm the humanity and perpetuity of the Caribbeans. Without shedding amnesia, the culture is found to emerge in the contact zone of differences and inequities. Michael Dash, in his monograph on Edouard Glissant, has pointed out that the narrative or story-telling through imaginative reflection generates a cross-cultural transaction or intra-cultural relation. Through the theatrical experience, what emerges is a cultural pattern of cohesion- a productive counter to the mechanistic, systematizing view of the world or homogenisation of the imperial ideology; "opacities can coexist, converge, weaving kinds of fabric whose true meaning would be related to interweaving of this weft and not to the nature of its component threads... It would be a grand act of generosity to launch such a movement, whose referent would not be Humanity but the exuberant divergence of Humanities" (*Relation* 204).

The experience of creolisation of all his inheritances in Walcott's dramas, no doubt, turns "the gaze of the discriminated back upon the eye of power" (154). As different cultures grapple with each other, the outcome is often unpredictable. This dialogue retells the story of contact, clash and confrontation from a non-adversarial angle; the identity of his characters undergoes mutation and is reposited in a network of relations. The cross-pollination of different performance styles adds a new dimension to the theatre as an inventive form of negotiation and dialogue. As drama and performance have always been shaped by dynamics across time and space, their narratives migrate across cultural contexts and the ontological stability of "native" is displaced with resultant formations of identity and nation with all fissures, like an infinite, multiple networks of branching roots.[3] The anthropologists' quest for "pure" and "authentic" native is revised and reconfigured in creole theatre. In Benitez Rojo's postulate, a Caribbean text is "a polyrhythmic ensemble"; in Walcott's *oeuvre* we find this "ensemble" which displaces binary discourse by increasing entanglement of worldviews, cultural customs. In the creole culture, every product is a transactional aggregate. Its radical assimilatory power helps to reclaim what is home-grown or native and hitherto subjugated and minor; what happens here is that the native is invested with a new significance which emerges as a potent counter to normative and universalist knowledge systems. Walcott's dramaturgic tricks underscore how Eurocentric or any other totalitarian signifying system and explanatory beliefs and their ignorance of non-Western did only destabilize the cultural authority and all colonialist perceptions - "For generations now, philosophers and thinkers shaping the nature of social science have produced theories embracing the entirety of humanity; as we well know, these statements have been produced in relative, and sometimes absolute, ignorance of the majority of humankind i.e., those living in non-Western cultures" (Chakrabarty 3). The charge of "Eurocentric humanism" often levelled against Walcott is countered in the space of theatre where a profound mingling of tradition corroborates a new egalitarianism regardless of nationality or race. The

---

[3] Boidun Jefiyo offers a nuanced reading of *A Dream* and *Pantomime* as response of the "native" as the Object of Eurocentric discursive, signifying and explanatory system.

reductive opposition of self and other in Nativist discourses or mere circumventing of the colonial authority paves the way open for the emergence of subject position which embodies the ongoing inter-mixture of cultural and racial identities. By erasing the essentialized notion of "nativeness" or mere fetishization of "local" and home-grown his stage narratives collapse different national-racial formations. At the site of the theatre, by eluding rootedness and fixity and xenophobic overtones of "native", his plays reimagine new identities, multiple subject position with cultural affiliations. His dramaturgy, language experiment, performance style underscores a new ontological reformulation of the "native" as a hybrid and fluid figure rather than a liberal human subject. The values of relation with other cultures and peoples upheld in Walcott's theatre practices, no doubt, reflect the access of both regional and global audiences. This is how the alternative version of reality fills the void of non-history of the Caribbean region and breaks down the boundary of indigenous worldview and knowledge system. The narratives and protagonists stand out to claim equality and human community. The dominance of one ideology over another could only encourage nation-based forms of collective belonging. And in staging Caribbean cultural lives all man-made borders melt away to forge solidarity of a community of interrelated beings. This alternative theatre has no mooring on its soil, culture, race or any such uniformization. Yet it proffers ethics of conviviality by an endless transformation of the pattern of social and historical experiences and identities. In face of dynamic transformation of performance, the effects of fixity and boundary look vulnerable. And new possibilities are generated through "cosmopolitical" theatre that speaks across North and South without making claim to be a universal practice.

Bibliography

Primary Texts

Dream on Monkey Mountain and Other Plays. Farrar, Straux and Giroux. 1970.
Another Life. Farrar, Straus and Giroux, 1974.
The Joker of Seville, and O Babylon. Farrar, Straux and Giroux, 1978.
The Star-Apple Kingdom. Farrar, Straus and Giroux, 1979.
Remembrance and Pantomime. Farrar, Straux and Giroux, 1980. Kindle.
Three Plays [The Last Carnival; Beef, No Chicken; A Branch of Blue Nile]. Farrar, Straux and Giroux, 1986. Kindle.
Collected Poems, 1948-84. Farrar, Straux and Giroux, 1986.
Omeros. Faber and Faber, 1990.
The Odyssey. Farrar, Straux and Giroux, 1993.
What the Twilight Says: Essays. Farrar, Straux and Giroux, 1998.
The Haitian Trilogy [Henri Cristophe; the Haitian Earth; Drums and Colours]. Farrar, Straux and Giroux, 2003.

Secondary Texts

Ahern, Megan K. "Insubordinate speech: Mimicry as Bourdieuian Heterodoxy in Walcott's Pantomime." *Ariel: A Review of International English Literature,* 2007.
Allen, Graham. *Intertextuality.* Routledge, 2007.
Anderson, Benedict. *Imagined Communities.* Verso Books, 2016.
Angelou, Maya. *I know why the Caged Bird Sings.* Hatchette Digital, 2010.
Armah, Ayi K. *The Beautyful Ones Are Not Yet Born: A Novel.* Heinemann, 1969.
Ashcroft, Bill, Gareth Griffiths, and Helen Tiffin. *The Empire Writes Back.* 2nd ed., Routledge, 2002.
Awam, Ampka. *Theatre and Postcolonial desire.* Routledge, 2004.
Bada, Valeri. "Cross – Cultural Dialogues with Greek Classics: Walcott's The Odyssey and Soyinka's The Bacchae of Euripides". *Ariel: A Review of International English Literature,* vol. 31, no. 3, 2000, pp. 7-28.
Baer, Williams, ed. *Conversations with Derek Walcott.* University Press of Mississippi, 1996.
Baker, Joseph K. "Dreams, Deliriums and Decolonization in *Dream on Monkey Mountain*". *Small Axe,* vol. 2, no. 14, 2010, pp. 1-16.
Bakhtin, Mikhail. *The Dialogic Imagination: Four Essays.* University Press of Texas, 1982.
Baldwin, James. *The Fire next Time.* Dial Press, 1963.
Banham, Martin, et al. *The Cambridge Introduction to African and Caribbean Theatre.* Cambridge University Press, 1994.

Baugh, Edward. *Derek Walcott. Cambridge Studies in African and Caribbean Literature.* Cambridge University Press, 2006.

———. "Of Men and Heroes"- Walcott and the Haitian Revolution. *Callaloo,* 2005, pp. 45-54.

Bhabha, Homi K. *Location of Culture.* Routledge, 2006.

Bhatia, Nandi. *Acts of Authority/Acts of Resistance: Theater and Politics in Colonial and Postcolonial India.* University Press of Michigan, 2004.

Bhattacharya, Baidik. *Introduction of Postcolonial writing in the era of World Literature.* Routledge, 2018.

Bloom, Harold. ed. *Derek Walcott.* Chelsea House Publishers, 2003.

Bohemer, Elleke. *Colonial and Post-colonial Literature.* Oxford University Press, 2005.

Brah and Coombes ed. *Hybridity and Its discontents Politics, Science and Culture.* Routledge, 2000.

Breiner, Laurence A. *An Introduction to West Indian Poetry.* Cambridge University Press, 1998.

Breslin, Paul. *Nobody's Nation: Reading Derek Walcott.* The University Press of Chicago, 2001.

Breslow, Stephen. "Trinidadian Heteroglossia. A Bakhtinian View of Derek Walcott's Play *A Branch of the Blue Nile*". *World Literature Today: A Literary Quarterly of the University of Oklahoma,* vol. 63. no. 1, Winter 1989, pp. 388-393.

Broadsky, Joseph. "The Sound of The Tide". *Derek Walcott,* edited by Harold Bloom. Chelsea House Publisher. 2003, pp. 25-34.

Brown, Lloyd. "Dreamers and Slaves - The Ethos of Revolution in Walcott and Leroi Jones", edited by Hamner Robert. D. *Critical perspective on Derek Walcott.* Lynne Rienner Publisher. 1993, pp. 193-201.

Brown, Stewart. ed. *The Art of Derek Walcott.* Seren Book, 1991.

Bucknor, Michael. A, and Alison Donnell. *The Routledge Companion to Anglophone Caribbean Literature.* Taylor and Francis, 2011.

Burian, Peter. "You Can Build a Heavy-Beamed poem out of This": Derek Walcott's *Odyssey*". *The Classical World,* vol. 93, no. 1, 1999. www.JSTOR.org/stable/4352372. Accessed on 19th Nov. 2020.

Burnett, Paula. *Derek Walcott: Politics and Poetics.* The University Press of Florida, 2001.

Burns, Lorna. *Contemporary Caribbean Writing and Deleuze: Literature between Postcolonialism and Postcolonial Philosophy.* Bloomsbury, 2012.

Canefield, Rob. "Theatralizing the Anglophone Caribbean". *History of Literature in the Caribbean. English and Dutch Speaking Regions,* vol. 2, edited by A. James Ronald, Julio Rodriguez-Louis. J. Mitchell Dash. John Benjamin Publishing Company, 2001.

Cesaire, Aime. *Discourse on Colonialism.* Monthly Review Press. 2000.

Chakraborty, Dipesh. "Postcoloniality and the artifice of history: who speaks for "Indian" Pasts?", *Representations,* no. 37, winter 1992, pp. 1–26.

Chambers, Iain. *Migrancy, Culture and Identity.* Routledge, 1994.

Chew, Shirley, and David Richards. *A Concise Companion to Post-colonial Literature.* Willey Blackwell, 2009.

Cixous, Helene, Keith Cohen, and Paula Cohen. "The Laugh of the Medusa". *Signs*, vol. 4, no. 1, pp. 875-893.

Colson, Theodre. "Derek Walcott's Plays: Outrage and Compassion". *Critical Perspective on Derek Walcott.* Lynne Rienner Publisher, 1993.

Cooper, Carolyn. "A language Beyond Mimicry: language as metaphor and Meaning in Derek Walcott's oeuvre." *The Literary Half-Yearly*, vol. 26, no. 1, pp. 23-40.

Cooppan, Shalini. *Cultural Memory in the Present: Worlds Within: National Narratives and Global Connections in Post-Colonial Writing.* Standford University Press, 2009.

Crow, Brian, and Chris Banfield. *An Introduction to Post-colonial Theatre.* Cambridge University Press, 1996.

Dabydeen, David, and Nana Wilson-Tagoe. *A Reader's Guide to West Indian and Black British Literature.* Hanshib Publications, 1997.

Dash, J. Michael. *Edouard Glissant.* Cambridge University Press, 2009.

Dawson, Ashley. *Mongrel Nation: Diasporic Culture and the making of Post-Colonial Britain.* University Press of Michigan, 2007.

Edmondson, Belinda. "Race, Tradition and the construction of the Caribbean Aesthetic. New *Literary History*, vol. 25, no. 1, Winter 1994, pp. 109-120.

Fanon, Frantz. *The Wretched of the Earth.* Trans. Richard Philcox. Grove Press, 2004.

———. *Black Skin, White Mask.* Pluto Press, 2008.

Ferguson, James, Akhil Gupta. "Space, Identity and the politics of Difference", *Cultural Anthropology*, vol. 7, no. 1, Feb. 1992, pp. 6-23.

Figueora, J. John. "Creole in Literature: Beyond Verisimilitude: Texture and varieties in Derek Walcott". *The Yearbook of English Studies*, vol. 25, 1995, pp. 156-162.

Fischer-Lichte, Erika. *The Routledge Introduction to Theatre and Performance Studies.* Routledge, 2014.

Fischer-Lichte, Erika, Torsten Jost, and Saskya Iris Jain. *The Politics of Interweaving Performance Culture Beyond Postcolonialism.* Routledge, 2018.

Fly, Richard. "The evolution of Shakespearean metadrama: Abel, Burckhardt, and Calderwood". *Comparative Drama*, vol. 20, no. 2, 1986, p. 124.

Fox, Robert. E. "Big Night Music": Derek Walcott's *Dream on Monkey Mountain.* And Splendors of Imagination. edited by Robert. D. Hamner. *Critical Perspective on Derek Walcott.* Lynne Rienner Publisher, 1993, pp. 201-211.

Froude, Anthony J. *The English in the West Indies. Or: The Bow of Ulyssess.* C. Scribner's Sons, 1900.

Gandhi, Lila. *Postcolonial Theory: A Critical Introduction.* Allen Unwin, 1998.

Gaskell, Ian. "Theatrical Representation and National Identity in Fiji." *The Nation Across the world: Postcolonial Literary representations.* Ed. Trivedi Harish, Meenakshi Mukherjee, C. Vijayshree, T. Vijay Kumar. Oxford University Press, 2007.

Gibbons, Rawle. "Theatre and Caribbean Self-definition". *Modern Drama*, vol. 38. no. 1, Spring 1995, pp. 52-59.

Gikandi, Simon. *Maps of Englishness: Writing identity in the Culture of Colonialism.* Columbia University Press, 1996.

Gilbert, Helen, editor. *Postcolonial Plays: An Anthology.* Routledge, 2001.

Gilbert, Helen, and Joanne Tompkins. *Post-colonial Drama: Theory, Practice, Politics.* Routledge, 1996.

Gilroy, Paul. "British Cultural Studies and the Pitfalls of Identity". Curran, James, David Morley and Valerie Walkerdine eds. Cultural Studies and Communications, 1996.

———. *The Black Atlantic: Modernity and Double Consciousness.* Harvard University Press, 1993.

Glissant, Edouard. *Poetics of Relation.* Trans. Betsy Wing and Ann Arbor. University Press of Michigan, 2003.

———. *Caribbean Discourses: Selected Essays.* University Press of Virginia, 1992.

Greenwood, Emily and Barbara Graziosi. *Homer in the Twentieth Century: Between World Literature and the Western Canon.* Oxford University Press, 2007.

Gregory, D. Alics. "The Greek in the Caribbean, Reflections on Derek Walcott, Homer and Syncreticism". *Historical reflections.* vol. 3 no. 27, Fall 2001, pp. 425-452.

Guillén, Nicolas. *Man-Making Worlds: Selected Poems Of Nicolas Guillen.* University Press of Massachusetts, 2003.

Hall, Stuart. *"Who Needs Identity"? Identity A Reader.* Edited by DuGay, P. Evans, Jand Redman. Sage, 2000, pp. 15- 30.

———. "Cultural Identity and Diaspora". *Identity, community and Difference.* Edited by Jonathan Rutherford. Lawrence and Wishart, 1990.

Hamner, Robert. D. *Critical perspective on Derek Walcott.* Lynne Rienner Publisher, 1993.

———. "Mythological aspects of Derek Walcott's Drama". ariel.ucalgary.ca/ariel/index.php/ariel/article/viewFile/1133/1107. Accessed on 20th Nov 19.

———. "Bruce King, Derek Walcott and West Indian Drama." *Modern Drama*, vol. 39, no. 1.

Haney, S. Willam. "Hybridity and Visionary Experience": Derek Walcott's *Dream on Monkey Mountain*". *Mystics Quarterly*, vol. 3, no. 41, September/December 2005, pp. 81-108.

Hardwick, Lorna, and Carol Gillespie. *Classics in Postcolonial World.* Oxford University Press, 2007.

———. "Classical Texts in Postcolonial Literatures: Consolation, Redress and New Beginnings in the Work of Derek Walcott and Seamus Heaney." *International Journal of the Classical Tradition*, vol. 9, no. 2, Fall 2002, pp. 236-256.

Harris, Wilson. *Selected Essays of Wilson Harris: the unfinished genesis of the Imagination.* Routledge, 1999.

———. *Tradition, the Writer and Society: Critical Essays.* New Beacon, 1967.

Heaney, Seamus. "The Sound of the Tide". *Derek Walcott*. Chelsea House Publisher, 2003.

———. "The Murmur of Malvern". *Derek Walcott*. Chelsea House Publishers, 2003.

Higgins. M. Kathleen. *Rebaptizing Our Evil: On the Revaluation of All Values. A Companion to Nietzsche*. Blackwell Publishing, 2006.

Hill, Errol. *The Trinidad Carnival: Mandate for National Theatre*. University Press of Texas, 1972.

Hirsch, Edward. "The Art of Poetry xxxvii: Derek Walcott." *Paris Review*, vol. 28. Winter 1986, pp. 197-230.

Hoggan, Patrick Colm. "Mimeticism, Reactionary Nativism and the Possibility of Post-colonial identity in Derek Walcott's *Dream on Monkey Mountain*". *Research in African Literatures*, vol. 25, no. 2, https://www.jstor.org/stable/4618266. Accessed on 25th Nov. 2019.

Ibekwe, Chinweizu. *Decolonising the African Mind*. Prop Press, 1987.

Ismond, Patricia. "Women in Walcott's Theatre". *Literature in the African Diaspora*. vol. 5, no. 1, 2004, pp. 139-151.

———. "Woman as Race-containing Symbol in Walcott's poetry". *Journal in West Indian Literature*. vol. 8, no. 2, April 1990, pp. 83-90.

———. "Walcott's Later Drama: from. 'Joker' to 'Remembrance'". *Ariel*, vol. 16, no. 3. http://ariel. journalhosting.ucalgary.ca/ariel/index. Accessed on 20th Sept. 2019.

James, C.L.R., and Michael Anthony. "Discovering Literature in Trinidad: Two Experiences." *The Journal of Commonwealth Literature*, vol. 4, no. 1, March 1969.

Josephs, Kelly Baker. "Dreams, Delirium and Decolonization in Derek Walcott's *Dream on Monkey Mountain*". *Small Axe*, vol. 14, no. 2, June 2010, pp. 1-16.

Justine, McConnel. "You had to wade this deep in blood"? Violence and Madness in Derek Walcott's "The Odyssey". *The Intertexts*, vol. 16 no. 1, 2012, pp. 43-56.

Kelly, Oliver. *Colonialization of Psychic Space: psychoanalytic Theory of oppression*. University Press of Minnesota, 2004.

Kincaid, Jamaica. *A Small Place*. Farrar, Straux and Giroux, 1988.

King, Bruce, editor. *Derek Walcott: A Caribbean Life*. Oxford University Press, 2006.

———. *Derek Walcott and the West Indian Drama*. Clarendon Press, 1995.

———. Editor. *Postcolonial English Drama: Commonwealth Drama since 1960*. St. Martin Press, 1992.

Kristeva, Julia. *"Powers of Horror: An Essay on Abjection"*. Trans. Leon S. Rudies. Columbia University Press, 1902.

Lamming, George. *In the Castle Of my Skin*. University Press of Michigan, 1991.

———. *The Pleasures of Exile*. University Press of Michigan, 1960.

Lazarus, Neil. "Introducing Postcolonial Studies", *The Cambridge Introduction to Postcolonial Studies*. Cambridge University Press, 2004.

Lefevere, André. *Translation, Rewriting, and the Manipulation of Literary Fame.* Routledge, 1992.

Lehmann, Hans-T. *POSTDRAMATIC THEATRE.* Translated by. Karen Jurs Munby, Routledge, 2006.

Leiter, Brian. *Nietzsche on Morality.* Routledge, 2014.

Letisser, George, editor. *Rewriting/Reprising: Plural Intertextualities.* Cambridge Scholars publishing, 2009.

Loichot, Valerie. "Renaming the Name: Gilssant and Derek Walcott's Reconstruction of the Self". *Journal Of Caribbean Literature.* vol. 3, no. 2:1-1-12. https://www.jstor.org/stable/40986126. Accessed on 20th Feb. 20.

Lovelace, Earl. *The Dragon Can't Dance.* Longman Publishing Group, 1995.

———. *Jestina's Calypso and Other Plays.* Heineman Educational Books, 1984.

Lowell, Fiet. "Mapping a New Nile: Derek Walcott's Later Plays". *The Art of Derek Walcott.* Edited by, Stewart Brown. Wales, 1991.

Manoni, Octave. *Prospero and Caliban: The Psychology of Decolonisation.* University Press of Michigan, 1990.

Marx, John. "Postcolonial Literature and the Western Canon." *The Cambridge Companion to Postcolonial literary Studies.* Cambridge University Press, 2006, pp. 83-97.

Mbembe, Achille. *On the Postcolony.* Cornell University Press, 2001.

McConnel, Justine. "You had to wade this deep in blood? Violence and madness in Derek Walcott's *The Odyssey*". *Intertext*, vol. 16, no. 1, Spring 2012, pp. 43-54.

Minford, Paul. "Resisting Narrative Orderings; Defoe's Crusoe and some of his Postcolonial Incarnation in Mitchell, Walcott and Coetzeee". Repository. mushshi.ac.jp/dspace/handle/11149/810. Accessed on 20th Aug. 19.

Morgan, C. John and Tejumola Olaynian. *African Drama and Performance.* Indiana University Press, 2004.

Mukherjee, Ankhi. *What is a Classic?: Postcolonial Rewriting and Invention of the Canon.* Stanford University Press, 2014.

Naipaul, V.S. *Mimic Men.* AndreDeutsch, 1967.

———. *Middle Passage.* Vintage Book, 2002.

———. *The loss of El Dorado: A Colonial History.* Pan Macmillan.

———. *A Bend in the River.* Vintage Press, 1980.

Narsimmah, C. D. *Swan and the Eagle: Esaays on Indian English Literature.* Indian Institute of Advanced Study Simla, 1969.

Ngugi, Wa T. *Decolonising the Mind: The Politics of Language in African Literature.* Heinemann, 1986.

Nietzsche, Fredrich. *On the Genealogy of Morality: A Polemic,* trans. Carol Diethe. Cambridge University Press, [1887] 2000.

———. *Thus Spake Zarathustra,* trans. R.J. Hollingale. Penguin, [1885] 1969.

———. *The Gay Science: With a Prelude in Rhymes and an appendix of songs,* trans. Walter Kauffmann. Vintage, [1882] 1974.

———. *The Birth of Tragedy: Out of the Spirit of Music.* Penguin, 1993.

Olaniyan, Tejumola. "Dramatizing Postcoloniality: Wole Soyinka and Derek Walcott". Disciplines of Theatre: Theory/Culture/Text. *Theatre Journal,* vol.

44, no. 4, pp. 485-499. https://www.jstor.org/stable/3208770. Accessed on 15th June 20.

———. *Scars of Conquest/Masks of Resistance: The Invention of Cultural Identities in African, African-American, and Caribbean Drama*. Oxford University Press, 1995.

O'Neill, Eugene, and William-Alan Landes. *The Hairy Ape*. Players Press, 2008.

Pathke, Rajiv S. *Postcolonial Poetry in English*. Oxford University Press, 2006.

Pfeffer, Rose. "Eternal Recurrence in Nietzsche's Philosophy". *The Review of Metaphysics*, vol. 19, no. 2, Dec 1965, pp. 276-300.

Poyner, Jane. *J. M. Coetzee and the Paradox of Postcolonial authorship*. Ashgate Publishing Ltd., 2009.

Prabhu, Anjali. *Hybridity, Limits, Transformations, Prospects*. State of Albany University Press, 2007.

Punter, David. *Postcolonial Imaginings: Fictions of A New World Order*. Edinburgh University Press, 2000.

Puri, Shalini. *Caribbean Postcolonial: Social Equality: Post-nationalism and Cultural Hybridity*. Palgrave Macmillan, 2004.

Radhakrishnan, Rajagopalan. "Postcoloniality and the Boundaries of identity". *Callaloo*, vol. 16, no. 4, 1993, pp. 750-771.

Rich, Adrienne. "When We Dead Awaken: Writing as Re-vision". *College English*, vol. 34, no. 1, pp. 18-30. https://www.jstor.org/stable/375215. Accessed on 2nd Feb 21.

Richards, David. "*Framing Identities*"- *Concise Companion to Literature and Culture*. Wiley Blackwell, 2010.

Robinson, David. *Nietzsche and Post- modernism*. Worldview Publications, 2008.

Rojo, Benitez. *The Repeating Islands*. Duke University Press, 1996.

Rorty, Richard. *Contingency, Irony and Solidarity*. Cambridge University Press, 2012.

Rowan, Richard Philip. "Derek Walcott: Imagination, Nation and Poetics of Memory". *Small Axe*, vol. 6, no. 1, March 2002, pp. 112-132.

Said, Edward W. *Culture and Imperialism*. Vintage Books, 1994.

Samad, Daizal.R. "Cultural Imperatives in DREAM ON A MONKEY MOUNTAIN". *Postcolonial Literatures: Achebe, Ngugi, Desai, Walcott*. ed. Michael Parker and Rorger Starkey. Palgrave Macmillan, 1995.

Sardar, Ziauddin. *Orientalism*. Buckingham Open University Press, 2000.

Selvon, Sam. *A Brighter Sun*. Allan Wingate, 1952.

Singh, R. Raj. *Schopenhauer: A Guide for the Perplexed*. International Publishing, 2010.

Sinnewe, Dark. *Divided to the Vein? Derek Walcott's Drama and the Formation of Cultural Identities*. Königshasuen and Neumann, 2001.

Spark, Muriel. *The Public Image*. Knopf, 1968.

Spinks, Lee. *Friedrich Nietzsche*. Routledge, 2003.

Soyinka, Wole. "Aesthetic Illusions: Prescriptions for suicide of poetry, Art, *dialogue* and outrage": *Essays on Literature and Culture*. New Horn Press Ltd., 1988.

———. *Shakespeare and the Living Dramatist.* Cambridge University Press, 1983.

Stevens, Camilla. "ThefutureofoldTrinidad.Theperformanceofnationalcultural identity. in two plays by Derek Walcott". *Modern Drama.* Vol. 46, no. 3, Fall 2003, pp. 450-469.

Stone, Judy. *Theatre: Studies in West Indian Literature.* Macmillan, 1994.

Taylor, Patrick. *Postcolonial Discourses and changing Cultural Contexts. Theory and Criticism.* Greenwood Press, 1995.

Tejumola, Olaniyan. *Scars of Conquests/Masks of Resistance; The Invention of cultural Identities in African, African-American and Caribbeean Drama.* Oxford University Press, 1995.

———. "Dramatizing Postcoloniality. Wole Soyinka and Derek Walcott". *Theatre Journal.* vol. 44. no. 4, 1992, pp. 485-499.

Thieme, John. *Derek Walcott.* Manchester University Press, 1999.

Thomas, Ned. *Derek Walcott-Poet of the Islands.* Welsh Arts Council,1980.

Tompkins, Joan. *Theatre's Heterotopias: Performance and the Cultural Politics of Space.* Palgrave Macmillan, 2014.

Trecsenyi, Katalin and Bernadette Cochrane, editors. *New Dramaturgy: International Perspectives on Theory and Practice*, 2014.

Venn, Couze. *The Postcolonial Challenge: Towards Alternative Worlds.* Sage, 2006.

Viola, Julia D. *Derek Walcott; Dramatist-creole drama for Creole acting-critical essays.* Interlock International, 2008.

Waugh, Patricia. *Metafiction: The theory and Practice of Self- consciousness.* Methuen, 1984.

Welshon, Rex. *Philosophy of Nietzsche.* GBR Acumen, 2004.

Wilson, Kathleen, editor, *A New Imperial History: Culture, Identity and Modernity in Britain and the Empire, 1660-1840.* Cambridge University Press, 2004.

Young, J.C. Robert. *Empire, Colony and Postcolony.* Willey Blackwell, 2015.

Yousaf, Nahem. *Chinua Achebe.* Atlantic Publisher (Indian reprint), 2010.

For Further Reading

Achebe, Chinua. *The Arrow of God.* Heinemann, 1964.

Atwood, Margaret. *The Penelopiad.* Penguin Books, 2006.

Ashcroft, Bill, et al. *The Post-Colonial Studies Reader.* 2nd ed., Routledge, 2005.

Bourdieu, Pierre. *Distinctions.* Routledge, 1984.

Brathwaite Edward. "The African Presence in Caribbean Literature". *Dedalus,* 103: 2, 1974, pp. 73-109.

———. *The Arrivants: A New World Trilogy.* Oxford, 1981.

Dash, Michael J. "Framing bones and Writing Rocks: Rethinking a Caribbean Poetics of (dis) location". *Shibbloeth: Journal of Caribban Theory.* Vol.4 no. 1, pp. 64-71.

Dunn, Robert G. *Identity Crises: A Social Critique of Postmodernity.* Minnesota University Press, 1998.

Derrida, Jaques. *Préjugés: Before the Law*, Translated by Sandra Van Reenen and Jaques de ville. University Press of Minnesota, 2018.

Gainor, J Allen. *Imperialism and Theatre: Essays on World Theatre, Drama and Performance*. Routledge, 1995.

Jeyifo, Biodun. *Wole Soyinka: Politics, Poetics and Postcolonialism*. Cornell University Press, 2004.

Msiska, Mpalive- H. *Wole Soyinka*. Northcote house Publisher, 1998.

Reginster, Bernard. *The Affirmation of Life: Nietzsche on Overcoming Nihilism*, Harvard University Press, 2006.

Sanders, Julia. *Adaptation and Appropriation*. Routledge, 2004.

Wright, Elizabeth. *Postmodern Brecht: A Re-presentation*. Routledge, 1989.

Index

A

Achebe, xviii, 2, 72, 74, 116, 143, 144
Achille Mbembe, 72
Adaptations, 73
Adriene Rich, 71
Another Life, 6, 8, *16*
Antony and Cleopatra, 89, 90, 92, *128*
Arkansas Testament, 67

B

Badal Sircar, 6
Bakhtin, 128
BBC, xvii
Benitez Rojo, 9
Bhabha, xii, xv, xxii, 45, 55, 95
Bim, xvii
Black Nationalism, 98
Black Nationalist Movement, 109
Black Power, xix, xxii, xxiii, 96, 100, 104, 109
Black Skin, 5
Blackconsciousness, xxv
Brathwaite, xvii, xviii, xxiii, xxix, 51, 67, 72, 122, 144
Brecht, 77
Bruce King, xi

C

C.L.R James, xx, xxiii
Calypso, 79
carnival, xiii
Carnivaleque, 75
Cesaire, xxiv
Coetzee, 79
Creole- continuum, 117
Crusoe, 74, 76

D

Defoe, 70, 76, 78, 89, 93, 125
Dialogue, 83
Dipesh Chakraborty, 88

E

Earl Lovelace, 55, 101, 109, 127
Errol Hill, xiii, xxi, 9
Eugene O'Neill, 23, 63

F

Fanon, 41, 54, 55, 95
Frederic Jameson, 71
Friday, 76
Froude, xv, xvi

G

George Lamming, 117
Gilroy, xix
Glissant, 56, 61, 70
Gray, 96, 102

H

Hall, xxvi
Harris, xxvi, 3, 56, 70, 71, 72, 81
Helene Cixous, 16
Henri Cristophe, xviii, *119*
Heraclitus, 6

Homer, 71, 72, 80, 81

I

In a Green Night, 97

J

Jamaica Kincaid, 43
Joseph Broadsky, 43
Joyce, 71, 72

K

Kamau Brathwaite, 12
Kristeva, 47
Kuroswa, 27

L

Lamming, xviii, xxiii, 4, 15, 40, 67
Lefebvre, 67
Little Carib Dance Company, xii
Little Theatre Movement, xxi

M

Malcochon or, The Six in the Rain, 6
Manichean, x
Marcus Garvey, xx
Maya Angelou, 49
Mc Kay, 130
Metafiction, 89
Middle Passage, xv, 8, 9
Mimicry, 78
Mulatto, 130
Muriel Spark, 91

N

Naipaul, xv, xviii, 40, 59, 105, 116, 127

Native, 70
Nativism, xxv
Nativist, 95
Negritude, xix, xxii, 96
New World, xxi, 7
Nicolás Guillén, 118
Nietzsche, xxviii, 17, 20, 22, 25, 28, 31, 32, 37, 38

O

OBabylon, 129
Octave Manoni, 48
Odyssey, 67
Omeros, 6, 8, *29*, *31*, 82, 86

P

Patricia Ismond, 14, 15
Peter Carey, 79
Postdramatic Theatre, 77

R

Radhakrishnan, 51
Rashoman, 17, *26*
Reid, 130
Revisions, 73
Rhys, 71
Richard Rorty, 33
Root, 95

S

Said, xxvii, 70
Saint Beauve, 73
Sam Selvon, 118, 127
Schopenhauer, 15, 30
Seamus Heaney, 117
Selvon, xviii, 59
Shabine, 85
Shakespeare, 72, 89
Shalini Puri, xxvi

Society and the Artist, 40
Soyinka, 8, 72, 116
St. Lucian Arts Guild, xx
St. Lucian Theatre Guild, xxi
Star Apple Kingdom, xxiv
Stuart Hall, xxv, 103
Synge, 8, 27, 70

T

T.S. Eliot, 86
The Branch of Blue Nile, 90
The Rockefeller Foundation, xvii
The Sea at Dauphin, 4
Thiong'o, x, 4, 116

Ti-Jean and His Brothers, 6, 10, 23, *119*
Trinidad Guardian, xxv
Trinidad Theatre Workshop, xii, 1
Twilight, 4

W

Walter Benjamin, 87
What the Twilight Says, 3
Wilson Harris, xxvi, 64, 81
Wole Soyinka, 68

Z

Ziauddin Sardar, 32

www.ingramcontent.com/pod-product-compliance
Lightning Source LLC
Chambersburg PA
CBHW050638300426
44112CB00012B/1853